P9-CAN-698

YANKEE ACCENT
23 Wianno Avenue
Osterville, Massachusetts 02655

Mystic Seaport Museum

WATERCRAFT

Mystic Seaport Museum

WATERCRAFT

by Maynard Bray

MYSTIC SEAPORT MUSEUM, INCORPORATED
MYSTIC, CONNECTICUT

Copyright © 1979 by Mystic Seaport Museum, Incorporated
ISBN 0–913372–16–1 (Cloth)
ISBN 0–913372–17–X (Paper)
Manufactured in the United States of America
FIRST EDITION

To Anne, who kept me going straight

Contents

CHAPTER TWO
Sloop Rigged

CHAPTER THREE
Ketch Rigged

CHAPTER FOUR
Schooner & Square Rigged

ROWING CRAFT

CHAPTER ONE
Flat Bottom

CONTENTS

POWER CRAFT

CANOES & SPECIALIZED CRAFT

Foreword

Except for a defective and obsolete forerunner of this work which is no longer in print, this is the first of a new kind of watercraft catalog, and as such is bound to have a profound and far-reaching influence on the current revival of classic watercraft which is now a rising tide.

It is true that a catalog of the U.S. National Watercraft Collection, prepared by Carl W. Mitman, appeared as early as 1923, and that it has since been superceded by an enlarged and completely rewritten catalog of the National Collection, compiled by Howard I. Chapelle and published in 1960. But these catalogs are lists of models, not actual vessels such as constitute the Mystic Seaport collection.

This difference is fundamental. Models, even the best of them, are only secondary sources of historic information and design detail, often defective and unreliable, while primary authority resides nowhere else but in the actual boats themselves. Moreover, this difference between a collection of models and a collection of boats relates directly to changes now taking place in maritime museums, and historical museums in general, and in the philosophy upon which museum practice is based.

Museums in the past have used models almost exclusively for displays and exhibits. The educational effect of the limited visual experience that such exhibits offer the casual museum visitor is, in most cases, both superficial and transitory. New hands-on, in-depth programs undertaken by maritime museums to interest and involve the public in activity directed to the preservation and utilization of our heritage watercraft and their adaptation to present needs and future use offer much more, and these must start with the collection and preservation of surviving examples of traditional watercraft.

Our rich heritage of classic design, which reached its peak late in the nineteenth century and for a brief interval thereafter, still survives in part in boats from that period that have survived. In great part these boats were not built from drawn designs and architects' plans, but were fabricated in accordance with an inherited trade experience and tradition which was never written down. The boats that have survived are more than repositories of unique technical information, however. They are irreplaceable historic documents, and in addition, objects of folk art as implicitly recognized by this catalog.

The models cataloged by Mitman existed as a jumbled hodgepodge packed together in the cases and on the walls of the old Watercraft Hall at the Smithsonian in Washington. Apart from such collections of models, there was not a museum in North America fifty years ago with anything that could be called a watercraft collection. The first collection of boats was started at The Mariners Museum in Newport News, Virginia in 1932 when a variety of small craft from all over the world, including an open, flatbottom Portuguese fishing boat of 51-feet, were brought together for display. Beyond displaying them, nothing else was done. In 1950 these boats, numbering eighty-five in all, were still the largest collection of boats in this country.

From its inception, Mystic Seaport, incorporated as the Marine Historical Association in 1929, has been actively involved in numerous ways with a variety of watercraft, both large and small, but during its first twenty-five years the number of boats acquired was meager. Up to 1950 no more than fourteen boats were accessioned. But by 1959 the number, exclusive of large vessels, had increased to fifty-three, as listed in *Small Craft At Mystic Seaport*, published that year. Although designated as "small," boats as large as the Friendship sloop *Estella A.* and the 45-foot Lubec carry-away boat *Regina M.* were among the boats listed.

During the 1960s, Mystic accessioned 53 more boats. From 1970 to date the collection has increased by an additional 109, nearly as many as the total number acquired over the previous thirty years. Including Mystic Seaport, there are now nine maritime museums in eastern United States with watercraft collections of boats and/or vessels of sufficient number to be considered here. In aggregate these nine collections will probably total close to 1000 boats, although an exact count has not yet been made. In 1950 only three of these museums were in existence, and one of them had not

begun to collect boats. During the 1950s two more were founded, and the remaining four in the 1960s. Of these, three now have extensive collections, namely Bath Marine Museum, 1963; Thousand Islands Museum, 1964; Chesapeake Bay Maritime Museum, 1965.

What has happened in the East is now beginning to take place on the West Coast. A classic wooden boat museum is in the process of formation on Lake Union in Seattle, and several West Coast museums are actively seeking out and acquiring examples of local watercraft.

Activity inside museums involving boats cannot be considered apart from what is occurring outside. There is continual interaction as the one influences and affects the other. Museum involvement stimulates outside interest which in turn feeds museum involvement.

Museums are now providing instruction in seamanship and boat handling, in navigation, and in boatbuilding and boat design. They furnish building plans and information derived from their collections. They organize workshops, meets, and conferences. All such activities relate to the museum's watercraft collection, and are involved with it to a greater or lesser degree.

Meets, regattas, boat shows, and boating festivals are organized in turn outside the museums. Amateurs, apart from museums, collect and restore antique boats, and build replicas and adaptations of classic watercraft both for use and for the rewards of craftsmanship. Aesthetic appreciation also enters in. Beyond mere utility as means of transportation or of sport, the best of classic working craft over many past centuries have achieved a delicacy, grace, and purity of form which lift them into the realm of art. The beauty of boats in and of themselves is a precious part of our maritime heritage which this catalog, funded in part by the National Endowment for the Arts proclaims and exemplifies.

Certainly one effect to be expected from this catalog of what is the largest collection of classic boats in North America, will be to stimulate further collecting, serving as an example and setting standards for achievement. Other museums will use it to gauge the strengths and weaknesses of their collections. Other catalogs for other collections almost certainly will result. Museums not involved with watercraft programs will be encouraged to enter the swim.

More than anything else, what this catalog will do will be to turn the flood lights on a development within the museum field which, up to now, has been proceeding quietly and in relative obscurity. The extent of what has been achieved will come as something of a revelation to many, and can only serve to reinforce and extend impressive gains already made.

John Gardner

Preface

In the 1970s those of us on the staff at Mystic Seaport witnessed the awakening of interest in traditional small craft. We were aware of what the Mystic Seaport Museum had acquired in its early decades and we became increasingly aware of possible treasures that might exist in boathouses, basements, and barns, wherever boats had been stored away. Motivated by their own keen interest, Maynard and Anne Bray began gathering information on the small craft collection at Mystic Seaport in order to make the information available to researchers at the museum. It was only a matter of time before it was clear that this material should be brought together in the form of a book.

As plans for the publication developed, a decision was made to depart from conventional museum catalog concepts to include, in addition to the small craft in the collection, the larger vessels and other watercraft at the museum. It was felt that the workboats used on the waterfront as well as reproductions of traditional designs, built by Seaport craftsmen, were worthy of notice, and ought to be included.

While the Brays worked on gathering the information, others of us began to puzzle over where funds for this publication could be found. It was evident to some of us that what we were dealing with was not simply a collection of boats, but the evidence of a very significant American art form. Boatbuilders, on coming to this continent, adapted traditional designs and construction techniques from their native lands to the waters and materials of America. A remarkable quality was attained in both design and construction of these watercraft. And yet this achievement had not been widely recognized. The National Endowment for the Arts, which is most often thought of in the context of its support for exhibits of paintings, or for performing arts programs, had grants available to encourage the publication of catalogs of significant collections. An application was submitted and the authorities at the Endowment were sufficiently perceptive to recognize the importance of the watercraft collection at Mystic Seaport and its potential for a worthwhile catalog. They awarded the museum a grant to cover half of the publication costs. With this base we set about matching the NEA funds.

While we drew on a variety of sources for the needed assistance, a number of individuals contributed to the project and deserve to be recognized for their role in supporting this publication. These people, whose names are listed below, along with the National Endowment for the Arts, the author, and all those involved in the production of this book, have brought about a fine publication which will be of benefit to future generations of boat enthusiasts, boatbuilders, and scholars. To all I extend my thanks and appreciation for this accomplishment.

J. Revell Carr
Director Mystic Seaport Museum

THESE INDIVIDUALS ASSISTED IN THE PRODUCTION OF THIS VOLUME THROUGH THEIR CONTRIBUTIONS:

Adirondack Historical Association
Mr. and Mrs. William Andrews
Mr. Thomas C. Arcand
Mr. Dana C. Armour
Mr. Robert W. Attenborough
Mr. Donald P. Aupperle
Mr. William A. Baker
Bath Marine Museum
Virginia Biddle, M.D.
Mr. William G. Blanding
Mrs. Brooke H. Brakenridge
Lt. Lawson W. Brigham
Mr. William R. Bronner
Mr. W. Tallmadge Bullock
Joseph L. Conboy & Associates
Mr. Daniel S. Connelly
Mrs. Hollister B. Cox
Mr. Robert D. Culler
Mr. Howard W. Davis
Mr. Henry Dixon
Mr. J. Newton Dunbar
Mr. Marc Evenkow
Mr. Bernard L. Faber
Mrs. Charles F. Flint
Mr. George B. Flynn
Mr. Ronald A. Ginger
The family of G. Philip Green,
in his memory
Mr. Daniel S. Gregory
Mr. Lee Harrison
Mr. Bolling W. Haxall
Mr. R. J. Holt

International Marine
Publishing Company
Mr. Thomas E. Jannke
Mr. James Jolpin
Mr. and Mrs. Godfrey W. Kauffmann
Mr. Frank M. Keese
Mr. George B. Kelley
Mr. George King
Mr. Jerome L. Kligerman
Mr. Donald G. Kreuzburg
Mr. Julian Langer
Mr. Lance Lee
Mr. Robert E. Logan
Mr. Clinton F. Loyd
Mr. and Mrs. J. H. McLuckie
Mr. Thomas F. Madigan
Mr. Warren P. Manger
Mr. James Means
Mr. John J. Molloy
Mr. Charles L. Morse, Jr.
Mr. James T. Mulvey
Mr. John H. Myers
National Fisherman
Lt. Cdr. J. S. Neal, U.S.N.
Mr. Edward F. O'Dwyer
Mr. George G. Palfrey
Mr. and Mrs. George A. Palmer
Mr. Donald Pearson
Mr. William M. Peterson
Professor Michael H. Porter
Mr. Fourtin Powell
Mr. and Mrs. E. Tyler Proctor, Jr.

Mr. Andre E. Rheault
Mr. Stephen J. Robinson
Dr. John L. Roche
Mr. Donald C. Rosencranz
Mr. Mitchell Ryerson
Mr. Peter Seeger
Mr. Philip P. Sharples
Mr. Warren Sherburne
Mr. Peter A. Silvia
Dr. Nora H. Spens
Mr. George H. Stadel, Jr.
Mr. E. Zell Steever
Mr. George Surgent
John H. Sutphen, M.D.
Mr. Richmond H. Sweet
Mr. Leo J. Telesmanick
Mr. Robert T. Todd
Mr. William G. Tyler
Mr. Peter H. Vanderwaart
Mr. John S. Van Dyke
Mr. Burritt N. Wakeman
James W. Wallace, M.D.
Mr. D. Reid Weedon, Jr.
Mr. Charles Welsh
Mr. Thomas R. Wilcox, Jr.
Mr. Harry A. Wilmshurst
Mr. Erwin N. Wilson
Mr. Nathaniel S. Wilson
Mr. Richard Wogisch, Jr.
Mr. Vagn Worm
Mr. Christian M. Yost
Mr. Caesar N. Youtchas

Introduction

When I joined Mystic Seaport about ten years ago, one of the first orders of business was to learn about the watercraft for which I had become responsible. I studied books, magazine articles, museum files, drawings, and photographs intently, but at great inconvenience since they were scattered all over the place. Sharing my own interest in old boats and wanting as ever to help out, my wife, Anne, volunteered to collect and compile photocopies of all available information about the least familiar boats into little reference booklets. By the time files for the first dozen or so small craft were put together, we found they were used not only by other staff members, but by a few interested people outside the museum as well.

By this time, we had become convinced that a published catalog of the entire watercraft collection was needed. That belief was reinforced by the traditional small craft revival of the 1970s. With less than half the boat collection on exhibit at any one time, we felt almost guilty about keeping the others under wraps in their storage sheds, away from public view. These sheds were opened on special occasions, such as the annual Small Craft Workshop, and persons having a special interest could always make arrangements to see the boats in storage, but most museum visitors never even knew of their existence. They never laid eyes on the majority of the watercraft in our collection, which is undoubtedly the finest in the country.

More exhibit space for boats is being considered but will not be available for awhile at least. And even if all the boats were on public display, one would still need to visit Mystic to take advantage of the fact. Thus, this catalog will serve as the primary means of acquainting people with the collection and kindling their interest and enthusiasm in traditional watercraft. Perhaps it will even cause some of them to build and use reproductions of boats contained herein.

I often think how nice it would have been to have included the compilations of source material that Anne put together, along with similar treatments for all the other watercraft. The result would have been an encyclopedic work of great convenience, but of prohibitive expense. Instead, this catalog must rely on a list of further reading for each entry which, in many instances, I have annotated to indicate the prime sources and to describe what some of the more obscure items contain.

It is my hope that readers who are enthused by a particular craft will find some measure of contentment in the pages of the books and articles on the reading lists.

By its nature, this catalog will require revision occasionally since boats are still being acquired by the Seaport and new material relating to those already there is always coming to light. Both historically relevant watercraft and information about them are always welcome. Limited indoor storage space causes us to turn down many boats that are offered, but we do try to undertake the preservation of the more significant types from Northeastern waters and the museum encourages inquiries from potential donors.

Maynard Bray

Acknowledgements

Many, many individuals and institutions have helped with this catalog. I'd especially like to thank the following who went out of their way to do so:

Adirondack Museum, Robert H. Baker, William A. Baker of the Hart Nautical Museum, Anne Bray, Lois Darling, Jack Deupree, Roger Dunkerley of the Suffolk Marine Museum, Waldo Howland, W. H. Dyer Jones, John Kochiss, John M. Leavens, Lance Lee of the Apprenticeshop, Bath Marine Museum, Edmund E. Lynch, Director, Bureau of Historic Sites, New York State, Keith MacArthur, Helen Mark, Brian Mogel, William Morris, Dan Phalen, Robert A. Pittaway, Gainor Roberts, Charles Sayle, Major William Smyth, Charles Sylvester, Roger Taylor of International Marine Pub-

lishing Co., Leo Telesmanick of Concordia Co., Thousand Islands Museum, Claibourne Van Zandt, Jr., Muriel Vaughn, William D. Wilkinson of the Mariners Museum, Jonathan Wilson of *WoodenBoat* magazine:

and from the Seaport staff: Robert C. Allyn, Willits D. Ansel, Kathy L. Bray, Philip L. Budlong, J. Revell Carr, Janice Charles, Oraleah Dice, John Gardner, Andrew German, Margaret Grisham, Rodi Hamilton, Jonathan Harley, Waldo C. M. Johnston, Behri P. Knauth, William Kramer, Kenneth Mahler, William Peterson, Donald P. Robinson, Mary Anne Stets, Barry Thomas, Joan Vermilya, Peter Vermilya, Claire White Peterson, Nancy Zercher.

Cataloging Conventions

ORGANIZATION

The Table of Contents displays the organization of this catalog. You will note that watercraft are divided into three basic sections, based on motive power: sail, oars, or engines. Canoes and specialized craft are placed in a separate section at the end. Within each section, there is a further typological subdivision by chapter. For instance, under Sailing Craft, single-masted craft are divided into chapters on cat rig and sloop rig. Under Rowing Craft, flat bottom craft are differentiated from round bottom craft.

A rather full index serves to locate watercraft by name, alternate names, or alternate type names. Proper names, place names, and such categories as Mystic Seaport built boats, reproduction boats, and specific rig types as they occur in the text can also be found in the index.

DIMENSIONS

Dimensions represent the overall length and maximum beam of the hull proper. Length is measured on deck to the outer face of the stem (or extended stem of clipper bowed craft). Beam measurements exclude guard rails and mouldings.

ACCESSION NUMBERS

Accession numbers uniquely identify all objects in the museum's collections, eg. 73.75. The first two digits signify the year acquired (1973 in the example) and those after the decimal point show in what order an object, be it boat or scrimshaw, was received by the museum during that year. Occasionally there is a second decimal point with numbers after it. They indicate that an object has related pieces which are serially cataloged along with it.

FURTHER READING LISTS

Because individual entries could by no means be comprehensive in a work of this scope, further reading lists have been provided. These lists were selected from the best published material available and known to the author at the time of writing; however current revival of interest in traditional watercraft produces new information almost daily.

PHOTOGRAPHS

Photographs in this catalog include historic views of specific watercraft or watercraft types, record shots of watercraft in storage or under restoration, and recent views made specifically for this catalog. Record shots vary in quality as they were not produced under optimum conditions and were intended primarily for files.

Even though all photographs are held in the photofiles of Mystic Seaport Museum, reproductions can only be provided of those which are the property of Mystic Seaport Museum. Those which are not are clearly acknowledged in the captions accompanying the photos. Again our thanks to the people and institutions who furnished these views; their generous cooperation has added immeasurably to this publication.

General Notes
Regarding The Watercraft Collection

Carefully preparing drawings of the Seaport's watercraft and making them available to scholars, modelers, and amateur builders is important business and keeps several staff members busy much of the time. Edson Schock did this work in earlier years and the plans for certain boats have been solicited from Robert H. Baker as well. Accurate and detailed measured drawings take an enormous amount of time and it will be years before even the most significant boats in the ever-expanding collection are committed to paper. An up-to-date list of plans available for sale, including those in the appendix, is maintained by the Curatorial Department and requests for copies of it and orders for the drawings themselves should be directed to: Curatorial Department, Mystic Seaport Museum, Mystic, Connecticut 06355.

Readers wanting to see or examine boats which are not currently on public display may do so by making arrangements with the Registrar's Office, in advance if possible.

Mystic Seaport has about two dozen boats which are geographically outside its field of interest which are not listed in this catalog. These craft were taken in during the museum's early years, when few other institutions were set up to preserve them. Good homes in responsible museums are now being sought for these boats.

Even at this writing, several recently accessioned boats arrived too late to be included. It is inevitable that more will follow and will, before long, necessitate a revision of this catalog.

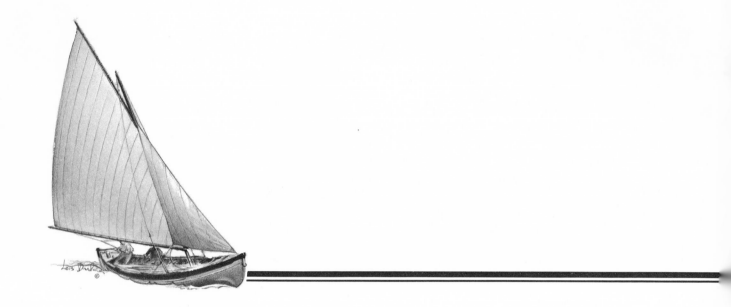

SAILING CRAFT

Chapter One
CAT RIGGED

THE CAT RIG
AND THE
CATBOAT

Great South Bay Catboats **Daphne,**
#9, and **Blue Wing,** *#55*
(Courtesy: Suffolk Marine Museum)

The word cat, where sailboats are concerned, has come to mean two distinct things: a kind of rig, the *cat rig*, and a hull form, the *catboat*.

The cat rig calls for a single fore and aft sail on a single mast set "well up in the eyes" or bow of the boat. Traditionally, the sail should be gaff headed and laced to a boom, but Marconi, and leg- or shoulder-of-mutton sails can also be considered to be cat rig when the other elements are present. For the purposes of this catalog, the spritsail has also been so classified. A boat can be cat rigged without being a catboat, but a catboat is always cat rigged.

The catboat is an able, weatherly, shoal-draft boat with a broad-beamed hull. The classic Cape Cod catboat has a beam-length ratio of 2:1, the beam being half the waterline length.

The catboat can have either a centerboard or a keel, a counter or transom stern, an underslung or barn-door outboard rudder. It can be tiller steered or wheel steered, of clinker (lapstrake) or carvel construction, have a stayed or unstayed mast. Cat sloops, and two masted cat ketches, and cat yawls are recognized catboat variants if they are shoal draft and broad of beam.

The origin and meaning of the words "cat" and "catboat" are obscure. However, from ancient times they have signified heavy-duty use, as in the case of a work boat.

The cat rig in its gaff-headed form derives from the square sail through intermediate transitional rigs, such as the lug sail. It antedates the catboat.

The catboat developed in the northeastern United States prior to 1850, probably from earlier hull forms. The likelihood is that the catboat developed more or less spontaneously and at the same time, in various places between Cape May, New Jersey, and Cape Ann, Massachusetts. Catboats also developed independently elsewhere before the 1880s: the Biloxi catboat along the Mississippi Gulf Coast, and the plunger or "oyster sloop," as it was called, on San Francisco Bay. Catboats also exist in Europe where they are known as Unaboats. This name was derived from the American catboat *Una* built in New Jersey in 1852 as a 16-foot racing boat. She was later taken to England where she inspired the building of catboats there. Eventually, the Unaboat spread to France and Germany.

Early clinker-built catboats 12 to 18-feet in length were used in fishing and lobstering. Later, carvel construction replaced clinker construction as larger catboats were built for fishing, ferrying people, packeting goods, partying, day sailing, racing and pleasure. Catboats now come in sizes from 12 to 30-feet with extreme examples ranging to 40-feet. However, beyond 40-feet the cat rig becomes inefficient and unmanageable for the catboat hull form.

1

Catboats come as completely open boats, as open-cockpit half-decked boats with and without a cuddy, and as cabin boats with and without a self-bailing cockpit.

The catboat reached its highest perfection of form around 1900 at which time it was also the most familiar and common sight in any New England harbor. The decline of the catboat as a work boat occurred shortly thereafter when the gasoline engine came into general use for boats. Power enabled new and more efficient hulls to be built for fishing. A few catboats fitted with power survived as work boats until the mid 1930s, but after the hurricane of 1938 not many were left.

After the catboat fell into disuse as a work boat, it continued to be popular for racing, pleasure sailing, and cruising for many decades because of its safety, comfort, and rig simplicity. A gradual decline in the importance of the catboat after World War II has been sharply reversed by two unrelated events: the establishment of The Catboat Association in the summer of 1962 and the development of the fiberglass cruising catboat hull in the winter of 1962–63. These two events once again brought to the fore the excellent qualities of the catboat as a pleasure, racing, and cruising boat.

John M. Leavens

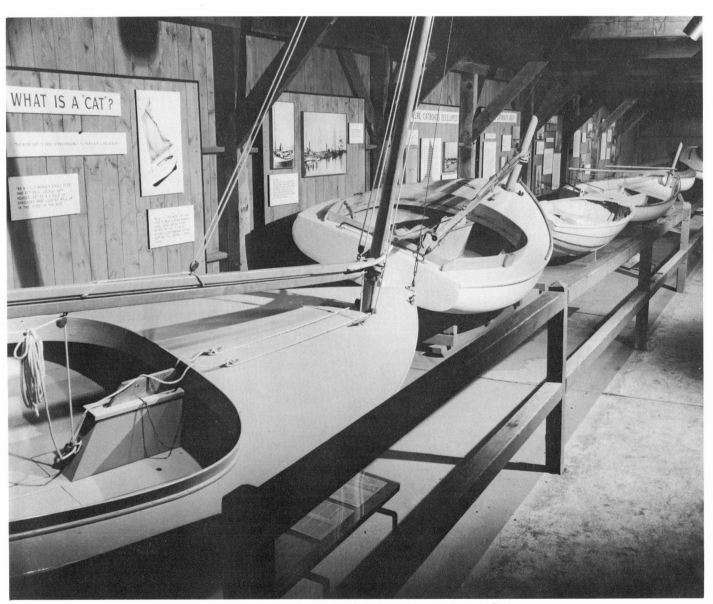

Catboat Exhibit at Mystic Seaport Museum (Photo: Author)

Planking a Beetle Cat at the Concordia Co. (Photo: Author)

Leo Telesmanick, father of more than 3000 Beetles, with boat presented to the Seaport (Photo: C. White Peterson)

Beetles have been sailed since 1921. They are still being built (Courtesy: Norman Fortier)

BEETLE CAT CLASS
HULL # 1448

12′4″ x 6′0″   1971

Beetle Cats are one of the last traditional wooden boats still being built in quantity in the country. Virtually no changes have been made since the first one came out of John Beetle's shop in New Bedford in 1921. Since then more than 3,000 Beetle Cats have been built with a current (1977) annual production of about 60. They are thoroughly enjoyed by sailors of all ages.

STATUS:
Unused, excellent condition.

DONOR:
Concordia Co., Inc.

FURTHER READING:
Blanchard, Fessenden S. *The Sailboat*

Classes of North America. New York: Doubleday & Co., 1973.

Coffey, Burton T. "Traditional Beetle Cat." *National Fisherman*, March, 1971.

Leavens, John M., ed. *The Catboat Book.* Camden: International Marine Publishing Co., 1973.—*Chapter 8 is written by Waldo Howland on the history of the Beetle Cat.*

New England Beetle Catboat Association Handbook.

Pinney, William. "Fifty Years of Beetles." *Classic Boat Monthly*, November 1971.

A compilation of material relating to Beetle Cats has been prepared by Joan Vermilya and is on file in the Seaport's G. W. Blunt White Library. The entire building process has been videotaped and may be viewed at the Seaport.

ACCESSION NO. 71.308

Sanshee *on exhibit (Photo: Author)*

Sanshee *under sail (Courtesy: Ingersoll Cunningham)*

Sanshee (ex-*Kim*)
CAPE COD CATBOAT
14′4″ x 6′7″ ca. 1900–1925

Sanshee is one of about forty such boats built by Charles A. Anderson in his Wareham, Mass., shop. Being small and simple they were easily handled; yet there was a good bit of room in their cockpits for a sailing party of several persons. These catboats for daysailing and racing were shrunk-down versions of the working catboats of the Cape Cod area. As one can gather from reading *The Catboat Book*, there were many different models of small catboats by many different builders; and it was rare for a builder not to be the designer as well. *Sanshee*'s builder did build boats to the designs of others on occasion. The well known 59-foot motorsailer, *Nor'Easter*, which he built in 1927, was designed by William H. Hand, Jr.

Upon her arrival at Mystic, *Sanshee* was sailed in the Seaport's youth training program for a few seasons before being restored as part of the formal catboat exhibit.

STATUS:
Rebuilt and refinished 1971, approximately 80% original, good condition.

DONOR:
Ingersoll Cunningham

FURTHER READING:
"A Catboat for Everyman." *Rudder.* July 1923.—*Shows plans for a 22-foot raised deck cat by Anderson with shape and construction like* Sanshee.

Leavens, John M., ed. *The Catboat Book.* Camden: International Marine Publishing Co., 1973.—*The catboat lover's bible. The basic reference book for catboat lovers since it contains not only much information in itself but has a complete and annotated bibliography of other sources as well.*

The Catboat Association, Bulletin, No. 5, October, 1963 and No. 11, May 1965.—*Contains information about Charles A. Anderson.*

ACCESSION NO. 70.646

Curlew
CAPE COD CATBOAT
13'11" x 6'9"   ca. 1900–1925

Curlew is much like *Sanshee* and was used, no doubt, for pleasure as well. Little is known about her, but there is a claim that she was built by one of the Crosbys. Boats like this one were not large enough to be listed in a yacht register and except for unusual cases they have no recorded history whatsoever. *Curlew* has not yet been examined in detail for those subtleties of construc-

tion which sometimes give a clue to a boat's origin. An old boat in need of repair when she arrived in Mystic; she was exhibited afloat until it was necessary to retire her to storage ashore.
STATUS:
Unrestored, poor condition.

(Photo: Author)
DONOR:
Moses Hay Teaze
FURTHER READING:
Leavens, John M., ed. *The Catboat Book.* Camden: International Marine Publishing Co., 1973.
ACCESSION NO. 60.537

Catboat **Trio** *(Photo: Author)*

Trio
CAPE COD CATBOAT
14'10" x 6'8"   ca. 1880–1912

When information from two reliable sources conflicts, as it does concerning *Trio*'s age, there are but two things to do: the issue can be confronted and resolved if possible (time permitting) or the conflicting information can be passed on in its raw form, as is the case here. In a letter to Mystic Seaport dated February 16, 1960, Wilton B. Crosby (nephew of the builder) says of *Trio*: "Stored here in our yard we have a 15' catboat which was built in 1880 by Wilton Crosby. We believe this boat to be

the oldest Crosby catboat in existence today." Later, during a taped interview with John M. Leavens on August 3–4, 1963, Capt. Malcolm (Uncle Max) Crosby, who was also closely related to the builder, stated: "*Trio* was built in 1912 by Wilton Crosby for Jack Adie."

Regardless of when *Trio* was built, she is a good boat. Huskily built, trimmed with varnished cypress and oak, she is like many of the Crosby

boats. With her high freeboard she should be quite dry and comfortable in a chop, in spite of her small size.
STATUS:
Minor repair, substantially original, good condition.
DONOR:
Wilton B. Crosby
FURTHER READING:
Leavens, John M., ed. *The Catboat Book,* Camden: International Marine Publishing Co., 1973.
ACCESSION NO. 60.499

Frances after restoration, 1970 (Photo: L. S. Martel)

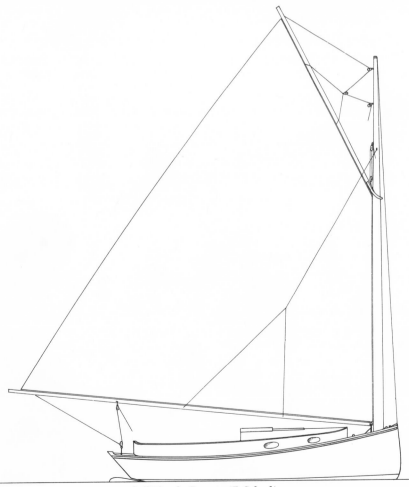

Sail Plan for **Frances** *(E. Schock)*

Frances
(ex-*Buddy*, ex-*Nantucket*)
CAPE COD CATBOAT

20'10" x 9'8"   1900

Frances was designed and built by Wilton Crosby of Osterville, Mass., whose family name is almost synonymous with catboats. She is a classic example of the cruising type with her "punkin" bow, oval cabin and coaming, and natural cypress interior. Her inboard rudder was preferred at Nantucket where *Frances* spent most of her life.

STATUS:
Restored 1971, approximately 70% original, good condition.

DONOR:
Stephen Peabody

FURTHER READING:
Barnard, William Lambert. "The Working Boats of New England, The Cape Cod Catboat." *Boating*, 1907. Reprinted in *WoodenBoat*, Vol. 1, No. 3, 1975.

Leavens, John M., ed. *The Catboat Book.* Camden: International Marine Publishing Co., 1973.—*Has chapters on restoration of* Frances *and on building a new boat to her design.*

The Classic Boat. Alexandria: Time-Life Books, 1977.—*Contains wonderful perspective drawings of* Frances' *building sequence.*

ACCESSION NO. 59.1221

WOODS HOLE SPRITSAIL BOAT

Spritsail boats started out as working craft and are related to the well known catboats of Cape Cod. The Woods Hole fishermen, working in an area known for its fierce current, often had to row rather than sail in order to work the eddys and slack waters in a calm. Thus the boats are proportionally narrower and generally smaller than the typical Cape Cod cat. Many spritsail boats were kept in the Eel Pond at Woods Hole and frequently had to douse their rigs to get under the bridge; the spritsail itself and an open cockpit with a hinged bale at the mast partners made this easier.

The Woods Hole Yacht Club sponsored races for spritsail boats with the fishing type in Class B while those designed especially for racing were in Class A. Nathanael G. Herreshoff designed *Gee* to race in Class A. To give her the largest sail that the rules allowed, he stepped the mast in a socket mounted on the stem head.

WOODS HOLE SPRITSAIL BOAT

13′4″ x 6′0″   1913 or 1914

This boat was built by E. E. Swift, a Cape Cod cabinetmaker, for his brother, who died before Swift completed his work. The nearly finished boat lay in the family barn for fifty-one years before the donors obtained her. (Mrs. White is Swift's grandniece.) The boat is exquisitely built, has never yet been used, and still shows the priming coat of paint on her hull. Along with her came Swift's tools and toolbox, his molds, patterns, and half models; one of which is probably of this boat. Another may be of *Suzie,* built a few years earlier and now (1977) owned by Mr. Robert H. Baker of Warren, R. I.
STATUS:
Uncompleted, original rig missing, excellent condition.
DONOR:
Mr. and Mrs. John E. White
ACCESSION NO. 68.2

Woods Hole Spritsail Boat as she appeared in 1975 (Photo: Author)

FURTHER READING: FOR 68.2, 60.196 & 73.40:

Costelloe, Sylvester. "The Building of the Woods Hole Spritsail Boat." Paper for Work Study Class, 1972, on file in Registrar's Office at Mystic Seaport.

Haln, Jan. "One of the Last Spritsail Boats Leaves Home as a Museum Piece." *Maine Coast Fisherman*, May 1960.

Herreshoff, L. Francis. *The Compleat Cruiser*. New York: Sheridan House, 1963.

Palmer, H. V. R. "Those Handy Little Boats." *Skipper*, December, 1968.

Mystic Seaport has considerable unpublished material relating to spritsail boats which has been compiled in a booklet of source material by Anne and Maynard Bray and is on file in the G. W. Blunt White Library.

Cockpit of Woods Hole Spritsail Boat **Explorer** *in 1970 after refinishing (Photo: L. S. Martel)*

Explorer (ex.-*T. C.*) WOODS HOLE SPRITSAIL BOAT

13'3" x 5'11"   ca. 1890

Crosby of Osterville built this boat for Oliver Grinnell or Henry Dyer (records conflict) and she is doubtless more typical of the working spritsail boats than Swift's boat (68.2) is. Nearly destroyed by the 1938 hurricane, she was purchased in 1943 by the donor.

To economize on material, the slot for her centerboard was formed by wedging open a saw kerf in the keel timber, which is softened first by steaming. This feature as well as the half-dovetailed frame ends are familiar Crosby innovations.

STATUS:
Restored 1960–1970, approximately 75% original, rig missing, good condition.

DONOR:
Dr. Alfred C. Redfield
ACCESSION NO. 60.196

Sandy Ford WOODS HOLE SPRITSAIL BOAT REPRODUCTION

13'3" x 5'11"   1973

Sylvester Costelloe of Mystic Seaport's Small Craft Laboratory duplicated

Carrie, *Woods Hole Spritsail Boat much like* **Explorer** *and* **Sandy Ford,** *underway off Woods Hole near the turn of the century (Photo: Source unknown)*

Sandy Ford *launching, 1973 (Photo: M. A. Stets)*

Explorer and named her after his home town in Ireland. She is fitted with a small Marconi mizzen as described for the working spritsail boats by one source. But in sailing, it is more of a nuisance than help and often is left ashore.

STATUS:
In use, excellent condition.

DONOR:
Mystic Seaport built reproduction of 60.196.

ACCESSION NO. 73.40

Kingfisher II *in 1975 (Photo: K. Mahler)*

Kingfisher II
NEWPORT CATBOAT
17'0" x 8'3"　　　　　　　ca. 1895

One of two extant Newport-type catboats, *Kingfisher II* was built on Long
Wharf in Newport, Rhode Island, by
either T. Stoddard or one of the Barker
brothers. Edward W. Smith, Sr., her
original owner, sailed her as a yacht
and used her when he made the wonderful glass plate negatives of Newport's
waterfront scenes. These plates, many
of which are published in his son's book
Workaday Schooners, are preserved at
Mystic Seaport.

Traded to Lars Larson in 1905, she
was later rebuilt by him with a cuddy
cabin and vertically staved coaming for
a day charter boat in Newport Harbor.
In 1941 Henry A. Wood III, nephew of
E. W. Smith, Sr., purchased the boat
from Larson's estate and she remained
in the family until she was donated to
the Seaport.

STATUS:
Unrestored, approximately 50% original, fair condition.

DONOR:
John Benson

FURTHER READING:
Smith, Edward W., Jr., compiler. *Worka-
day Schooners*. Camden: International
Marine Publishing Co., 1975.

ACCESSION NO. 75.5

Kingfisher II *at Newport, Rhode Island, ca.
1900 (Photo: Edward W. Smith Collection)*

Unidentified Lady at the helm of
Kingfisher II *(Photo:
Edward W. Smith Collection)*

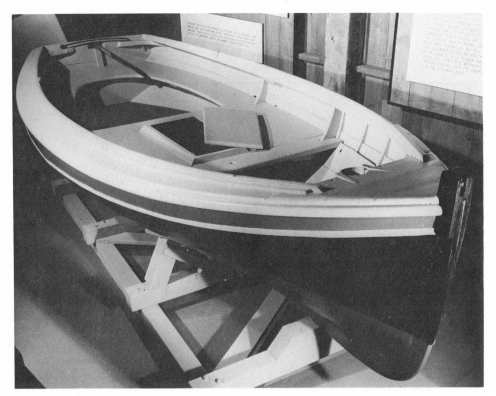

Button Swan after restoration, 1975 (Photo: Author)

Button Swan
NEWPORT FISH AND LOBSTER BOAT
12′3″ x 5′4″   ca. 1880

"The *Button Swan* is an excellent example of the type of boat that originated on Long Wharf in Newport. Here, since the early 1800s, and perhaps even earlier, were congregated the simple shops of a dozen or more Newport small boat builders who specialized in pull boats, skiffs, ship's yawl boats and similar craft.

"Historically, the *Button Swan* is unique. She is a well-preserved, well-documented example of a small working catboat with roots reaching back 125 years or more. She was made by a man who is known to have built boats of this very type at Newport over 100 years ago for commercial fishing in Narragansett Bay and the offshore waters of the open ocean around Brenton's Reef and from Sakonnet to Point Judith. She represents an evolution in small boat design from earlier types built at Newport and

the surrounding area .... Certainly no existing catboat in the Mystic Seaport collection or elsewhere can equal her in importance and she deserves to be ranked with Bob Fish's famous 1851 catboat *Una* that gave her name to the unaboat as catboats are known in England and on the continent.

"Button Swan [who built the boat and for whom she was later named] was born at Newport in 1833. Although his real name was William Henry Munroe, being short of stature, he readily acquired the nickname of 'Button.' From youth he was closely associated with his uncle John Swan, a well-known Newport fisherman, and this association led to his nickname 'Button Swan,' a name by which he was universally known in Newport all his life." *John M. Leavens, The Catboat Association Bulletin, No. 46, March, 1975.*

STATUS:
Restored, approximately 75% original, rig missing, good condition.

DONOR:
Given in memory of Capt. Fernando Fowler by the children of Cyrus P. Brown.

FURTHER READING:
Brewer, John Peter. "Button Swan Revisited." *The Catboat Association Bulletin,* No. 52, March 1977.—*Description of the thorough restoration by Robert H. Baker of* Button Swan *during 1974–75. This work was sponsored by The Catboat Association.*

Chapelle, Howard I. *American Small Sailing Craft.* New York: W. W. Norton & Co., 1951.—*Appears as Providence River Catboat.*

————. *The National Watercraft Collection.* Washington: Government Printing Office, 1960.—*Appears as Providence River Catboat.*

LaFarge, Christopher Grant. "Button Swan." *Scribner's Magazine.* October 1921, Vol. LXX No. 29. Reprinted in *The Catboat Association Bulletin,* No. 46, March 1975.

A rigged model of a similar boat is in the Seaport's collection.

ACCESSION NO. 49.145

Kingfisher, shown here, was a Newport Fish and Lobster Boat similar to **Button Swan** *(Photo: Edward W. Smith Collection)*

CONNECTICUT RIVER DRAG BOAT

15'7" x 5'9"

With two men in boats like this, shad fishing was carried on in the lower Connecticut River. At night a drift net was set from each boat which was carried by the current to the end of the reach, then hauled back aboard, hopefully loaded with fish. The shad would then be removed and the boat rowed upstream to the head of the reach where a new set would be made. Sail was not used during the fishing process, but most boats were fitted with centerboards and sailing rigs. It is believed these craft did do considerable racing and daytime sailing. Drag boats were undecked aft since the net is worked over the stern.

STATUS:
Restored, approximately 60% original, rig missing, good condition.

DONOR:
Marshall Watrous

FURTHER READING:
Barten, Isabel. "The Search for the Shad Boat." *The Log of Mystic Seaport,* January, 1976.

Connecticut River Drag Boat as she appeared in 1975 (Photo: Author)

Chapelle, Howard I. *American Small Sailing Craft.* New York: W. W. Norton & Co., 1951.

Morris, E. P. *The Fore and Aft Rig in America.* New Haven: Yale University Press, 1927.

Several half models of drag boats are in Mystic Seaport's collection, one of which has been drawn up by Chapelle and appears on p. 202 of his *American Small Sailing Craft.*

ACCESSION NO. 59.808

Drag Boats and gear at Hamburg Cove on the Connecticut River, from an old postcard (Courtesy: Mrs. Kenneth D. Plimpton, Jr.)

Old Indian *(Photo: Author)*

Old Indian *when acquired by Paul Stubing. Steam-bent coaming both forward and aft complimented her wineglass stern wonderfully (Courtesy: Paul Stubing)*

Old Indian
CONNECTICUT RIVER DRAG BOAT

16′3″ x 6′1″   ca. 1882

Guilford, Connecticut was reported to be the birthplace of this boat, built there by a man named Hall. After a short working career, fishing for bluefish as well as shad, she was purchased in 1893 by a divinity professor from Yale University. It is likely that she was used by him as a pleasure boat until World War I. Her history after that is cloudy until she was purchased by the donor in 1957, at which time she was still in the Guilford area. Somewhere along the line there was considerable repair which replaced the keel, floor timbers, and most of the frames. A new transom, centerboard trunk, and after deck have also been installed. In spite of her age and all the repair, she has retained her handsome shape and is a pleasure to look at.

STATUS:
Considerable repair including that noted above, fair condition.

DONOR:
Mystic Seaport purchase from Paul Stubing.

FURTHER READING:
(Same as for 59.808)

ACCESSION NO. 76.33

Owner Paul Stubing hauling a lobster trap aboard Old Indian *from waters off Noank (Photo: J. E. Swedberg)*

CONNECTICUT RIVER DRAG BOAT

16′3″ x 6′5″   ca. 1947

This boat was designed by George Stadel and built by Tim MacDonald in Old Lyme, Connecticut. Although of comparatively recent construction, it is evident that she has undergone a number of repairs and alterations.

STATUS:
Considerable repair, poor condition.

DONOR:
Michael Murray

FURTHER READING:
(Same as for 59.808)

ACCESSION NO. 76.56

Connecticut River Drag Boat in 1978
(Photo: Author)

George W. Shiverick (1870–1943), builder of Baclaju *(Courtesy: Mr. and Mrs. Roger Shiverick)*

The Shiverick Shop at Kingston, Mass. (Courtesy: Mr. and Mrs. Roger Shiverick)

Baclaju *(Photo: P. Vermilya)*

Baclaju
DUXBURY CATBOAT

17′0″ x 6′9″   ca. 1922

George Shiverick was a fussy builder and some exquisite yachts of all shapes and sizes left his Kingston, Mass., shop. In his day, however, he wasn't particularly unique because there were many boatbuilders who did superb work in wood. The tragedy is that too few received attention in ways that would record their efforts. Although only a few

Shiverick boats have survived, *Baclaju* and *Vireo* (59.455) being examples, it is fortunate that his builder's half models and some photographs were saved. These were turned over to the Seaport a few years ago by his son, and are worthy of careful study.

Baclaju herself is one of about forty or fifty such boats that once raced from the Duxbury Yacht Club. It is quite certain that she was modeled by her builder who, although living quite close

to the Cape, chose to depart from the standard Cape Cod catboat shape.

STATUS:
Unrestored, approximately 85% original, fair condition.

DONOR:
John W. Fellows

FURTHER READING:
Leavens, John M., ed. *The Catboat Book.* Camden: International Marine Publishing Co., 1973.

ACCESSION NO. 73.726

Great South Bay Catboat in 1975 (Photo: Author)

*Gilbert Smith as a young man
(Courtesy: Suffolk Marine Museum)*

GREAT SOUTH BAY CATBOAT

21′5″ x 7′0″   ca. 1890

This is one of the many catboats designed and built by Gil Smith of Patchogue, Long Island, notable builder of racing sailboats. The catboats of Great South Bay are generally narrower with less freeboard than those of Cape Cod, doubtless because of the smoother water of Great South Bay. Smith usually did away with the plumb stem in his later boats giving them a rounded profile sometimes called a knockabout bow.

STATUS:
Unrestored, some repair, fair condition.

DONOR:
Thomas H. Anderson

FURTHER READING:
Bigelow, Paul. "Gil Smith, Master Boatbuilder." *Long Island Forum*, June–July, 1966.

DeFontaine, W. H., and Paul Bigelow. "Gilbert (Gil) Smith, a Great South Bay Legend." *Yachting*, March, 1966.

Massa, George Farragut. "South Bay Cats." *Rudder*, January, 1897.—*Contains drawings of Smith-built cat* Lucile *drawn by C. G. Davis.*

ACCESSION NO. 60.4

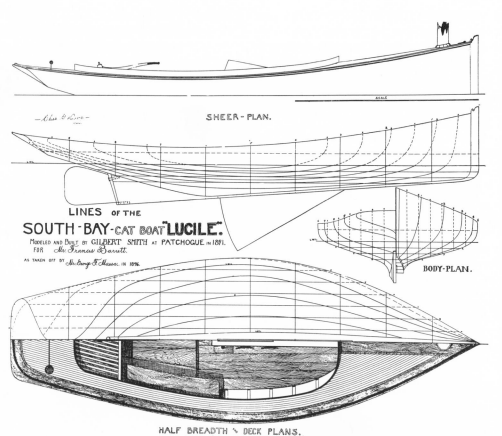

SHEER-PLAN.

LINES OF THE
SOUTH-BAY-CAT BOAT "LUCILE".
MODELED AND BUILT BY GILBERT SMITH AT PATCHOGUE IN 1891.
FOR *Mr. Francis Barrett.*
AS TAKEN OFF BY *Mr. George F. Massa* IN 1896.

BODY-PLAN.

HALF BREADTH & DECK PLANS.

Lines of similar boat appeared in the January, 1897 **Rudder** *(Courtesy:* **Rudder** *magazine)*

Brand new Great South Bay Cats at Gil Smith's boat shop, ca. 1900 (Courtesy: Suffolk Marine Museum)

"Dress ship" on a Great South Bay Catboat, ca. 1900 (Courtesy: Suffolk Marine Museum)

Blue Wing, *similar to the boat in the Seaport's collection (Courtesy: Suffolk Marine Museum)*

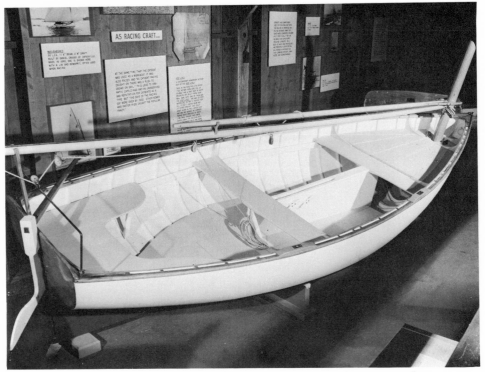

North Haven dinghy in 1975 (Photo: Author)

NORTH HAVEN DINGHY
14'3" x 4'10"

These dinghies are considered the oldest one-design class in the country, having been first raced in 1887. They still compete each summer in their home waters, the Fox Island Thoroughfare between the islands of Vinalhaven and North Haven, Maine. The origin of this particular boat is uncertain but she was probably built sometime after 1900. Another boat of this class is preserved at Penobscot Marine Museum, Searsport, Maine.

STATUS:
Restored 1972, approximately 90% original, excellent condition.

DONOR:
George Lewis

FURTHER READING:
Blanchard, Fessenden S. *The Sailboat Classes of North America.* New York: Doubleday & Co., Inc., 1968.

Brown, C. Pennington. "The North Haven Dinghies." *Down East,* August, 1974.

Slaughter, Sam C. "Age Before Beauty." *Yachting,* July, 1952.

———. "Three Score and Ten." *Yachting,* April, 1959.

White, Anne B. "Over the Years." *Down East,* August, 1974.

ACCESSION NO. 71.383

North Haven dinghies racing in 1973 (Photo: Author)

FOUR HERRESHOFF DINGHIES

(1) JOB #3403

11'6" x 4'1"   1905

"Job 3403 was an '11'6" Boat for Sailing and Rowing. Model of *Columbia*'s Lifeboat Reduced 10/12 scale'; it was ordered on 6 February 1905 for W. B. Duncan, Jr. As far as I can make out 50 boats were built to this design, the first in 1901 and the last in 1922." *From a letter—William A. Baker, Hart Nautical Museum, to J. Revell Carr, Mystic Seaport, 24 September 1974.*

A replica was built by Barry Thomas of Mystic Seaport's Small Craft Lab in 1975, utilizing the Herreshoff Co.'s construction methods. The monograph by Thomas (see Further Reading) describes this building process in detail.

STATUS:
Original including sail, excellent condition.

DONOR:
George Nichols, Jr., M.D.

FURTHER READING:
Herreshoff, L. Francis. *The Common Sense of Yacht Design.* New York: The Rudder Publishing Co., Inc., 1946.—*See chapter entitled "Small Craft."*

Thomas, Barry. *Building the Herreshoff Dinghy: The Manufacturer's Method.* Mystic: Mystic Seaport, Inc., 1977.

ACCESSION NO. 74.930

Herreshoff sailing dinghy Job #3403 in 1975 (Photo: K. Mahler)

Barry Thomas tries out his replica of a Herreshoff dinghy (built in 1975) (Photo: K. Mahler)

17

(2) JOB #18152

12′9″ x 4′7″   1928

This dinghy was modeled by N. G. Herreshoff and built by the Herreshoff Manufacturing Co. The original half model, now in possession of the donor, has pencilled on its back "12 ft sailing dinghie for *Shuttle.* NGH. Coconut Grove 1928." *Shuttle* was a 70-foot twin screw commuter launched in 1928 by the Herreshoff Manufacturing Co. for the donor's father, Junius S. Morgan.

STATUS:

Unrestored, mostly original, fair condition.

DONOR:

John P. Morgan II

FURTHER READING:

Yachts by Herreshoff. Herreshoff Manufacturing Company. Bristol: Privately printed, probably 1935.—*Shows photograph of* Shuttle *with what appears to be this boat on deck.*

ACCESSION NO. 73.89

Herreshoff sailing dinghy Job #18152 in 1975 (Photo: Author)

Herreshoff sailing dinghy #1318 in 1975. Note custom wood frame trailer and provision for stowing spars and oars while in transit (Photo: Author)

(3) HULL #1318

14′1″ x 4′11″   19

Conceived by N. G. Herreshoff 1934, one of his last designs (at a eighty-six), and built especially for M Morgan early in 1935, this boat featu a free-standing two-piece pivoting ma rope steering, and wishbone boom w lever-operated draft control for the sa

STATUS:

Unrestored, original, excellent con tion, on its original Herreshoff traile

DONOR:

Henry S. Morgan

FURTHER READING:

Correspondence between N. G. Herresh and Henry S. Morgan containing much the rationale for the design of this boat a her fittings is on file in the Registrar's Off at Mystic Seaport.

ACCESSION NO. 74.1058

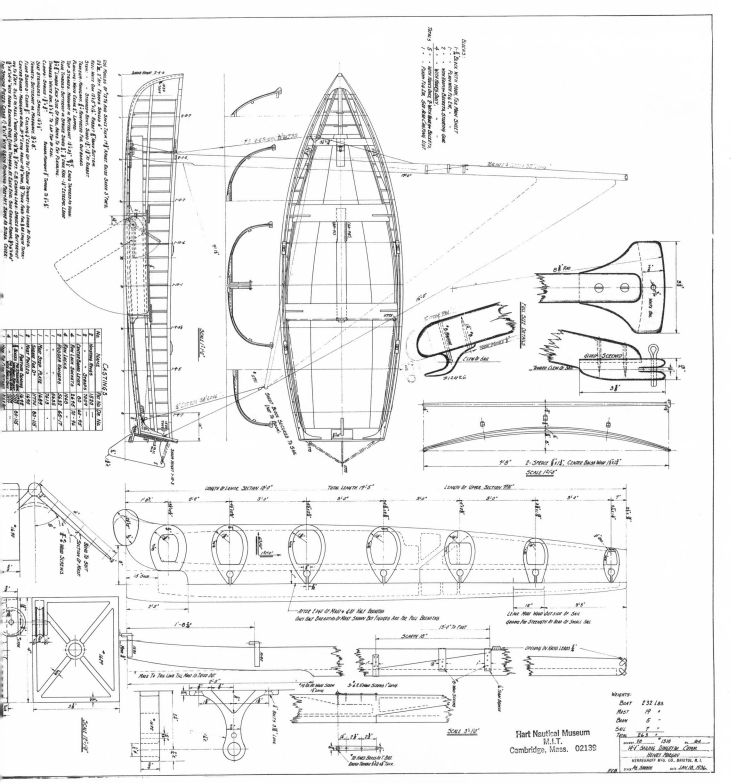

Herreshoff Manufacturing Co. plan for Hull #1318
(Courtesy: Hart Nautical Museum, M.I.T.)

19

Amphi-Craft, Hull #1388 on her custom trailer (Photo: Autho...

Amphi-Craft in 1976 (Photo: J. Deupree)

(4) AMPHI-CRAFT, HULL #1388

13′1″ x 4′9″   ca. 1936

The Great Depression was in full swing when, in the later years of its existence, the Herreshoff Mfg. Co. turned most of its effort to the building and promotion of smaller boats. This Amphi-craft is an example; she could be sailed, rowed, or fitted with an outboard motor and the fact that she was sold with a custom trailer made her an appealing item for "Mr. Everyman." Such a concept was indeed a far cry from earlier times when wealthy yachtsmen came to the Herreshoffs for 40-foot daysailers and 72-foot one-designs. The Amphi-crafts were designed by N. G. Herreshoff's oldest son, Sidney, who developed a number of other interesting boats for the Herreshoff Co. during this time.

STATUS:
Original, complete with its Herreshoff trailer, good condition.

DONOR:
Rudolf F. Haffenreffer IV

FURTHER READING:
Yachts by Herreshoff. Herreshoff Manufacturing Company. Bristol: Privately printed, probably 1935.—*Contains advertising material for the Amphi-craft.*

ACCESSION NO. 75.461

A page from the Herreshoff Manufacturing Company catalo...

The **Amphi-Craft** trailer is designed to minimize the lifting and simplify the fastening required to secure this boat for transportation.

All spars, rigging and gear can be safely and easily secured inside the hull beneath the canvas tarpaulin which covers the open cockpit when the boat is on the trailer.

The boat was designed for power as well as sail, and is fitted with a re-enforced transom to take an outboard motor. It makes it adaptable for fishing, hunting, camping and picnicking on inland or seacoast waters. A light-weight hooded outboard motor is furnished as an extra.

The **Amphi-Craft** has a centerboard and an adjustable rudder which permits its use in shallow as well as deeper waters.

Oars are conve... stored for those wh... the exhilaration of r... or for auxiliary po... cal...

Herreshoff AMPHI-CRAFT

This recent Herreshoff creation adds a new thrill to your week-ends, opens up thousands of miles of water-ways hitherto inaccessible, and gives those who must live in the city a chance to vagabond at will on their holidays, at such yachting centers as Newport, Lake Placid, or to fish from secluded mountain streams; suitable for hunting, ideal for fishing, the camper or picnicker will find countless recreational and practical uses for this all-purpose boat.

Page Thirty-eight

RATSEY INTERNATIONAL DINGHY

11'4" x 4'9"   ca. 1939

The design is English and the first boats built were called Lymington pram dinghies. In 1930 G. Colin Ratsey brought over the first one which quickly became so popular that many others were imported before the year's end. Henry B. Nevins of City Island, N.Y. was ultimately licensed to build them in this country and this particular boat was built by the Nevins yard. Frostbiting originated with this class and the North American Dinghy Association was organized around these boats in 1932.

STATUS:

Unrestored, original, good condition.

DONOR:

Roberts Parsons

FURTHER READING:

North American Dinghy Association, Yearbook

ACCESSION NO. 65.812

Ratsey International Dinghy in 1975 (Photo: Author)

DYER DINK, #D-223

10'0" x 4'4"   ca. 1937

Philip L. Rhodes designed these dinghies in 1934 to serve both as yacht tenders and to frostbite in Class D of the North American Dinghy Association. About 850 had been built by The Anchorage, Inc., Warren, Rhode Island, when wooden production ceased in 1952.

STATUS:

Unrestored, original, including sail, excellent condition.

DONOR:

Given in memory of Alfred L. and Grace L. Fish by Edith P. Osborne, Doris T. Little, and Winifred T. Gelinas.

FURTHER READING:

Davis, Arthur W. "Jeff." *Yachting in Narragansett Bay 1921–1945.* Providence: Providence Journal Co., 1946.

North American Dinghy Association, Yearbook.

ACCESSION NO. 72.47

Dyer Dink #223 as she appeared in 1975 (Photo: Author)

DYER DHOW, #1–9

9'0" x 4'5"   ca. 1949

In 1942, to fulfill a Navy contract for lifeboats, Bill Dyer, of The Anchorage, Inc., designed this 9-footer built of moulded plywood. Conversion was made to fiberglass in 1949. As of March 1975, nearly 5,000 boats of this type had been built. This Dyer Dhow is believed to be the first boat of the fiberglass series. The Seaport Mariner Training Program uses about 30 of these craft in its sailing activities.

STATUS:

Unrestored, original, rig missing, good condition.

DONOR:

Anonymous

FURTHER READING FOR 65.392 AND 65.391:

Blanchard, Fessenden S. *The Sailboat Classes of North America*. New York: Doubleday & Co., 1968.

ACCESSION NO. 65.392

Dyer Dhow #1–9 in 1975 (Photo: Author)

Dyer Dhow in 1975 (Photo: M. A. Stets)

INTERNATIONAL TWELVE-FOOT CLASS
1–12

11'6" x 4'9"   ca. 1940

"The International 12 was designed by an Englishman whose name, I believe, was Hall. I believe the first boats were built early in 1941 and went to the U.S. Coast Guard Academy. Much like the other boats, the 12' International was converted to fiberglass production during the 1950s, and about the only boats which have been built have been to occasionally replace the Coast Guard Academy fleet, and the most recent ones have been delivered in 1969. In all, only about 150 boats have been built." *From a letter—W. H. Dyer Jones of The Anchorage, Inc. to Maynard Bray, 21 March 1975.*

STATUS:

Unrestored, original, rig missing, good condition.

DONOR:

Anonymous

ACCESSION NO. 65.391

International Twelve-Foot sailing dinghy in 1975 (Photo: Author)

Connecticut River Duck Boat shown without rig in 1975 (Photo: Author)

CONNECTICUT RIVER DUCK BOAT

12'5" x 3'5"

Used for bird shooting, this boat has a centerboard trunk and mast step so it could be sailed to and from the hunting area.

STATUS:

Unrestored, original, good condition, rig missing.

DONOR:

George P. P. Bonnell

ACCESSION NO. 59.208

Barnegat Bay Sneakbox shown here without rig (Photo: Author)

BARNEGAT BAY SNEAKBOX

12′1″ x 4′2″   **ca. 1910**

The sneakbox is another of the many boats designed for bird shooting. This type is unique in hull shape because of its overhanging or so-called "spoon" bow and rounded deckline. Along with a pair of bottom runners, the spoon bow supposedly makes the sneakbox amphibious so that it can sail on ice as well as water. The low freeboard can be easily concealed with grass to hide the boats from the birds.

Either Samuel Perrine of Barnegat, New Jersey, or his son Howard built this particular boat. Sneakboxes in later years have been adapted for racing by yacht clubs in the Barnegat area.

STATUS:

Unrestored, original, rig missing, good condition.

DONOR:

Mr. and Mrs. Ernest H. Fontan

FURTHER READING:

"A Perrine Sneakbox, Famous Boat of Barnegat in Maritime Museum." *Beach Haven Times* (N.J.), May 9, 1962.

Bishop, Nathaniel H. *Four Months in a Sneakbox.* Detroit: Gale Research Press, 1976. Reprint of 1879 edition.

Blanchard, Fessenden S. *The Sailboat Classes of North America.* New York: Doubleday & Company, Inc., 1968.

Chapelle, Howard I. *American Small Sailing Craft.* New York : W. W. Norton & Co., 1951.

Gardner, John. *Building Classic Small Craft.* Camden: International Marine Publishing Co., 1977.

Guthorn, Peter J. *The Seabright Skiff and Other Jersey Shore Boats.* New Brunswick: Rutgers University Press, 1971.—*Well researched history of sneakboxes, both for gunning and racing. Also covers Nathaniel Bishop's influence on its development.*

Herreshoff, L. Francis. *The Compleat Cruiser.* New York: Sheridan House, 1963.

Schock, E. P. "The Barnegat Sneakbox." *Rudder,* February, 1907.

Schoettle, Edwin J., ed. *Sailing Craft.* New York: The MacMillan Co., Inc., 1927.—*Two chapters on history of sneakboxes and their development into racing boats.*

ACCESSION NO. 61.915

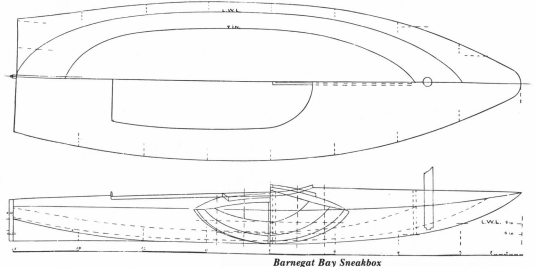

Barnegat Bay Sneakbox
from W. P. Stephens's book **Canoe and Boat Building,** *1889 edition*

DELAWARE DUCKER

15'0" x 4'0"

Known also as Rail-Bird boats, rail gunning skiffs, reed bird skiffs, push skiffs, and pole skiffs, Chapelle has proclaimed these altogether delightful little boats as being the most able of all gunning skiffs for use in rough water. Some were fitted for sail and not a few, beautifully built, came out of high-class boatshops near Philadelphia. Marshes south of that city and further down Delaware Bay abounded with small birds known as rail; market-gunners and sports alike used these boats for their pursuit.

After sailing or rowing from shore two men, one poling from the stern, the other poised to blast away up forward, hunted for a brief two-hour high tide period when the rail birds were flooded out of their hiding places. Then, as Sandys tells us, "The amount of shooting to be obtained largely depends upon the height of the tide and the skill of the boatman. But whether the gun is kept busy for hours or mostly rests upon its owner's knees, the experience is a pleasant one. Properly propelled, the light draught boat steadily glides through or over the yielding cover; a rail flutters up within a few yards and goes wobbling away, its feet hanging as if reluctant to leave their accustomed footing; the flush is indicated by the pusher's automatic cry of 'Mark,' and the squib of the light charge punctuates a kill or a miss—usually the former if the sportsman possesses a moderate amount of skill. The performance may be repeated until from twenty to one-hundred shells have been exploded and the outgoing waters have uncovered so much lush growth that the rail cannot be compelled to rise. It is an easy, restful form of sport, with just enough of sunshine, of the salt strength of the marshes and of mild excitement to do a tired man a great deal of good."

Hermann Simon painting
from the cover of Outing *magazine, September, 1896*

Delaware Ducker, also called a Delaware Bay rail-bird boat,
as she appeared in 1975 (Photo: Author)

These boats' hulls, being symmetrical, pushed with equal ease in either direction. In profile they were much like the contemporary sailing canoe, but being a shooting platform for two standing men when on location, greater beam was needed. Three or four wooden prongs on the dirty end of the push pole kept it from sticking too far into the mud. The Chesapeake Bay Maritime Museum at St. Michaels, Maryland, has another fine boat of this type and interested persons would do well to examine it.

This was John B. York's boat and was given to the Seaport, fully equipped even to an awning and tent for her cockpit, by his grandson.

STATUS:
Original, good condition.

DONOR:
John J. York, Sr.

FURTHER READING:
Chapelle, Howard I. *American Small Sailing Craft.* New York: W. W. Norton & Co., Inc., 1951.

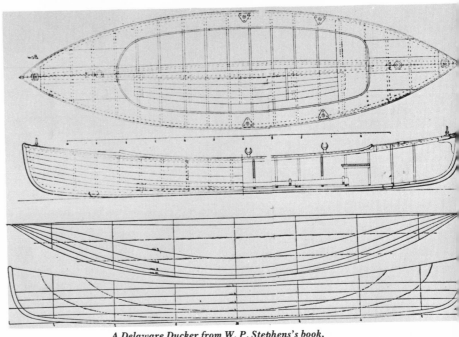

A Delaware Ducker from W. P. Stephens's book,
Canoe and Boat Building, *1889 edition*

Guthorn, Peter J. *The Sea Bright Skiff and Other Jersey Shore Boats.* New Brunswick: Rutgers University Press, 1971.

Sandys, Ed. W. "Rail and Reed Bird." *Outing,* September, 1896.

Stephens, W. P. *Canoe and Boat Building.* New York: Forest and Stream Publishing Co., 1889.

ACCESSION NO. 69.821

Oriole as she appeared in 1975 (Photo: Author)

Oriole
DELAWARE DUCKER

15'1" x 3'8"

Some very fine workmanship went into this boat and it wasn't wasted either, because her shape was worth all the time it took fussing over her. Her history and builder are not known.

STATUS:
Original, fair condition.

DONOR:
Samuel W. Burgess

FURTHER READING:
(Same as for 69.821)

ACCESSION NO. 69.208

DELAWARE DUCKER FROM DELAWARE BAY

14'10" x 3'10"

Unlike the other two boats of this type in the Seaport's collection, this boat is not rigged for sail; perhaps this is why she needed no side decks or coamings. It is this boat that Peter Guthorn pictures in his *Sea Bright Skiff* on page 184, and which he says was found at Cape May, New Jersey in 1968 by the donor.

STATUS:

Original, fair condition.

DONOR:

John Dubois

FURTHER READING:

(Same as for 69.821)

ACCESSION NO. 69.98

Delaware Ducker in 1975 (Photo: Author)

Brownie
SEAFORD SKIFF

12'7" x 4'2"   ca. 1883

Brownie and her once-numerous sisters were used by guides and New York sportsmen in the waters of Great South Bay, New York, and environs for hunting and fishing. In spite of a small sail area these boats are fast due to their exquisitely modeled hulls. Charles Verity is believed to have built this boat.

STATUS:

Unrestored, original, good condition.

DONOR:

G. Gorton Baldwin

ACCESSION NO. 62.674

Brownie as she appeared in 1975 (Photo: Author)

Ro Ro
SEAFORD SKIFF

13'6" x 4'4"

In spite of being heavily built, this hunting skiff is a very handsome model. Although the Seaford skiff took its name from and is supposed to have originated near Seaford, Long Island, most surviving boats bear a close resemblance to the melon seed type of boat from New Jersey waters. This boat with its skeg construction seems particularly like the melon seed. Her building date is not known, but her framing method with the frame faces being square to the boat's centerline would indicate that she is a very old boat.

Seaford skiff **Ro Ro** *in 1978 (Photo: Author)*

STATUS:
Hull has been stripped of paint and is dried out and weak, poor condition.

DONOR:
Morgan Bowman MacDonald III
ACCESSION NO. 76.149

SEAFORD SKIFF
REPRODUCTION

14'7" x 4'3"   ca. 1948

This is one of about forty reproductions of an 1880 boat by Samuel Gritman all built by Paul A. Ketcham, Amityville, L.I. They provided residents with an inexpensive and lively racing craft, and one of local historic origin.

STATUS:
In use, excellent condition.

DONOR:
John O. Zimmerman

FURTHER READING FOR 62.674, 72.264 AND 76.149:
Martin, Humbert O. "The Seaford Skiff." *The Amityville Record*, October 11, 1962.

Thomas, Barry. "The Melon Seed and the Seaford Skiff." *The Log of Mystic Seaport*, Summer, 1974.

Weeks, George L., Jr. "The Seaford Skiff." *Yachting*, January 1952.—*Good history by one who was there during some of it.*

ACCESSION NO. 72.264

The Seaford Skiff reproduction is frequently in use during the sailing season (Photo: Author)

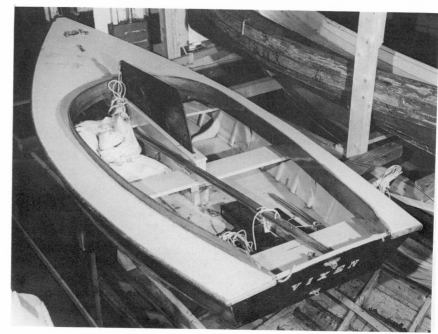

Cotuit skiff **Vixen** *in 1975 (Photo: Author)*

Vixen
COTUIT SKIFF

14'6" x 5'5"   1948

These are the class boats of the Cotuit
(Mass.) Mosquito Yacht Club and have
been raced there each summer by
young people since before 1910. Although *Vixen* was built by Cecil Bigelow
(the famous schooner *Niña* was built by
his father) to plans drawn up by J. Murray Watts, the original fleet was built
without any drawings at all. Stanley
Butler produced most of them and later
on Watts measured one of his boats, the
Scamp, from which his drawings were
made.

STATUS:
Unrestored, complete, good condition.

DONOR:
Dr. Benjamin V. White

FURTHER READING:
Cotuit Mosquito Yacht Club. *Summary of
Yachting Activities.* Cotuit: Privately printed
by C.M.Y.C.

ACCESSION NO. 73.407

Cotuit skiffs racing (Courtesy: Benjamin V. White)

W. B.
SHARPIE-SKIFF

15′9″ x 5′1″   ca. 1888

W. B. looks like the working sharpie-skiffs once used by the oystermen of Fair Haven, Conn., but the donor, who owned her since new, always used her for pleasure. He states she was scaled down from the large (35-foot) sharpies. *W. B.* is fitted with three mast steps for either a one- or two-masted rig.

STATUS:

Approximately 75% of the bottom was replaced and other repairs were made in 1967, fair condition.

DONOR:

Winchester Bennett

FURTHER READING:

Connecticut, State of. *Shell Fish Commission Report, 1901.—Page 47 shows photographs of commercial sharpie skiffs under sail.*

ACCESSION NO. 51.4206

W. B. rigged as a small oyster sharpie-skiff (Photo: K. Mahler)

*Under original ownership, **W. B.** was sailed either as a cat or a cat-ketch, the latter with two masts (Courtesy: Mrs. W. E. Hoblitzelle)*

SHARPIE-SKIFF

14'6" x 4'4"

Although at first glance this boat appears to be a cross-planked flat iron skiff, she is not. Her bottom planking runs fore and aft, like a dory. Nevertheless, she would be an easy boat to build and would be quite weatherly on account of her high freeboard and wide afterbody. She was built to sail as well as row, once having had a centerboard trunk (now removed) and is fitted with three mast steps so she could be rigged either with one or two masts.

STATUS:
Some repair, fair condition.

DONOR:
Edward A. Ackerman

ACCESSION NO. 76.73

Sharpie-skiff in 1978 (Photo: Author)

WHITEHALL-TYPE

11'0" x 4'1"

Unfortunately, nothing is known about the origin or original appearance of this beautifully shaped craft, but it is interesting to speculate and her sail plan has been developed on just that basis.

STATUS:
Relic, hull only.

DONOR:
Russell Clark

FURTHER READING:
Gardner, John. "Comments Here & There." *National Fisherman*, February, 1973.— *Describes acquisition by Mystic Seaport.*

ACCESSION NO. 73.22

*Cat-rigged Whitehall type
in 1975 (Photo: Author)*

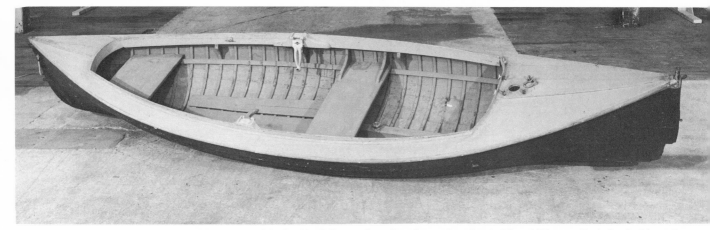

Double-ended sailboat in 1978. The trunk for her "radix" centerboard can be seen just ahead of the middle seat. She is fitted with outrigger oarlocks (Photo: Author)

HALF-DECKED DOUBLE-ENDED SAILBOAT

13'11" x 3'9"   ca. 1900

With her two quite different rigs, a boat like this must have been a fun one to own. In addition to the lug rig shown, she has a big gaff sloop rig which requires a bowsprit for the tack of its jib. Whether she is one of a kind or part of a class or type is not known, although perhaps further research will turn up more someday. In his *Canoe and Boat Building*, W. P. Stephens shows a similar, but larger, boat in Plate XLVIII called *Clio*. She was the 1887 champion of her class, unnamed in the book, at Toronto Bay on Lake Ontario.

STATUS:

Some repair has been made, poor condition.

DONOR:

Thomas C. Sutton

FURTHER READING:

Stephens, W. P. *Canoe and Boat Building.* New York: Forest and Stream Publishing Co., 1889.

ACCESSION NO. 75.22

In addition to the small lugsail rig shown here, this boat came with a much larger sloop rig carrying a big gaff mainsail and a jib set from a removable bowsprit (Courtesy: Thomas C. Sutton)

Snarleyow in 1975 (Photo: Author)

Sail plan of the catboat Dodge (an almost identical craft to Snarleyow) from C. P. Kunhardt's book Small Yachts, published in 1887. The author had this to say: "The horns of the boom extend some distance forward of the mast. If a tripping line is taken from the fore end of these horns, passed through a block slung at the hounds of the rigging and from thence through a leading block or bullseye at the deck on one side of the boom, the tripping line acts as a purchase to keep the boom down at the outer end when the main sheet is slacked for the purpose of running before the wind. For steering, tiller ropes lead from a yoke forward to a footboard, canoe fashion, leaving the crew with both hands free. An oscillating seat low down accomodates the skipper and this can be slid fore and aft to trim with a passenger on board."

Snarleyow
CUTTER-TYPE

14'11" x 3'8"   1882

This toy-like cutter was designed by John Harvey, one of the leading English designers of the fashionable and larger "plank-on-edge" cutter yachts, and was owned for a number of years by the author-boatbuilder-yachting historian, W. P. Stephens. *Snarleyow* was built in New York by John C. Smith in 1882. It is believed she first appeared looking much like the catboat *Dodge* illustrated in C. P. Kunhardt's book, *Small Yachts;* and that sometime later Stephens changed her rig to that of a cutter. In hull form, *Snarleyow* represents the typical English cutter of the 1870s and 1880s only very much reduced in size.

STATUS:

Unrestored, rig missing, fair condition.

DONOR:

Eleanor Stephens

FURTHER READING:

Kunhardt, C. P. *Small Yachts*. New York: Forest and Stream Publishing Co., 1887.

Stephens, W. P. *Traditions and Memories of American Yachting.* New York: Hearst Magazines, 1945.—*Contains good description of sloop and cutter controversy.*

Yachting, February 1944.—*Contains an obituary of W. P. Stephens.*

ACCESSION NO. 52.498

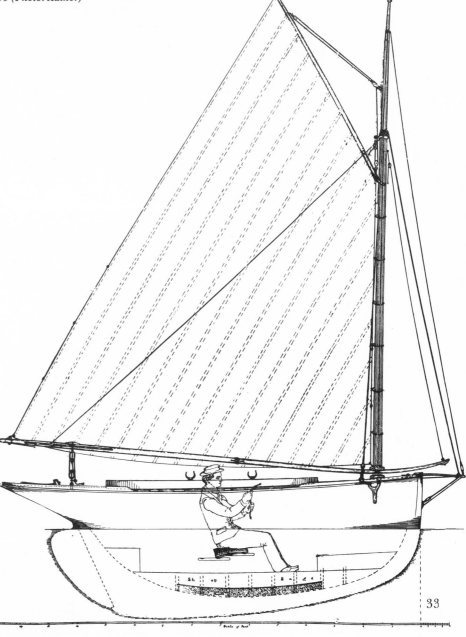

33

Wanda, *similar in appearance to Nixie (Courtesy: Hart Nautical Museum, M.I.T.)*

Nixie in 1975, stripped to her original structure (Photo: Author)

Nixie
CUTTER-TYPE

23′4″ x 7′7″   1885

Nixie is one of the last survivors of Edward Burgess' work. This famous designer developed the successful defenders of the America's Cup, *Puritan*, *Mayflower*, and *Volunteer*, and a great many other yachts during his short but brilliant career. Built originally by William B. Smith, South Boston, Mass., *Nixie* later was rigged as a cutter and was rebuilt for cruising in 1939 by Captain Charlton Smith.

STATUS:
Hull stripped to original, cabin, deck, cockpit, and rig are missing, fair condition.

DONOR:
Given in memory of Edward Burgess by his grandson, Dr. Frederic Tudor.

FURTHER READING:
Atkin, William, and John. *The Book of Boats*. Camden: International Marine Publishing Co., 1976.

Smith, Charlton. "The Re-birth of Nixie." *New England Yachtsman*, 1939.

Yachting, March 1951.—*Contains a biography of Edward Burgess.*

ACCESSION NO. 73.714

Nixie as she looked after her rig was altered the first time, from H. A. Mott's Yachts and Yachtsmen of America, *published in 1894*

Chapter Two
SLOOP RIGGED

Views of Alerion's cockpit and deck layout taken in 1973 (Photo: L. D. Olin)

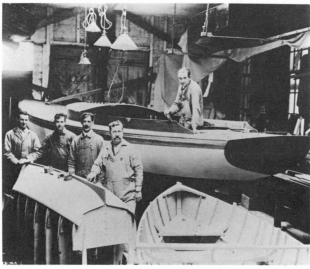

Alerion *in the small boat shop of the Herreshoff Mfg. Co. before launching. The partly planked dinghy was designed to fit upside down over* **Alerion's** *centerboard trunk for shipment to Bermuda. Charlie Sylvester, second from the left, has identified the other workmen, left to right, as Ernest Adler, Sylvester, Henry Vincent, James Clarkson, and Willard Kenney (Courtesy: Clarence Herreshoff)*

Alerion *being weighed on a steelyard before being put overboard at Bristol, Rhode Island (Courtesy: Mrs. Muriel Vaughn)*

Alerion
drawn by S. H. Lincoln, 1978

Alerion as she looked in 1973 at Mystic Seaport (Photo: L. D. Olin)

Alerion III
HERRESHOFF MANUFACTURING CO.
HULL #718

26'0" x 7'7"   1912

The beautiful *Alerion!* She is the favorite of many, and a number of people have told me they return just to see her again. Indeed, she is one of Herreshoff's most exquisite creations. "Mr. Nat" or "Capt. Nat" as N. G. Herreshoff was called, was sixty-four years old when he designed this boat (the third of that name) for himself. His career was perhaps at its zenith and *Alerion*'s beauty and simplicity reflect his genius every bit as much as one of his cup defenders did. After being built by the Herreshoff Manufacturing Co. in Bristol, Rhode Island, she was shipped to Bermuda where "Capt. Nat" spent part of each winter. Just what inspired her shape is not known, but she was a rather distinct departure from his previous designs, most of which had the

longer overhangs and full keels typical of the Universal Rule racers. *Alerion* became an inspiration for her designer, and within the next year or two he came out with the 12½-footers, Newport 29-footers, Fish class, and Buzzards Bay 25s—all with somewhat similar hull shapes. One other boat, *Sadie*, was built in 1914 using *Alerion*'s offsets but with some minor changes. She is now (1977) part of the fleet at the Chesapeake Bay Maritime Museum.

"Mr. Nat" discarded *Alerion*'s original gaff rig after a few years and put a sliding gunter mainsail on her which had a sprit equal in length to the boom and which, when raised, became almost an extension of the mast itself. It is with this rig that she is exhibited.

STATUS:

Refastened and refinished in 1972,

otherwise mostly original, excellent condition.

DONOR:

Isaac B. Merriman, Jr.

FURTHER READING:

Davis, Arthur W. *Jeff Davis's Log.* Providence: Providence Journal Publishing Co., 1937.—*Chapter 14 contains a sketch and anecdote about "Capt. Nat" and Alerion.*

Herreshoff, L. Francis. *The Writings of L. Francis Herreshoff.* New York: The Rudder Publishing Co., 1943.—*Contains an account of an exciting sail from New York to Bristol in* Alerion.

————. *Capt. Nat Herreshoff, The Wizard of Bristol.* New York: Sheridan House, 1953.—*The authoritative biography of Alerion's designer.*

Skerry, Amory S. "Alerion, Capt. Nat's Favorites." *The Log of Mystic Seaport.* September 1969.—*A good write-up by one of her former owners.*

ACCESSION NO. 64.631

Fantasy returning from the Crosby yard in Osterville, Massachusetts where she was restored in the shop in which she was built 56 years before (Photo: L. S. Martel)

Fantasy
WIANNO SENIOR
KNOCKABOUT
CLASS #11

25'4" x 8'5"   1914

Not only are the "Senior boats," as Bill Crosby calls them, still racing in large numbers each summer, they are still being built of wood in the traditional way. H. Manley Crosby designed them and the first batch of 13 boats, which included the *Fantasy*, came out in 1914. Since then more than 150 have been launched from the Crosby Yacht Building and Storage Co. yard. Each winter a few more built in the same shop as the originals are usually added. It was here that *Fantasy* was taken for a restoration in 1970. She had been owned by the donor since new.

Perhaps the most famous Wianno Senior is *Victora #94* which belongs to the Kennedys of Hyannisport and was raced by JFK for many years.

STATUS:
Restored 1970, approximately 60% original, good condition.

DONOR:
James G. Hinkle

FURTHER READING:
Blanchard, Fessenden S. *The Sailboat Classes of North America.* New York: Doubleday & Co., 1968.

Farrell, Jane. *The History of Cape Cod's Own . . . The Wianno Senior.* Privately printed, August 1969.

Gray, F. C., Jr. "The Wianno Senior 1914–1964." *Yachting*, March 1965.

"The Wianno Y. C. One-Design." *Rudder*, April 1915.

ACCESSION NO. 65.820

Fantasy, in the foreground, seems to be doing well in this race with other Wiannos (Courtesy: Wilton Crosby)

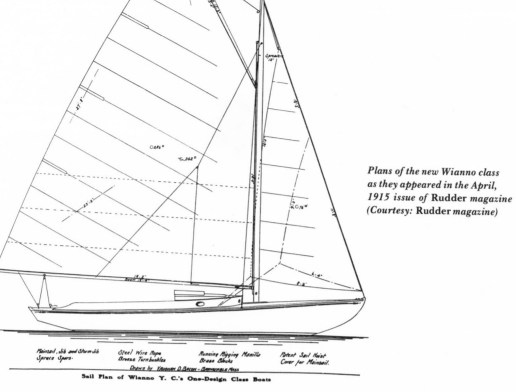

*Plans of the new Wianno class
as they appeared in the April,
1915 issue of* Rudder *magazine
(Courtesy:* Rudder *magazine)*

Mainsail, Jib and Storm Jib   Steel Wire Rope   Running Rigging Manilla   Patent Sail Hoist
Spruce Spars.   Bronze Turnbuckles   Brass Blocks   Cover for Mainsail.
Drawn by YAVONAH D. BACON - BARNSTABLE Mass

Sail Plan of Wianno Y. C.'s One-Design Class Boats

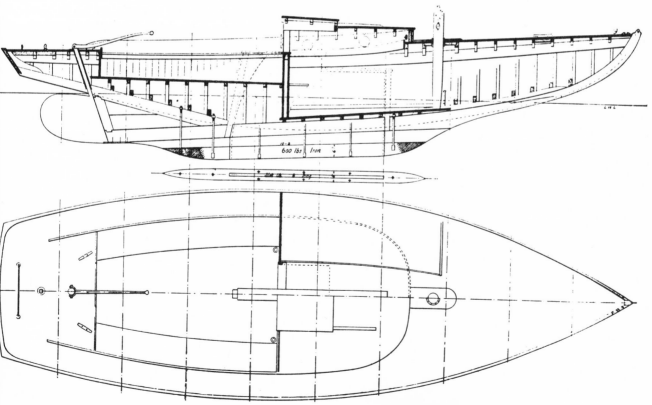

600 lbs Iron

12½ footers under construction in the Herreshoff shops sometime in the 1930s
(Courtesy: Charles Sylvester)

Nettle
BUZZARDS BAY
12½-FOOT CLASS,
HMCo HULL #762

15'10" x 5'10"   1914

In concept, these popular daysailers are not unlike the earlier Newport fishing boat (49.145) in that they do not have centerboards or after decks; the tiller penetrates the wineglass transom; the mast is held by a bail at the partners, and the side decks are unusually narrow. Whether or not her designer, N. G. Herreshoff, was influenced by these local fishing boats with which he was intimately familiar is problematical, but there can be no doubt that his own *Alerion*, modeled two years earlier, inspired the shape of this boat's forebody. The combination of a hollow waterline and full foredeck almost always creates a lovely shape. It was a common one for many nineteenth-century small craft but one which was abandoned when racing rules started to penalize long waterline lengths.

The 12½'s, as the class was usually called, were built in greater number (about 360) and over a longer time span (1914–1943) than any other Herreshoff boat. Since the first batch of boats, which included *Nettle*, a number of changes have been made. For example, some later 12½'s had Marconi rigs, mahogany trim, plywood decks, and alternate cockpit arrangements. The 12½'s are also called Buzzards Bay Boys Boats, Doughdishes and Bullseyes.

Nettle in 1978 *(Photo: M. A. Stets)*

Herreshoff 12½ footer under sail about 1950 (Courtesy: Norman Fortier)

After World War II, when the Herreshoff yard closed down, it first licensed the Quincy Adams yard to build 12½-footers. After 51 boats, that contract was canceled and Cape Cod Shipbuilding took over the building rights, patterns, molds, etc., and went on to build about 30 more wooden boats before switching to fiberglass in the early 1950s. Since then more than 800 fiberglass Bullseyes have been sold by Cape Cod and within the last few years another builder, Edey and Duff, has started production on a somewhat more traditional fiberglass version, called the Doughdish.

Nettle herself was purchased by Charles Francis Adams as a Christmas gift for his daughter, Catherine. Nearly fifty years later, after three generations learned to sail in her, *Nettle* was given to the Seaport by her original owner.

STATUS:
Restored 1975–77, approximately 85% original, excellent condition.

DONOR:
Mrs. Henry S. Morgan

FURTHER READING:
Blanchard, Fessenden S. *The Sailboat Classes of North America.* New York: Doubleday & Co., Inc. 1968.

Thomas, Barry. *Building the Herreshoff Dinghy—The Manufacturer's Method.* Mystic: Mystic Seaport, Inc., 1977.—*Has photos of 12½'s being built at Herreshoffs.*

Yachts by Herreshoff. Herreshoff Manufacturing Co. Bristol: Privately printed, probably 1935.—*Contains advertising material on the 12½'s.*

ACCESSION NO. 63.595

Kittiwake (ex-*Louise*)
HERRESHOFF MANUFACTURING CO.
HULL #678

30'9" x 8'2"   1907

No other boats were built to this model; she was a special boat, designed by N. G. Herreshoff for Louise Tiffany, and cost $1,875 when new. She was purchased in 1944 by W. B. Lockwood who, a few years later, outfitted her with a new Sparkman & Stephens-designed Marconi rig and put on a new deck and cabin. Then as *Kittiwake,* raced mostly by Mr. Lockwood's daughter, Mary, this boat became a consistent winner in eastern Long Island Sound. Her hull is double-planked above the waterline; an unusual feature for so small a boat, but one which has proven itself, since her topsides after all this time are still flawless.

STATUS:
Rig converted to Marconi, in use, good condition.

DONOR:
W. B. Lockwood   ACCESSION NO. 74.929

Kittiwake on her mooring in the Mystic River, 1975 (Photo: Author)

Kittiwake sailing in Gardiner's Bay at the eastern end of Long Island, her home waters for many years (Courtesy: Norman Fortier)

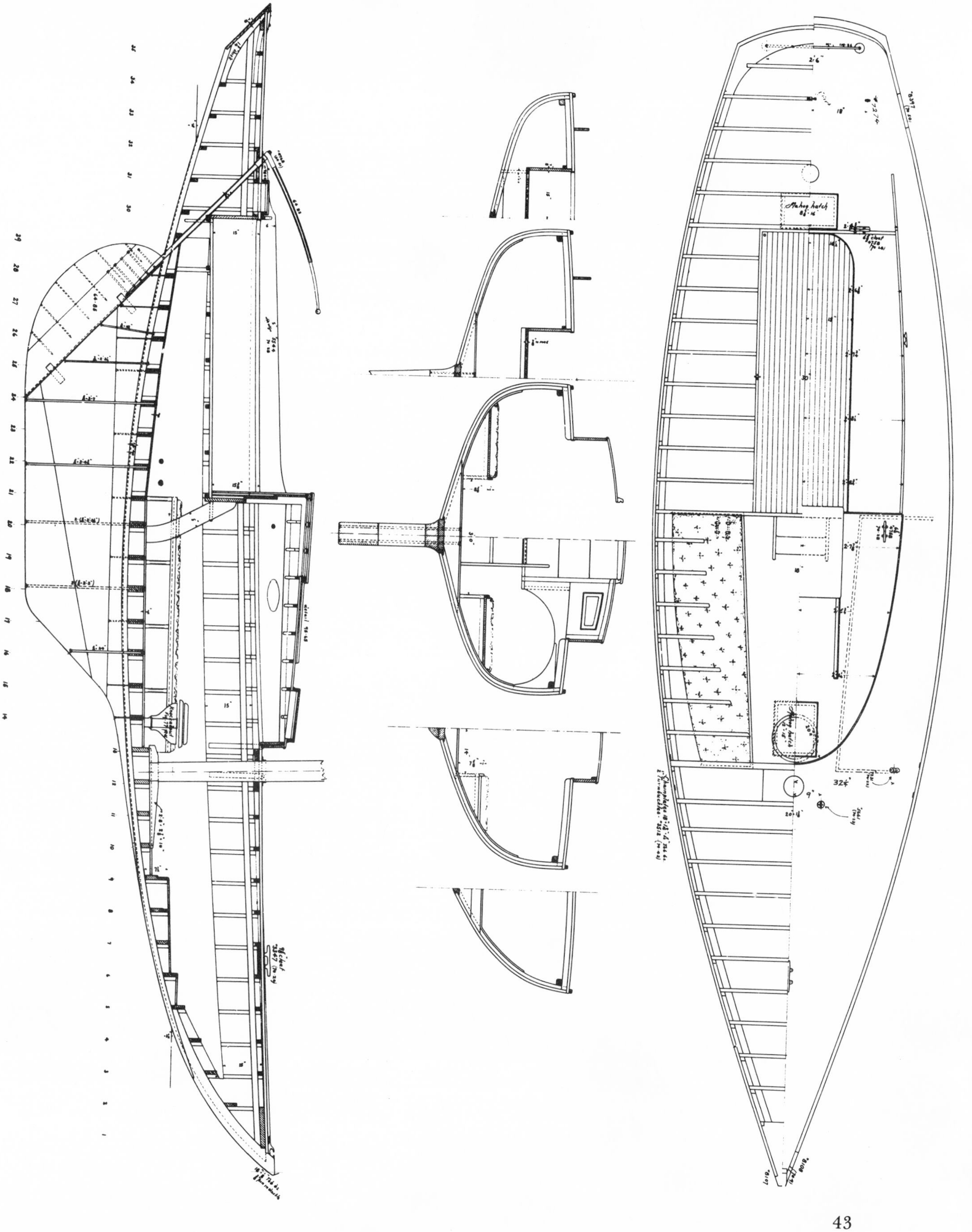

Original Herreshoff Manufacturing Co. construction plan for Hull #678 (Courtesy: Hart Nautical Museum, M.I.T.)

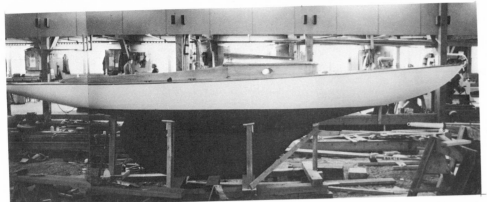

Northeast Harbor "A" #7 boat in 1976 being repainted at Mystic Seaport (Photo: J. Deupree)

NORTHEAST HARBOR "A" CLASS

27'9" x 7'3"   1911

Remarkable is the fact that this boat, which has never had a name, was owned by the Morris family from 1912 until she was given to the Seaport in 1975. Each summer they raced her with the others of her class; but the season was short, lasting usually from July 4th until Labor Day. She was under cover the rest of the year and was cared for by professionals, the reason for her wonderful condition today. This boat and twenty-three others were built for the Eastern Yacht Club of Marblehead, Mass., by the George F. Lawley & Son yard to the design of Edwin A. Boardman. Their racing days in Marblehead were brief, however. After several years they were sold as a class to members of the Northeast Harbor Fleet and other nearby clubs to become the Northeast Harbor "A" Class. As time went on, more boats were built, this time by the Rice Bros. yard in East Boothbay, Maine. With the new boats, the class numbered forty-five and racing was keen up until World War II. Since then the fleet has dwindled, although the class did sail its fiftieth anniversary race with six boats. This boat is perhaps the best remaining one of the class.

STATUS:
Original except for a deck overlay of plywood, excellent condition.

DONOR:
William B. Morris, Thomas D. C. Morris.

FURTHER READING:
Robinson, W. E. "From Knockabout to Raceabout." *Rudder*, May, 1900.

Welles, Edward R. III. "Grand Old One-Design Class Still Races off Northeast Harbor." *Down East*, September, 1964.

———. "A Grand Old One-Design." *Yachting*, July, 1961.

———., ed. *Mariner Notes and Antiques*, Vol. I, No. 4. Southwest Harbor Antique Boat Society, Inc., 1977.

ACCESSION NO. 75.452

"A" boat #7 strapped down in a stiff breeze (Courtesy: William B. Morris)

"A" boat #7 in Mount Desert waters (Courtesy: William B. Morris)

Vireo in 1975 (Photo: Author)

Vireo
KNOCKABOUT

25'5" x 7'0"   1914

Franklin Delano Roosevelt purchased *Vireo* in 1920 (he was then Assistant Secretary of the Navy) and took her to Campobello aboard the destroyer *Hatfield*. The exchange of letters between FDR and John G. Alden, the broker, tells the story:

FDR, June 10, 1920—"I am looking for a small sailboat for my children this summer . . . I do not want to pay more than six or seven hundred dollars."

JGA, June 15, 1920—"Small boats are in great demand and extremely scarce, but I have one little boat, owned by Mr. G. Herbert Yerxa, of Boston, which is available . . . The boat is beautifully built by Shiverick of Duxbury, Mass. . . . I am inclined to think an offer of around $550 or $600 would get the boat."

FDR, June 18, 1920—". . . have telegraphed you to offer $500.00 and go up to $600.00 if necessary . . . expect to go up to Campobello Island on a destroyer and my plan is to take the small boat up there on the destroyer's davits."

The above quotes were excerpted from letters on file at the FDR Library, Hyde Park, N.Y. The donor purchased *Vireo* from the Campobello estate of the late FDR. George Shiverick designed *Vireo* and built her to high standards of workmanship, as was his custom for the many other boats which came from his shop.

F.D.R., some of his children, and friends, aboard Vireo *off Campobello, probably in the summer of 1920 (Courtesy: F.D.R. Library, Hyde Park)*

STATUS:
Unrestored, original, fair condition.
DONOR:
Victor Hammer
FURTHER READING:
Robinson, W. E. "From Knockabout to Raceabout." *Rudder*, May, 1900.
ACCESSION NO. 59.455

Fiddler being moved into her exhibit, 1972 (Photo: L. D. Olin)

Fiddler
HERRESHOFF BUZZARDS BAY 15′CLASS

24′9″ x 6′9″   ca. 1902

N. G. Herreshoff designed this class in 1898 and the first boats sold for $666.66 according to the Herreshoff Manufacturing Co. records. *Fiddler* was built a few years later for Miss Caroline M. Dabney who was also her first skipper, and apparently a good one, for in 1904 she won the championship sponsored by the Beverly Yacht Club of Marion, Mass. As years passed, Miss Dabney became Mrs. Parker and in 1933 her son, Augustin, outdid his mother and the *Fiddler* won the Van Rensselaer Cup, presented to the champion "15" of all Buzzards Bay.

In all, about ninety boats were built to this model, some having ballast keels 6-inches lower and known as Newport 15-footers, and others with Marconi rigs and pointed coamings which came out in 1922 as the Watch Hill 15-footers.

STATUS:
Restored 1971, approximately 65% original, good condition.

DONOR:
Augustin H. Parker, Jr.

FURTHER READING:
Cheever, David. "The Herreshoff Fifteens." *The Log of Mystic Seaport*, Summer, 1972.

Yachts by Herreshoff. Herreshoff Manufacturing Company. Bristol: Privately printed, probably 1935.

ACCESSION NO. 59.1286

Fiddler *with her petticoat crew sailed by her original owner, Miss Caroline Dabney (Photo: Gift of A. H. Parker)*

Fiddler *and others of her class racing in light weather (Photo: Gift of A. H. Parker)*

Pantooset on exhibit in 1955 (Photo: L. S. Martel)

Pantooset
HALF RATER CLASS
26'5" x 7'0"   1907

Built in South Boston, Mass., by W. J. Edwards for use with the steam yacht *Pantooset*, this daysailer is equipped with lifting eyes at each end and was normally carried, along with a variety of other boats, on the larger yacht's davits. The big *Pantooset*, owned by the donor's uncle, came out in 1902. She was designed by W. J. J. Young and built by Bath Iron Works, Bath, Maine.
STATUS:
Unrestored, mostly original, poor condition.
DONOR:
Cleveland Bigelow
ACCESSION NO. 55.1201

When not in use, the Half Rater Pantooset was carried on the davits of the steam yacht whose name she bore. She is shown here with her rig still standing (Photo: Gift of Charles F. and Walter S. Almy)

DAYSAILER "PANTOOSET"

(Photo: C. White Peterson)

Annie
SANDBAGGER RACING CLASS

28'9" x 12'4"   1880

One of *Annie*'s distinctions is that she was the first boat in Mystic Seaport's collection, acquired in 1931. D. O. Richmond modeled her and she was built in his Mystic River shop for Henry Tift of Mystic, Connecticut, and Tifton, Georgia. Racing sandbaggers was a popular sport before 1885 when the overall length alone determined her racing handicaps and one could crowd on as much sail as he thought his craft could carry. With so great a spread of canvas, just to keep from capsizing was a challenge let alone winning the race. The idea was for the large crew to position themselves along with several fifty-pound sandbags far enough windward to balance the press of wind on the sails. Squally weather or frequent tacking called for quick and expert movement; it was exciting sport. Sandbaggers were raced in several classes according to their size; *Annie* raced in class A with the other large boats, while on the other end of the scale were the smaller boats of about 20 feet. Much of the racing and building took place near New York City where the sport originated, but *Annie*'s successful career was in eastern Long Island Sound near where she was built, and in Florida waters where she was shipped during the winter. Like many other aging and outbuilt sandbaggers, *Annie* became a working craft and was in this state when acquired by the museum.

Today she has the spectacular appearance of a sandbagger but can hardly be considered original. A number of changes were made during her early years to make her faster, and in 1902 she was totally rebuilt after a fire. At least twice since then, in 1950 and again in 1968, she was given an almost completely new hull, and her rig was, of course, restored to that of a typical sandbagger. While such major modifications are unfortunate and each time they occur reduce her value, *Annie* still illustrates in full scale an important era in yachting history—when the base of the sail plan was over twice the length of the hull itself!

STATUS:
Restored 1950 and 1968 after earlier modifications and rebuildings, little original, floating exhibit, good condition.

DONOR:
Dr. C. K. Stillman

FURTHER READING:
Chapelle, Howard I. *History of American Sailing Ships*. New York: W. W. Norton & Co., Inc., 1935.

Lynch, Edmund E. "Wood and Weather." *The Log of Mystic Seaport*. Winter, 1969.

Simmons, William E. "The Sandbagger." *Rudder*, March, 1906.

Smith, A. Cary. "Small Yacht Racing in 1861." *Rudder*, October, 1906.

Stephens, W. P. *Traditions and Memories of American Yachting*. New York: Hearst Magazines, 1945.

"The New Haven Boat Race." *The Log of Mystic Seaport*, September, 1968.—*Article reprinted from the* Mystic Press *of October 6, 1881.*

A half model, reputedly duplicating *Annie's* original builder's model, two rigged models, and several half models of sandbaggers are in Mystic Seaport's collection. The Seaport also has W. P. Stephens's collection of manuscripts and drawings, many of which relate to sandbaggers. South Street Seaport, Suffolk Marine Museum, and New York State University each has a sandbagger in its collection.

ACCESSION NO. 31.4

Annie, *or her sister* **Sweetheart,** *in front of her builder's shop on the Mystic River (Photo: Gift of Oscar Cottrell)*

Annie *getting ready to jibe off Race Rock light. Neither she nor her competitor are fitted with a boomkin at this time, indicating that their booms must be shorter and their mainsails smaller than with full racing rig (Photo: Source unknown)*

Galena, *then called* **Fox,** *at Mystic Seaport in 1958 (Photo: L. S. Martel)*

Galena (ex-*Fox,* ex-*Cockle*)
CUTTER-TYPE

18′9″ x 6′5″   1913

James E. Graves of Marblehead, Mass., built this boat to the design of James Purdon. *Cockle*, as she was first named, was to be used as a pleasure boat by a couple of boys. Later she belonged to W. Starling Burgess whose young son, Frederic, sailed her extensively around Provincetown where the family lived at the time. Purdon based his design on the English "plank-on-edge" cutters of the 1880s.

STATUS:
Restored 1969–72, approximately 60% original, floating exhibit, good condition.

DONOR:
James Geier

FURTHER READING:
Darvin, Tom. *The Rudder Treasury*, New York: The Rudder Publishing Co., 1953—*A reprint of pp. 246–47 of* Rudder, *March 1915.*

Tudor, Dr. Frederic. Letter published in *The Log of Mystic Seaport*, Spring, 1972.

ACCESSION NO. 57.537

Galena *under sail in Long Island Sound (Courtesy: Dr. Frederic Tudor)*

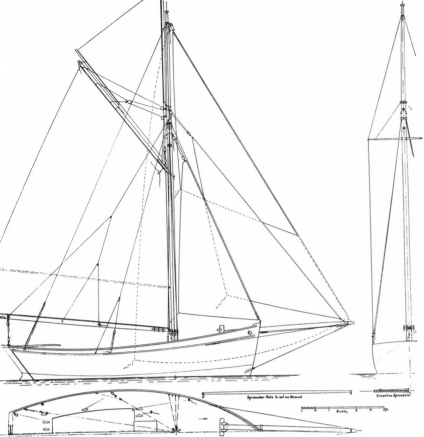

Sail Plan of Cockle, Sixteen-Foot Water-Line Cutter. Designed by J. R. Purdon

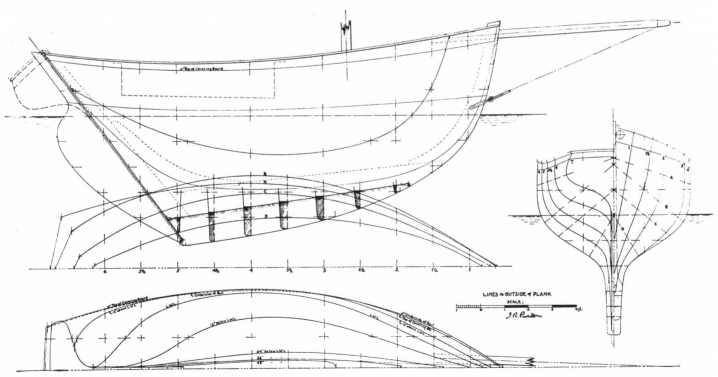

These drawings of Cockle *published in the March, 1915* Rudder *(Courtesy:* Rudder *magazine)*

51

The Star Class sloop Ace *as she appeared on exhibit in 1970 (Photo: L. D. Olin)*

Ace
INTERNATIONAL STAR CLASS #202

22′8″ x 5′10″   1925

When the International Star Class Yacht Racing Association was formed in 1922, there were 110 registered boats. Fifty years later there were 5,763 and today they are still going strong. Good going for a 1911 design!

Francis Sweisguth of William Gardner's office drew the plans, expanding the Bug class of 1906. Until 1921, Stars carried a sliding gunter mainsail and for the next eight years a Marconi sail was used of about the same proportions. The present sail plan was adopted in 1929. Over 500 different builders have produced registered boats.

Ace was built by the Purdy Boat Company of Port Washington, N.Y., for Adrian Iselin II who sailed her to victory in the world's championship her first year and again eleven years later in 1936.

STATUS:
Unrestored, has been extensively rebuilt and rerigged by owner, good condition.

DONOR:
C. Oliver Iselin, Jr.

FURTHER READING:
"One Design Classes." *Rudder*, December, 1911.—*Contains construction and sail plans for original boats.*

Blanchard, Fessenden S. *The Sailboat Classes of North America.* New York: Doubleday & Co., 1968.

Elder, George W. *Forty Years Among the Stars.* Port Washington: Schanen and Jacque, 1955.—*Elder is considered the "father" of the Star Class Association.*

Log of the Star Class. ISCYRA annual publication.

Lucke, Charles E. Jr. "A Quarter Century for the Stars." *Motorboating*, November, 1936.—*Contains photo of Ace.*

———. "The Stars Come of Age." *Yachting*, January, 1932.

Ogilvy, C. Stanley, "50 Years of Stars." *Motorboating*, May, 1961.

Schoettle, Edwin J., ed. *Sailing Craft.* New York: The MacMillan Co., 1927.

"The Star, 61 Years Old and Still in the Olympics." *Sailing*, October, 1972.

ACCESSION NO. 61.912

Ace, early in her racing career before the new rig was put in (Photo: by Morris Rosenfeld Gift of Mrs. C. O. Iselin)

When class was new, plans of Star One-Design Class appeared in December, 1911 issue of Rudder *(Courtesy:* Rudder *magazine)*

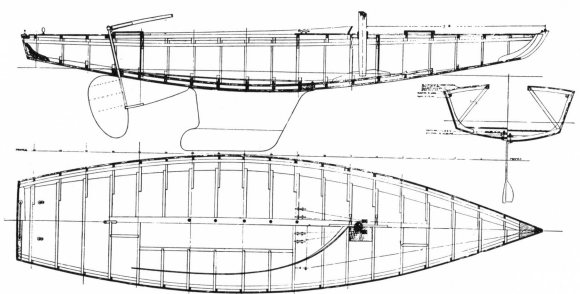

Construction Plan of Star One-Design Class. Dimensions: 22.7 Ft. O. A., 15.4 Ft. W. L., 5.8 Ft. Breadth, 3.4 Ft. Draught, Sail Area 280 Sq. Ft., Ballast 830 Lb. on Keel

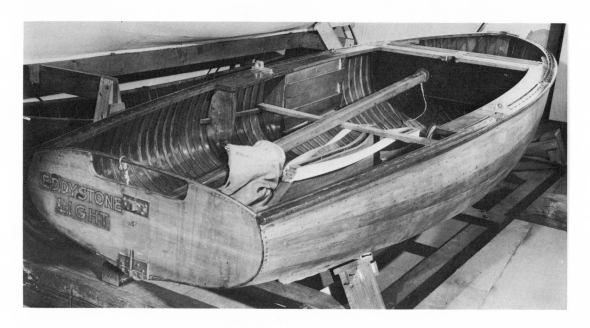

Eddystone Light in 1975
(Photo: Author)

Eddystone Light
INTERNATIONAL 14 FOOT CLASS

14′0″ x 4′6″   1935

The International 14s were probably the first high-performance planing sailboats and held that distinction from 1923, when they were first recognized as a class, until the middle 1950s when other types were introduced. The modern 14-footers originated in England when Uffa Fox became interested in the National 14s, as they were called in 1927, and came out with a radical new design the following season. That year his new *Avenger* won the Prince of Wales Cup and went on to win many other races, at one time having a record of fifty-two wins out of fifty-seven starts. About this time the class became an international one and boats began appearing in other countries. In the United States one of the first four boats built to race in this class was *Eddystone Light*. She and the three others were modeled after one of the Uffa Fox boats and built by the Rochester Boat Works. The International 14 Class is still very active and has about 4000 boats on its register.

STATUS:

Unrestored, substantially original, excellent condition.

DONOR:

Howard V. R. Palmer, Jr. and Richard V. Palmer

FURTHER READING:

Blanchard, Fessenden S. *The Sailboat Classes of North America.* New York: Doubleday & Co., 1968.

Fox, Uffa. *Sailing, Seamanship, and Small Yacht Construction.* New York: Charles Scribner's Sons, 1934.

Palmer, H. V. R. "It Was a Matter of Love at First Sight." *Skipper,* February, 1955.

Schoettle, Edwin J., ed. *Sailing Craft.* New York: The MacMillan Co., 1927.

Vaughan, T. J. *International Fourteen Foot Dinghy 1928–1964, Handbook and History.* London: International Fourteen Foot Dinghy Class Association of Great Britain, 1964.

ACCESSION NO. 74.1030

Eddystone Light under sail in home waters near Rochester, New York about 1935
(Courtesy: H. V. R. Palmer)

Good News III
INTERNATIONAL SNIPE
CLASS #6025

15'8" x 5'1"   1947

In 1931 the Florida West Coast Yachting Association conceived a "trailer class" boat, whose length was not to exceed 16 feet or its sail area 100 square feet, and asked William F. Crosby to draw the plans. Crosby went one better; he not only produced the drawings but published them as a 'How to Build' article in *Rudder* Magazine for which he was editor. It was the Depression; people were turning to smaller boats, particularly ones they could build themselves. Within a year 150 Snipes were built (the name "trailer class" was abandoned in favor of a sea bird, the magazine's usual custom for its 'How to Build' series). When the Snipe Class International Racing Association was formed in November 1932, 250 boats were registered. Five years after Crosby's article, the Snipes were the largest one-design racing class *in the world* with 1,950 boats. In 1966 there were 16,000.

Good News III was a fast boat. Skippered by one-time SCIRA Commodore Ted Wells, she was a three-time winner and a five-time runner up in the national championships. She was built in California by Louis Varalyay.

STATUS:
Fiberglass covered, modern racing gear has been added, good condition.

DONOR:
August F. Hook

FURTHER READING:
Blanchard, Fessenden S. *One Design Classes of North America.* New York: Doubleday & Co., 1968.

Crosby, William F. "How to Build the Snipe." *Rudder,* July, 1931.

———. "The Snipe Story." *Yachting,* June, 1953.

Official Rule Book. The Snipe Class International Racing Association.

ACCESSION NO. 66.304

Good News III *in 1975 (Photo: Author)*

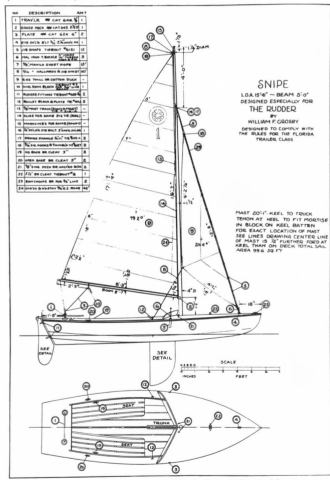

Five years after these plans appeared in the July, 1931 Rudder *magazine with a "How to Build" article, the Snipe Class was the largest one-design class in the world (Courtesy:* Rudder *magazine)*

Emma C. Berry, *rerigged as she was originally, at anchor in the Mystic River in 1971 (Photo: R. A. Fowler)*

Emma C. Berry
NOANK WELL-SMACK
Official No. 7971

45′9″ x 14′8″   1866

Mystic Seaport's interest in acquiring this vessel began in 1966 when, to celebrate her golden anniversary, Capt. Dayton Newton brought her back to the old Palmer yard (now Noank Shipyard) on the Mystic River where she was built. Newton had chartered her from F. Slade Dale for the occasion and shortly after returning to her home port of Bay Head, New Jersey, arrangements were made with Dale for the museum to have her. Once at the Seaport, the *Berry* underwent an extensive rebuilding and restoration, emerging in 1972 with the

Left: Emma C. Berry *arriving off the Mystic River in 1969 after being towed and sailed from Bay Head, New Jersey (Photo: R. A. Fowler)* **Right:** *Taking on a deckload of poles, probably in the Chesapeake in the 1930s (Courtesy: F. Slade Dale)*

sloop rig, wet well, and deck arrangement of her early days. Of her history, Willits Ansel says in his book:

"The *Berry* fished local waters for almost thirty years—some of the time as a fishcarrier rather than a fisherman—and was registered first in Stonington and then in New London. She was re-rigged as a schooner to divide the rig for easier handling in the 1880s. Then in 1894 she was sold to an owner in Maine, where she was to remain for many years. Here she worked as a wet well lobster smack and bait carrier, but as she gradually deteriorated, her employment became more humble. Once she was sold at a public auction in Portland. Finally in 1924 she seemed worn out, 'fished out,' and her owner abandoned her on the mud flats of Beals Island, Maine, where she lay, filling and draining with the tide.

"Many schooners ended thus, but the *Berry* was to be saved two years later by a new owner who afterward said he was attracted by her lines. He pulled her off the mud and patched her. . . . Now she began a new career as a coaster, hauling coal, salt, and dried fish along the coast of Maine. By 1931, with coastal trade suffering from the Depression, the *Berry* was again left in a state of neglect and disrepair."

It was at this time Slade Dale bought her, sailed her to Bay Head and had her rebuilt. He used her as a yacht but occasionally carried some cargo. For the nearly forty years of his ownership she was engineless.

STATUS:
Restored 1969–71, little original, floating exhibit, good condition.

DONOR:
F. Slade Dale

FURTHER READING:
Ansel, Willits D. "Reframing the *Emma C. Berry.*" *The Log of Mystic Seaport*, Winter, 1970.

————. *Restoration of the Smack* Emma C. Berry *at Mystic Seaport, 1969–1971.* Mystic: The Marine Historical Association, Inc., 1973.

Chapelle, Howard I. *The National Watercraft Collection.* Washington: Government Printing Office, 1960.

Dale, F. Slade. "Old Emma Comes Home to Barnegat." *Yachting,* June–July, 1933.

Goode, George Brown. *The Fisheries and Fishing Industries of the United States.* Washington: Government Printing Office, 1887.

Krause, Arthur et al. *"The Emma C. Berry,* June 5, 1866–   ." *The Log of Mystic Seaport,* September, 1969.

ACCESSION NO. 69.231

Billethead from the **Emma C. Berry** *during refinishing in 1970 (Photo: L. S. Martel)*

Oyster sloop **Nellie** *in 1975 (Photo: Author)*

Nellie
OYSTER DREDGING
SLOOP
Official No. 130578

32′7″ x 12′9″   1891

Working in deeper water than the tonging boats and manned with a crew of two or three, boats such as the *Nellie* towed their four or five dredges over the natural oyster beds off the shores of Long Island Sound. With slacked sheets they more or less drifted slowly over the beds with the tide. The boat's heading was controlled with the jib sheet and centerboard; the dredges were hauled back as they became full. During a drift from one end of the bed to the other there might be time for anywhere from two to six hauls; whereupon the boat would be sailed back against the tide to begin another drift. The oysters, dumped on deck from the dredges, were culled from the rocks and other debris between hauls. The oystering season opened in the fall and lasted until spring. Power was not permitted in the boats until 1921 and even then its use was restricted to running between the harbor and the oyster beds. The last sailing dredger had long gone in 1969 when the law was changed to permit dredging under power on natural beds.

Most of the oyster sloops were like *Nellie* with gaff mainsails, cabins aft, and low-sided shallow hulls with centerboards. Most were unlike her, however, in that they had square rather than round sterns. *Nellie* was built in Smithtown, Long Island, and had been converted to a power vessel when the Seaport acquired her. For most of her life she was owned by the Ryle family who oystered from Stamford, Connecticut.

STATUS:
Rig restored 1965, hull restored 1972, approximately 60% original, good condition.

DONOR:
Purchased for Mystic Seaport by Society for the Preservation of the *Nellie A. Ryle.*

FURTHER READING:
Chapelle, Howard I. *American Small Sailing Craft*. New York: W. W. Norton Co., Inc., 1951.

Ingersol, Ernest. *The Oyster Industry: Tenth Census of the United States*. Washington: Government Printing Office, 1881.

Kochiss, John M. *Oystering from New York to Boston*. Middletown: Wesleyan University Press for Mystic Seaport, Inc., 1974.

ACCESSION NO. 64.1551

Nellie *was operating as a powerboat when the Seaport acquired her (Photo: J. M. Kochiss)*

Oyster dredging at Port Chester, New York (Courtesy: Fred Lovejoy)

Estella A.
MAINE SLOOP BOAT

Official No. 201627

34′5″ x 11′9″   1904

Friendship sloops are what these boats are called now, but to the Maine fishermen who used them they were known simply as "sloop boats." Although the Muscongus Bay area was where most were built, other towns besides Friendship produced them. *Estella A.* herself came from Bremen Long Island, Maine. Her builder was R. E. (Rob) McLain whose son, Newell, of Thomaston was an indispensible source of information during the boat's restoration. Needless to say, the term "Friendship sloop" is not used by him.

These boats were built as lobsterboats and often were sailed by one man. Once there were hundreds of them, and they swung from moorings in most every Maine harbor just as the engine-driven lobsterboats do today. Engines were their undoing; as soon as they became dependable there was no need for a sailing hull. During the transition to power around the turn of the century, some of these boats carried small auxiliary engines which were rigged for hauling traps as well as for propulsion. *Estella A.* was so equipped when new, having a two cylinder 9 HP Knox engine.

Used sloop boats became somewhat of a glut on the market in the twenties and thirties as fishermen changed to the more modern power boats. The better ones—those not left on the beach to die—made economical yachts and were purchased and sailed "up to the west'ard" by their new owners. *Estella A.* herself was sold by her original owner, H. J. (Jack) Ames of Matinicus in 1930 to the donor's late husband who sailed her from his Jamestown, R.I. summer home for the next twenty-seven years. During this time her rig was converted to Marconi, outside lead ballast was added, and the cabin was enlarged.

The Gloucester sloop boats possibly were the forebears of these smaller but similar craft. In any event the charm of these boats still keep them popular and was the basis for forming the Friendship Sloop Society in 1961, whose annual Sloop Days have become a well-attended and much-publicized affair. Several stock models are now built of fiberglass and occasionally an amateur will even build one of wood.

STATUS:
Restored 1970–72 by Newbert & Wallace, Thomaston, Maine, little original, floating exhibit, excellent condition.

DONOR:
Mrs. Duncan I. Selfridge

FURTHER READING:
Barnard, William Lambert. "The Working Boats of New England, the Maine Sloop." *Boating,* 1907. Reprinted in *Woodenboat,* November–December, 1974.

Bray, Maynard E. "Good and Simple." Friendship Sloop Days Program, 1971.

Chapelle, Howard I. *American Sailing Craft.* Camden: International Marine Publishing Co., 1975. 2nd edition.

———. *American Small Sailing Craft.* New York: W. W. Norton & Co., 1951.

———. "The Friendship Sloop." *Yachting,* July, 1932.

Duncan, Roger E. "Sloops of Friendship." *Yachting,* February, 1965.

Jones, Herald A., ed. *It's a Friendship.* Rockland: The Friendship Sloop Society, 1965.

———., ed. *Ships That Came Back.* Rockland: The Friendship Sloop Society, 1962.

Kelly, Alice "Friendships Never Die." *Rudder,* July–August, 1946.

McKean, Robert B. "We Build a Friendship Sloop." *Yachting,* December, 1939.

"Old Time Yard and Builder's Son Help Restore '04 Fishing Sloop." *National Fisherman,* January. 1971.

Richards, Joe. *Princess. New York.* Indianapolis: Bobbs-Merrill, 1956.

Roberts, Al, ed. *Enduring Friendships.* Camden: International Marine Publishing Co., 1970.

Taylor, William H. "The Friendship Sloop is Back." *Yachting,* December, 1946.

Wasson, George S. *Sailing Days on the Penobscot.* New York: W. W. Norton & Co., 1949.—*Chapter VI,* Lobster Sloops and Tidal Bores, *describes the sloops used at Isle au Haut.*

Winslow, Sidney L. *Fish Scales and Stone Chips.* Portland: Machigonne Press, 1952.

Most Maine sloop boats were used by lobstermen for hauling traps, from Goode's **Fisheries Report,** *1887.*

Estella A. *sailing in Fishers Island Sound in 1974 after her restoration (Photo: K. Mahler)*

—*Pages 69 and 70 describe the adoption of gasoline engines by sloop boat owners.*

One rigged model of a small Friendship sloop is in Mystic Seaport's collection. Mystic Seaport has considerable unpublished material on sloop boats which, along with much of the above, has been compiled in a booklet of source material by Anne and Maynard Bray and is on file in the G. W. Blunt White Library. A comprehensive report on *Estella A*'s restoration is on file in the Registrar's office.

ACCESSION NO. 57.498

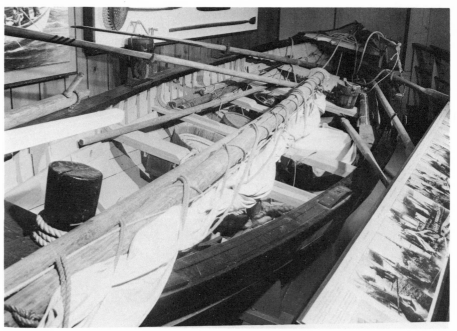

The Whaleboat on exhibit in 1975
(Photo: Author)

WHALEBOAT

28'11" x 6'6"   ca. 1920

This boat arrived aboard the *Charles W. Morgan* in 1941. Before that her history is unknown but it is likely she was off the *John Manta*, the *Wanderer*, or the *Morgan* herself, as these were the last vessels to sail from New Bedford in search of the whale. Every whaleship carried a few of these boats hung from davits and ready for lowering away whenever a whale was sighted. Whaleboats were developed and refined over many years and at the end became quite standardized. Each was manned by a boatsteerer (whose job it was to harpoon the whale) four other oarsmen, and one of the whaleship's mates who was in command. If the whale was to leeward and there was some wind, sail was hoisted and the whaleboats were sailed—oftentimes right up to the whale—to make their kill. The hinged mast partner made quick work of striking the rig, and oars could be quickly shipped for maneuvering, at which time a steering oar was run out to replace the rudder.

At first whaleboats were lapstrake, but it was later found best to have a boat with a smooth skin at the waterplane in order to sneak up on the whale without the chortling noise common to lapstrake craft. Battens fastened behind each of the flush-planked seams kept the hulls from drying out and leaking after long periods out of the water.

While the whaleboat itself is strong and flexible, it is also light in weight. But with six men, oars, paddles, a sailing rig, two tubs of line, harpoons, lances, and other gear it becomes much heavier.

STATUS:

Restored 1968, approximately 50% original, good condition.

DONOR:

Anonymous

FURTHER READING:

Ansel, Willits D. *The Whaleboat, 1850–1970: A Study of Design, Construction, and Use*. Mystic: Mystic Seaport, Inc., 1978.

Note: Mystic Seaport has three other original whaleboats in its collection, all in only fair condition and in most instances much repaired. They are similar in size and appearance to 68.60 above and are therefore not illustrated. Accession numbers of these whaleboats are 55.679, 58.690 and 72.327.

ACCESSION NO. 68.60

When not in use, mast, boom, and sprit were bundled up, along with the sail, and shoved under after thwart, leaving most of the rig overhanging the stern (Photo: Author)

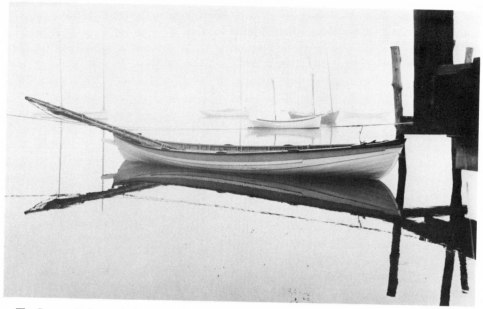

WHALEBOAT REPRODUCTIONS
(Leonard Model)

29'11" x 6'6"   1972–1973

This boat and two others like her were built by the staff of the Seaport shipyard with several purposes in mind. The *Morgan* needed to be outfitted with serviceable boats, having at least one for waterfront demonstration purposes. Will Ansel (who subsequently built the first boat) was underway with a book on whaleboats and felt the experience of building and testing one would add considerable validity to his project; and there was a need for some experience in boatbuilding skills. Although the *Morgan*'s normal complement of seven boats (five on davits and two spares on the boatskids) has not been satisfied—the other objectives have been in the construction of three Leonard and one Beetle designed whaleboats.

The Leonard shop is believed to have produced the boat from which R. O. Davis of William Hand's office drew up a set of plans sometime before 1930. These plans, now part of the Hand Collection at MIT, were used to build these boats.

STATUS:
In use, excellent condition.

DONOR:
Mystic Seaport built reproduction
FURTHER READING:
Ansel, Willits D. *The Whaleboat, 1850–1970: A Study of Design, Construction, and Use.* Mystic: Mystic Seaport, 1978.

Note: The other two boats built to this design are similar in size and appearance and are not illustrated individually. Their accession numbers are 73.449 and 73.488.
ACCESSION NO. 72.883

oto: C. L. White Peterson)   *(Photo: Author)*

Whaleboat race attracts onlookers among the Seaport's summer visitors

WHALEBOAT REPRODUCTION
(Beetle Model)

28'6" x 6'4"   1974

Peter Vermilya of the Seaport staff built this whaleboat, helped out from time to time by a number of persons, among them English boatbuilder, Harold Kimber. She duplicates, as closely as possible, the Beetle whaleboat at the Mariners Museum, Newport News, Virginia. That boat was one of the last built by the most prolific of all whaleboat builders, Beetle of New Bedford, specifically for Mariners Museum about 1930. She has never been used and is a really remarkable craft; so remarkable that Bob Allyn and Will Ansel traveled from the Seaport to Newport News to measure the boat and take pictures of her. Upon their return, detailed plans were drawn and this boat was built from them. It's easy to see why Beetle was so successful; this boat is unquestionably better looking than the Leonard model and, like the original, is superbly put together. Along with the three Leonard reproductions, she divides her time between the davits of the *Charles W. Mor-*

The Seaport built Beetle whaleboat was rigged with a sprit mainsail instead of the sliding gunter rig (Photo: K. Mahler)

gan and the waters of the Mystic River. She was rigged with a spritsail instead of the sliding gunter mainsail of the other boats.

STATUS:
In use, excellent condition.

DONOR:
Mystic Seaport built reproduction.

FURTHER READING:
Ansel, Willits D. *The Whaleboat, 1850–1970: A Study of Design, Construction, and Use.* Mystic: Mystic Seaport, Inc., 1978.

Howland, Llewellyn. *Sou'west and by West of Cape Cod.* Cambridge: Harvard University Press, 1948.

ACCESSION NO. 74.1027

On exhibit in 1951 (Photo: Mystic Seaport)

Fly
CHESAPEAKE BAY LOG CANOE

21'11" x 5'1"

As the name might suggest, the lower part of this canoe was hewed out of

three logs using only hand tools. Then, to achieve the desired freeboard and to fair out the sheerline, additional pieces were fastened onto the outer logs. This process of boatbuilding is unlike that for most watercraft and is described in quite a bit of detail by Brewington in his book on log canoes and bugeyes (see further reading).

Canoes of *Fly*'s type are called Poquoson Canoes, taking their name from a village on the York River on Virginia's western shore where many were built. Early history of this boat is not known, but the records show that she was repaired in 1930 by one Ed Leatherberry at which time she was known to be an old boat. It was then that Leath-

erberry renamed her *Fly.*

Anyone making a study of these canoes would do well to visit Chesapeake Bay Maritime Museum at St. Michaels, Md. and Mariners Museum at Newport News, Va.

STATUS:
Repaired, good condition.

DONOR:
Wells E. Hunt

FURTHER READING:
Brewington, M. V. *Chesapeake Bay Log Canoes and Bugeyes.* Cambridge: Cornell Maritime Press, Inc., 1963.

Chapelle, Howard I. *American Small Sailing Craft.* New York: W. W. Norton & Co., Inc., 1951.

ACCESSION NO. 51.4205

Chapter Three
KETCH RIGGED

The fishing camps on Noman's Land, from Goode's **Fisheries Report,** *1887*

Noman's Land boat in 1973 (Photo: M. A. Stets)

NOMAN'S LAND BOAT

19'9" x 6'2"   ca. 1882

The name came from a small island off the Massachusetts coast south of Martha's Vineyard, which in the summer (because of its nearness to the fishing grounds) became home to many fishermen and their families. Their colony has long disappeared and landing there is now prohibited since unexploded bombs, reminders of military target practice, cover the island.

Noman's Land never had much of a harbor and in bad weather the boats were hauled up on the beach over greased skids by oxen. The Noman's Land boat with its double-ended hull could be launched stern first into a surf and rowed into deep water where sail was set.

Josiah Cleveland built this boat and it remained in the Cleveland family until acquired by the Seaport. In later years an engine was installed, and the rig was changed to that of a catboat with a gaff sail. But her wet well was not disturbed and remains intact today.

STATUS:
Stripped to original structure, rig missing, fair condition.

DONOR:
Purchased from Rodney V. Cleveland with money from the Storrs fund.

ACCESSION NO. 52.1115

Josiah Cleveland, builder and original owner of the Noman's Land boat, in his shop around 1875 (Courtesy: Charles Sayle)

Rodney Cleveland aboard his Noman's Land boat (Courtesy: Mrs. Rodney Cleveland)

Orca
NOMAN'S LAND BOAT

19'9" x 6'5"   ca. 1882

Of batten seam rather than lapstrake construction, her hull was built in Fairhaven, Mass., by Delano for Onslow Stuart who took her to his Chilmark shop for finishing. She was never actually used at Noman's Land but fished until about 1920 from the Gay Head area of Martha's Vineyard. *Orca*, too, had an engine and single mast when the donor acquired her in the 1950s. *Orca* is now back to her original rig and is being used each summer at the donor's request. Thus rigged, both masts, being short, are easily unstepped. The foremast has a bale at its partners to make the task even easier.

STATUS:

Restored by donor in the 1950s, hull rebuilt by Seaport in 1970, approximately 75% original, in use, good condition.

DONOR:

Robert H. Baker

FURTHER READING FOR 52.1115 AND 63.592:

Allen, Joseph C. *Martha's Vineyard Boats*. New Bedford: Reynolds Printing, n.d.

Brewington, Dorothy E. R., and M. V. "Some Notes on the Boats of Noman's Land." *The Mariner*, July, 1932.

Cabot, David. "The New England Double Enders." *The American Neptune*, Vol. XII, April, 1952.

Chapelle, Howard I. *American Small Sailing Craft*. New York: W. W. Norton & Co., 1951.

———. *The National Watercraft Collection*. Washington: Government Printing Office, 1960.

Goode, George B. *The Fisheries and Fishery Industries of the United States*. Sect. V, Vol. II. Washington: Government Printing Office, 1887.

Herreshoff, L. Francis. *The Compleat Cruiser*. New York: Sheridan House, 1963.

Howland, Llewellyn. *Sou'west and by West of Cape Cod*. Cambridge: Harvard University Press, 1948.—*Vivid description of life at Noman's Land including use of a boat*.

Huntington, Frederick R. "A Noman's Land Double Ender." *Yachting*, April, 1932.

Huntington, Gale. "Nomansland, Salt Codfish and the Nomansland Boat." *The Dukes County Intelligencer*, November, 1975, Volume 17, No. 2.

Leavens, John M. "The Cat Rigged Island Double Ender." *National Fisherman*, August, 1976.

———. "The Noman's Land Boat." *The Log of Mystic Seaport*, October, 1976.

Morris, E. P. *The Fore and Aft Rig in America*. New Haven: Yale University Press, 1927.

Taylor, Roger C. *Good Boats*. Camden: International Marine Publishing Co., 1977.

Taylor, William H. "The Nomansland Sailboat." *Yachting*, March, 1932.

Wood, Annie M. *Noman's Land, Isle of Romance*. New Bedford: Reynolds Printing, 1931.

Mystic Seaport has considerable unpublished material on Noman's Land boats which along with much of the above has been compiled in a booklet of source material by Anne and Maynard Bray and is on file in the Seaport's G. W. Blunt White Library.

ACCESSION NO. 63.592

Orca as she appeared when first acquired by Robert Baker about 1952 (Courtesy: Robert H. Baker)

Orca under sail in the Mystic River in 1974 (Photo: K. Mahler)

Glory Anna II **sailing in the Mystic River after her restoration at Mystic Seaport**
(Photo: Russell A. Fowler)

The original Block Island Cowhorn Glory Anna **as she lay rotting on the beach near**
Cormorant Cove on Block Island about 1930 (Courtesy: Mrs. Paule Loring)

Glory Anna II
BLOCK ISLAND COWHORN REPRODUCTION

23'0" x 9'0"   1948

Proving that an open cockpit can be seaworthy, cowhorns were used both winter and summer in the rough waters of Block Island Sound. Only the Maine pinky seems to enjoy such a reputation for seaworthiness.

Before the Old Harbor breakwater was built in 1873, cowhorns (which they resembled because of their high ends) were numerous, as they could be hauled up on the beach during bad weather. Larger craft having the same appearance and known simply as Block Island boats gradually displaced the cowhorns after that date, however.

The originals had all vanished by the time artist Paule Loring became interested in them. But working from models and photographs and with the help of H. I. Chapelle and others, he conceived this reproduction, built in Wickford, R.I., by L. Howard. From the start her deck layout was different— altered to suit Loring's needs—and by 1970 she sported a high pilot house and a cut-down ketch rig. Saving only the hull, the Seaport modified her appearance to that of the original *Glory Anna*.

Paule Loring was best known and loved for his "Dud Sinker" cartoons which were published in each issue of *The National Fisherman*.

STATUS:
Rebuilt and restored to original configuration, in use, excellent condition.
DONOR:
Purchased for Mystic Seaport by Thomas R. Wilcox
FURTHER READING:
Ansel, Willits D. "Loring's Cowhorn Sails Again." *National Fisherman*, April, 1972.

Cabot, David. "The New England Double Enders." *The American Neptune*, Vol. XII, 1952.

Chapelle, Howard I. *American Small Sailing Craft*. New York: W. W. Norton & Co., 1951.

————. *The National Watercraft Collection*. Washington: Government Printing Office, 1960.

Davis, Charles G. *Ships of the Past*. Salem: The Maritime Research Society, 1929.— *Has chapter dealing with the larger Block Island boats, includes plans.*

Hall, Henry. *Report on Shipbuilding Industry of the United States*. Washington: Government Printing Office, 1884.

Herreshoff, L. Francis. *The Compleat*

Cruiser. New York: Sheridan House, 1963.

Hyslop, John. *Forest and Stream*, January 3, 1884.

Morris, E. P. *The Fore and Aft Rig in America*. New Haven: Yale University Press, 1927.

Nicholson, Paul C. *The Block Island Double Ender*. Rhode Island Historical Society Collections, October, 1923.

Ritchie, Ethel Colt. *Block Island Lore and Legends*. Block Island: Norman Associates, 1955.

Taylor, Roger C. *Good Boats*. Camden:

International Marine Publishing Co., 1977.

Thompson, Winfield M. "Adriaen Block, His Yacht and His Island." *Rudder*, March, 1912.

————. "Roaring Bessie." *Rudder*, April, 1912.

Most of the above material has been compiled in booklet form by Anne and Maynard Bray and is on file in the Seaport's G. W. Blunt White Library. There are three Block Island boat models in Mystic Seaport's collection.

ACCESSION NO. 70.763

Left: *Handlining for codfish off Block Island, from Goode's* Fisheries Report, *1887.* Right: *"Pole Harbor," Block Island, where Cowhorns* were kept. Cowhorns were replaced by larger Block Island boats after breakwater (background) was built (Courtesy: Mrs. Paule Loring)

Cadet as she arrived at Mystic Seaport in 1955 (Photo: Mystic Seaport)

Cadet
DOUBLE-ENDED HAMPTON BOAT

23'4" x 6'6"   ca. 1846

Rev. Elijah Kellogg (1813–1901) had this boat built, probably by Ebenezer Durgin of Birch Island, and owned her throughout his life. She was found stored in the old Kellogg barn in the mid 1950s, and damaged such that total rebuilding was thought necessary. For Kellogg, best known for his thirty-odd

adventure books for boys, this boat furnished transportation from his home in Harpswell, Maine, to the many islands in Casco Bay. Many others like her were used for fishing. In 1977 a working reproduction of this boat was built by The Restoration Shop of the Bath Marine Museum.

STATUS:

Restored, little original, good condition.

DONOR:

Olive French Kellogg

ACCESSION NO. 55.318

Cadet afloat off the Seaport waterfront after restoration (Photo: L. S. Martel)

Cuspidor
SQUARE-STERNED HAMPTON BOAT

17'4" x 6'0"   1902

Built by Capt. D. Perry Sinnett on Bailey's Island, Maine, *Cuspidor* is typical of hundreds of such boats used for fishing and hauling lobster traps along the coast. Later models, one of which, also by Sinnett, is in the collection of Bath Marine Museum, show transition to power as forerunner of the modern lobster boat. *Cuspidor* was built as a pleasure boat for the late Dr. Franklin P. Luckey of Paterson, N.J. and Bailey's Island.

STATUS:

Restored 1967, approximately 90% original, good condition.

***Hampton boat* Cuspidor *in 1975* (Photo: Author)**

DONOR:

Mrs. F. P. Luckey

FURTHER READING FOR 55.318
AND 61.916:

Audubon, John James. *Delineations of American Scenery and Character*, New York: 1926.

Bishop, W. H. *Fish and Men in the Maine Islands*. New York: Harper, 1885.—*Reprint from Harpers Magazine*, August–September, 1880.

Bodge, J. "Old Times at Harpswell." *Maine Coast Fisherman*, February, 1954.

Cabot, David. "The New England Double Enders." *The American Neptune*, Vol. XII, April, 1952.

Chapelle, Howard I. *American Small Sailing Craft*. New York: W. W. Norton & Co., 1951.

———. "The Hampden Boat." *Yachting*, July, 1938.

———. *The National Watercraft Collection*. Washington: Government Printing Office, 1960.

Doughty, Jean. "Muffin Goes From Fish to Boats." *National Fisherman*, July, 1968. —*A good write-up on Sinnett family history.*

Elden, A. O. "Power Boating in Casco Bay, Maine." *Yachting*, April, 1907.

Emerson, Charles. *The American Neptune*. April, 1941.—*Page 173 has a letter containing evidence that the square-stern Hampton boat descends from the double-ender.*

Hall, Carl F. "Looking Back One Hundred Years." *The Sea Breeze*, April, 1962.

Kellogg, Elijah. *The Young Shipbuilders of Elm Island*. Boston: 1870.—*Page 259 makes reference to a boat of this type.*

Malloy, Anne. "Elijah Kellogg of Elm Island." *Down East*, June, 1969.

Millet, W. H. "Original Hampton Boats." *Maine Coast Fisherman*, June, 1948.

Morris, E. P. *The Fore and Aft Rig in America*. New Haven: Yale University Press, 1927.

Soule, Phelps. "The Hampton Boat." *The American Neptune*, April, 1943.

The Apprenticeshop of the Bath Marine Museum. *The Crotch Island Pinky*. Bath: 1975.—*Useful as background because of the* close resemblance between Crotch Island pinkys and the double-ended Hampton boats.

Watson, Warren. "The Hampton Boat." *Motor Boat*, Vol. VI, 1909.

*Cuspidor under sail
at Bailey's Island
(Courtesy:
Mrs. F. P. Luckey)*

Mystic Seaport has considerable unpublished material relating to this Hampton boat which has been compiled in a booklet of source material by Anne and Maynard Bray and is on file in the Seaport's G. W. Blunt White Library.

ACCESSION NO. 61.916

David Perry Sinnet's boat shop at Bailey's Island, Maine (Courtesy: Mrs. F. P. Luckey)

KINGSTON LOBSTER BOAT

19'0" x 6'3"   ca. 1890

The nearby yacht-building yards of the Boston area influenced the lobstermen along Massachusetts' south shore to take up racing with their work boats. After 1885, when this fever took hold, the local builders started to adopt some of the speed-giving features of the larger yachts. They refined their products to become the speediest and most responsive of all commercial sailing watercraft, known commonly as the Kingston lobster boat. The boats of Edward Ransom were particularly fast and beautiful, as Chapelle's drawings show. Other builders, however, didn't succeed as well in producing superior boats, as was the case with William Bates who built this one. While her sailing qualities can only be guessed at, it is doubtful if, without the usual firmness to her quarters, she could lug enough sail to be very fast. Most of these boats were half-decked, necessary to keep them dry, no doubt. But

Kingston lobster boat in 1958 (Photo: L. S. Martel)

the deck eliminated one of the great conveniences of most other two-masted spritsail boats for it made it impossible to strike the foremast while underway and required a man to climb up out of the cockpit to shorten or furl the sail.

Like the *Annie A. Fuller*, this boat is strip planked. She has a wet well on either side of the centerboard trunk in which the "catch" was carried.

STATUS:
Restored 1969, approximately 80% original, rig missing, good condition.
DONOR:
Robert Hanckel
ACCESSION NO. 56.1544

Kingston lobster boat as found in 1956 near Scituate, Massachusetts (Photo: Mystic Seaport)

Annie A. Fuller
KINGSTON
LOBSTER BOAT

15'8" x 5'5"   1872

This was Capt. Parker Hall's first boat; the coasting schooner *Alice S. Wentworth* was his last. During his long career in the coasting trade he owned many others, which he usually sailed single-handed all up and down the New England coast. He was quite a character, as John Leavitt describes him, and was well known among coastermen. *Annie A. Fuller* was named for an early ladyfriend and it is reported that he gave the boat to another friend, Capt. Freeman Closson, in later years. The boat was built on the south shore of Massachusetts by Arthur Rogers and is an early version of what Chapelle calls the Kingston lobster boat. The more recent boats were longer and racier with counter sterns and hollow garboards.

STATUS:
Restored 1970, approximately 80% original, rig missing, good condition.

DONOR:
William Bell Watkins

FURTHER READING FOR 63.818 AND 56.1544:
Barnard, Wm. L. "The Lobster Boats of Plymouth." *Boating*, 1907. Reprinted in *Woodenboat*, Vol. 1 No. 1 September, 1974.

Chapelle, Howard I. *American Small Sailing Craft.* New York: W. W. Norton & Co., 1951.

Gardner, John. "Kingston Lobster Boats." *National Fisherman*, July, 1969.

Jones, Henry M. *Ships of Kingston.* Plymouth: The Memorial Press of Plymouth, Mass., 1926.

Leavitt, John F. *Wake of the Coasters.* Middletown: Wesleyan University Press for The Marine Historical Association, Inc., 1970.

A compilation of the above material is in a booklet prepared by Anne and Maynard Bray and on file in the G. W. Blunt White Library at the Seaport.

ACCESSION NO. 63.818

Annie A. Fuller *in 1975 (Photo: Author)*

Parker Hall at the helm of his first boat Annie A. Fuller *(Photo: Source unknown)*

73

New Haven Oyster Sharpie under sail in the Mystic River in 1974 (Photo: K. Mahler)

NEW HAVEN OYSTER TONGING SHARPIE

35′4″ x 6′11″   ca. 1890

Like the dugouts (46.643 and 46.644) the sharpies were used for oyster tonging; however, they were a refinement responsive to changing needs and advancing technology. The tonger had to travel further away for oysters as the beds near home became exhausted; so he needed a better sailing boat. Scarcity of large trees and an abundance of sawmills made a built-up boat more practical than one fashioned from a single log. Inexpensive, shallow, and easy to handle; the sharpies proved popular not only with the tongers of Connecticut, primarily of Fair Haven, but with the oystermen in the Chesapeake and southern Atlantic coast as well.

STATUS:
Rebuilt as a condition of gift in the 1950s; little original, in use, fair condition.

DONOR:
Ernest E. Ball

ACCESSION NO. 47.597

NEW HAVEN OYSTER TONGING SHARPIE

34′11″ x 7′4″   ca. 1880

This boat is much like 47.597, both representing the largest size of tonging sharpie, carrying 150–175 bushels of oysters and rigged with two masts. For winter work or in heavy weather, however, a single mast could be used, stepped just ahead of the cockpit. When the wind was too light for sailing, these sharpies could be either rowed or sculled.

STATUS:
Unrestored, original, structurally weak.

DONOR:
Exchange with the Mariners Museum, Newport News, Virginia.

ACCESSION NO. 74.1031

New Haven Oyster Sharpie on exhibit in 1975 (Photo: C. White Peterson)

FURTHER READING FOR 47.597 AND 74.1031:

Chapelle, Howard I. *American Small Sailing Craft.* New York: W. W. Norton & Co., 1951.

———. *Migrations of an American Boat Type. USNM Bulletin 22,* Washington: Government Printing Office, 1961.

———. *The National Watercraft Collection.* Washington: Government Printing Office, 1960.

———. "The New Haven Sharpie." *Yachting,* January, 1927.

Hall, Henry. *Report on Shipbuilding Industry of the United States.* Washington: Government Printing Office, 1881.

Ingersol, Ernest. *The Oyster Industry: Tenth Census of the United States.* Washington: Government Printing Office, 1881.

Kochiss, John. *Oystering from New York to Boston.* Middletown: Wesleyan University Press for Mystic Seaport, 1974.

———. "Some Aspects of the Sharpie and Its Work." *The Log of Mystic Seaport,* January, 1976.

Morris, E. P. *The Fore and Aft Rig in America.* New Haven: Yale University Press, 1927.

Stephens, W. P. "The Sharpie." *Yachting,* January, 1927.

Three rigged models of oyster sharpies are in Mystic Seaport's collection.

Canoe yawl **Half Moon** *in 1975 (Photo: Author)*

in W. P. Stephens' *Canoe and Boat Building* (see Further Reading). She is neither a canoe nor a yawl; however, the name canoe yawl was frequently used to describe this type of one-man cruising boat.

STATUS:

Unrestored, some parts missing, fair condition.

DONOR:

Captain Elwell B. Thomas

FURTHER READING:

Herreshoff, L. Francis. *The Compleat Cruiser.* New York: Sheridan House, 1963.

"Iris, Eighteen-Foot Canoe Yawl." *Yachting*, December, 1933.

MacGregor, John. *The Voyage Alone in the Yawl Rob Roy.* London: Rupert Hart-Davis, 1954.

Stephens, W. P. *Canoe and Boat Building: A Complete Manual for Amateurs.* New York: Forest and Stream Publishing Co., 1889.

———. *Traditions and Memories of American Yachting.* New York: Hearst Magazines, 1945.

Taylor, Roger C. *Good Boats.* Camden: International Marine Publishing Co., 1977. —*Contains chapter on the canoe yawl Iris with some material republished from* Yachting, *December, 1933.*

ACCESSION NO. 59.1209

Half Moon
CANOE YAWL

18'3" x 5'5"   ca. 1930

Half Moon was built by A. W. Barlow and Herbert Salisbury of Providence and Pawtucket, R.I., to old drawings of the *Iris* by J. A. Akester which appear

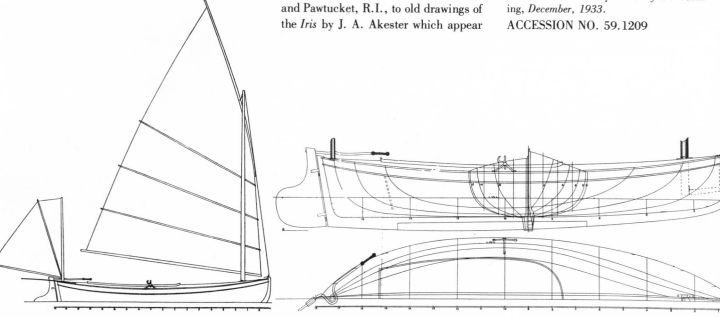

Plans of the canoe yawl Iris *taken from W. P. Stephens's* **Canoe and Boat Building,** *1889 edition.*
Half Moon *was built from these lines, although her rig was altered somewhat*

Chapter Four
SCHOONER & SQUARE RIGGED

As designed and built, **Brilliant** *was gaff-rigged on both masts and carried a fidded main topmast*
(Photo: Morris Rosenfeld; Courtesy: Stanley Rosenfeld)

Brilliant
SCHOONER-YACHT
Official No. 231472

61'6" x 14'8"   1932

"The schooner *Brilliant* is the seagoing emissary of Mystic Seaport. Although she has several fine records for speed, acquired in her early days, *Brilliant*'s great claim to fame lies in the program she has served for the past

eighteen years—a seagoing training ship for the Mystic Mariner Program. Eighteen voyages are made each year, with a crew of nine teenagers, an adult leader and a professional captain and mate."—Capt. F. E. ("Biff") Bowker in *The Log of Mystic Seaport*, Summer, 1971.

Luck has been with *Brilliant* all her life, and shows up particularly in the good care she has been given. No trace of a seam shows in her flawless topsides, her teak deck and varnished teak trim look like new, and below decks one would find things every bit as good. As she nears fifty years of age, *Brilliant*

Brilliant *leaves Latimer's Light astern, October, 1977 (Photo: M. A. Stets)*

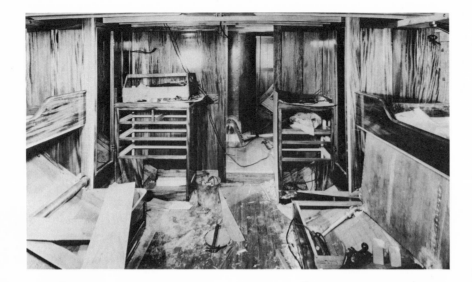

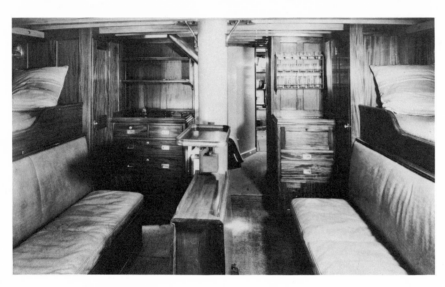

Three views of **Brilliant's** *interior during and after installation, giving an idea of the fine workmanship and materials which went into her. (Photos: Morris Rosenfeld; Courtesy: Stanley Rosenfeld)*

symbolizes, perhaps better than any other craft at the Seaport, the benefits of timely, intelligent, and unfailing maintenance. But her good luck reaches beyond; the bottomed-out stock market of 1932 didn't stop Walter Barnum from ordering a first class yacht; or from having the young and talented Olin Stephens prepare a custom design; or from encouraging the marvelously skilled workers at Henry B. Nevins' City Island yard to take whatever time needed to do the best work they knew how. Even in her day, *Brilliant* stood

out as superior. Now with the senses dulled by look-alike boats of fiberglass and aluminum, *Brilliant* turns heads wherever she goes, rekindling one's appreciation for beauty, good taste, and craftsmanship.

Staysail schooners with Marconi mainsails were the rage when *Brilliant* came out, but in spite of her old-fashioned gaff-headed rig, she won the 1933 transatlantic race to Plymouth, England, making more than 200 miles per day for several days on end. But the wholesome *Brilliant* was more of a

cruiser than racer and even though Briggs Cunningham had her masts lengthened and her sail area increased when he bought her after World War II, she was never a consistent winner until very recently when she began to bring home a few prizes from the A.S.T.A. races and the annual Seaport-sponsored schooner race. Perhaps the competition is no longer what she used to be up against, or maybe it is her Marconi mainsail (changed from gaff in the mid-1950s) or the eagerness of her crew; no one really cares, for beating

Photograph was taken inside the Nevins shop on October 18, 1931, **Brilliant's** *hull planked and about half caulked (Photo: Morris Rosenfeld; Courtesy: Stanley Rosenfeld)*

other boats, while good fun, is not of vital importance in her present role.

Brilliant's good life at the Seaport is due in great measure to the interest of her former owner, Briggs Cunningham, who subsidizes her expenses, and to Capt. "Biff" Bowker, who has conscientiously skippered her and superintended her care since 1962.

STATUS:

In use, mostly original, excellent condition.

DONOR:

Briggs S. Cunningham

FURTHER READING:

Bowker, Francis E. "To Know the Sea." *The Log of Mystic Seaport,* Summer, 1971.

Fox, Uffa. *Sailing, Seamanship and Yacht Construction.* New York: Charles Scribner's Sons, 1934.—*Contains some worthwhile comments about* Brilliant *in an entire chapter devoted to her. Her major plans, although redrawn by the author, are included as well.*

Loomis, Alfred F. "Two Hundred a Day." Yachting, October, 1933.—*A first-hand account of* Brilliant's *transatlantic race.*

Nevins, Henry B. "Economy Versus Cheapness." *Yachting,* September, 1933.—*Contemporary comments by* Brilliant's *builder on the fine points of high grade yachts.*

Since about 1940, **Regina M.** *has been rigged as a schooner, which, with other outward modifications, were to simulate a Maine pinky. This photo shows her in 1966 (Photo: L. S. Martel)*

Regina M.
LUBEC CARRY-AWAY BOAT
Official No. 206136

45′2″ x 13′6″   1900

Carrying herring or mackerel from Maine coastal weirs and seines to the canning factories was her trade. Now, this function is performed by Diesel-powered sardine carriers. Originally a sloop, *Regina M.* was first converted to an out-and-out powerboat; then just before coming to Mystic, she was converted to pinky schooner appearance. There is some uncertainty as to whether the boat was built with an engine, but she had one in 1909 when first listed in the Merchant Register. *Regina M.* was built in Perry, Maine. We hope in the future to restore her, outwardly, to her earlier sailing appearance.

STATUS:
Rebuilt 1955–64, little original, fair condition.

DONOR:
C. D. Mallory, Sr.

FURTHER READING:

Chapelle, Howard I. "The Lubec Carry-away Boats." *Yachting,* July, 1940.

Goode, George Brown. *The Fisheries and Fishery Industries of the United States.* Washington: Government Printing Office, 1887.

Rogers, Francis Day. "*Regina M.* to Mystic." *The Log of Mystic Seaport,* Autumn, 1966.

ACCESSION NO. 40.338

Above: Regina M. *under auxiliary power in Rockland Harbor, 1928*
(Photo: John F. Leavitt Collection)
Above right: Regina M. *at Bucksport, Maine about 1940 after being*
converted to a power boat (Photo: Gift of Mrs. C. D. Mallory, Sr.)

A carry-away boat being unloaded,
from Goode's **Fisheries Report,** *1887*

Carry-away boats under tow (Courtesy: James H. Allyn)

Australia sailing in Chester River, Maryland, in 1933 (Courtesy: The Mariners Museum)

Model of the *Australia* completed in 1975 by staff modelmaker, Ray Pendleton
(Photo: M. A. Stets)

Australia (ex-*Alma*)
COASTING SCHOONER
Official No. 25

72'5" x 19'4"   1862

When *Australia* came to Mystic in 1951 one story told was that she took part in the War of 1812 as the *Alma*. No such thing happened; this vessel is not that old. She was built in Patchogue, Long Island, in 1862 as a humble merchant vessel named *Alma*, but not the *Alma* of 1812. Since then she has been lengthened 10 feet and after an almost total rebuilding, she was used as a yacht by the donor and her husband on Chesapeake Bay. After arriving in Mystic the schooner was a floating barracks for the Seaport's Mariner Program for ten years, then in the early 1960s had to be hauled out because she leaked so badly. An attempt was made at restoration but then abandoned once the degree of prior rebuilding and change was realized. Today she is a relic through which visitors may walk and see how wooden vessels are constructed.

STATUS:
Relic, less than 50% original, poor condition.

DONOR:
Mrs. E. Paul duPont

FURTHER READING:
Leavitt, John F. *Wake of the Coasters.* Middletown: Wesleyan University Press for Mystic Seaport, 1970.

Lyman, John. *Log Chips.* Vol. 2, No. 7, pp. 76–80.

Smith, Edward W., compiler. *Workaday Schooners.* Camden: International Marine Publishing Co., 1975.

A very fine rigged model of *Australia* has been completed by Ray Pendleton, the Seaport's modelmaker.

Documentation of *Australia*'s history and her confusion as the *Alma* is available in the G. W. Blunt White Library as an information bulletin.

ACCESSION NO. 51.4509

Hulk of the Australia,
now used to illustrate wooden vessel construction and the effects of prolonged deterioration (Photo: M. A. Stets)

L. A. Dunton *at her Mystic Seaport berth in 1969 (Photo: R. A. Fowler)*

L. A. Dunton
GLOUCESTER FISHING SCHOONER
Official No. 221150

123′0″ x 24′11″   1921

The American fishing schooner, of which this vessel is almost the last surviving example, enjoyed a worldwide reputation for speed and beauty. She carried a large rig and lots of sail: perhaps inspired by racing yachts and sea stories. Yet once on the fishing grounds, she could be snugged down to carry only three fairly small sails, mak-ing it possible for the captain and cook alone to jog her back and forth while her "brood" of dories was off fishing.

There were ten of these dories, each manned by a crew of two. They were launched from the *Dunton*'s deck in the morning to set their baited trawls, and were expected to return before dark with a good load of fish. Fog and sudden snow squalls made for anxious times and lost dories were not uncommon.

The *Dunton*, built by the Arthur D. Story yard in Essex, Mass., — both names synonymous with the Gloucester fishing fleet — was designed by Thomas McManus. Felix Hogan had her built and was her first master. In a vain attempt to keep up with the times, an auxiliary engine was installed in 1928 but the schooners were on their way

L. A. Dunton *on the fishing grounds with crew aft baiting up trawls. The shortened rig, used for jogging, could be handled by very few men (Photo: Source unknown)*

out. In 1934 she was sold to Canadian interests and was able to fish only a few more years. She was ultimately repowered and became a freighter carrying just enough sail to steady her. Such was her state in 1963 when acquired by the Seaport.

Within a year her appearance had been altered to what it was originally and she was placed on exhibit. In the early 1970s the long task of "retopping" her began. It was completed in 1977 and resulted in nearly all new wood above the waterline.

STATUS:
Restored 1963–1977. Original below waterline. Good condition.

DONOR:
Mystic Seaport purchase

The **Dunton** *being launched in 1921 from A. D. Story's yard in Essex, Massachusetts (Courtesy: Dana Story)*

The shallow, narrow Essex River required that schooners be towed to Gloucester for fitting out. The **Dunton,** *shown below, under tow at Essex after launching (Courtesy: Dana Story)*

FURTHER READING:

Chapelle, Howard I. *American Sailing Craft.* Camden: International Marine Publishing Co., 1975.

——. *The American Fishing Schooner.* New York: W. W. Norton & Co., 1973.

——. *The History of American Sailing Ships.* New York: W. W. Norton & Co., 1975.

Church, Albert Cook. *American Fishermen.* New York: W. W. Norton & Co., 1940.

Goldie, George S. "A Winter's Fishing Trip to Georges." *Yachting,* November and December, 1910.—*A marvelous first hand account of a trip in the schooner* Lizzie M. Stanley.

Kleinschmidt, James. "Last Voyage of the *L. A. Dunton.*" *The Log of Mystic Seaport.* January, 1964.—*See also April 1964 issue for a description of the first phase of her restoration.*

McFarland, Raymond. *The Masts of Gloucester,* New York: W. W. Norton & Co., 1947.

Pidgeon, Roy W. "A Fishing Trip to the Western Banks on the Schooner *Mayflower.*" *Yachting,* April, 1922.

Pierce, Wesley George. *Goin' Fishin'.* Salem: Marine Research Society, 1934.

Story, Dana. *Frame Up: The Story of Essex, Its Shipyards and Its People.* Barre: Barre Publishing Co., 1964.

Thomas, Gordon W. *Fast and Able.* Gloucester: 350th Anniversary, Celebration, Inc., 1973.

ACCESSION NO. 63.1705

The **Dunton** *at Gloucester, about 1930 (Courtesy: Charles Sayle)*

The **Dunton** *as a freight vessel out of St. John's, Newfoundland, as she appeared when acquired in 1963 (Photo: Source unknown)*

Retopping the forward end of the **L. A. Dunton** *at Mystic Seaport during the winter of 1972–73 (Photo: L. D. Olin)*

89

The **Charles W. Morgan** *at sea (Photo: Source unknown)*

Charles W. Morgan
WHALESHIP
Official No. 5380

113′11″ x 27′8″   1841

In eighty years, from her launching in 1841 until the end of her last voyage in 1921, the *Morgan* made a record thirty-seven voyages which earned $1,400,000. Outlasting all others of her type she is now the treasured hallmark of Mystic Seaport.

The events in her long life have been quite well recorded and the more significant ones are listed below:

1841 (July)—Launched from the New Bedford shipyard of Jethro and Zachariah Hillman and named for her principal owner, Charles Waln Morgan. She was ship-rigged when new.

1841 (September)—Sailed on first voyage under the command of Capt. Thomas A. Norton.

1859 (October)—Sailed from New Bedford on her sixth and most profitable voyage from which she returned three and a half years later with a cargo worth over $165,000.

1863—Sold to J. & W. R. Wing who

From left to right: *The* Morgan *drying sails at New Bedford around 1906; on a Fairhaven railway in 1906; laid up in Fairhaven from 1913 to 1916*
(Courtesy: Kendall Whaling Museum)

were to be her principal owners for the next fifty-three years.

1864—Gimballed bed was built for Capt. Landers' wife who was aboard for the seventh voyage. A "gamming chair" was also fitted on the vessel for her.

1867—Vessel remeasured under the new tonnage rule; registered tonnage was changed from 351 to 313.75. Her rig was altered to that of a bark with removal of yards from the mizzenmast.

1874–75—The *Morgan* was extensively refitted and repaired.

1881—She underwent more refitting which included moving the anchor windlass forward, some new spars and rigging, and the fitting of double topsails on the mainmast.

1883—Double topsails were fitted on the foremast during the twelfth voyage.

1886 (June)—Returned from her longest voyage of nearly five years.

1886 (October)—Left New Bedford for her new home port of San Francisco. Before leaving she was refitted, repaired, and altered somewhat for arctic whaling with reinforcement of her bow and the addition of a steam deck engine.

1906 (June)—The *Morgan* returned to New Bedford after an absence of nearly twenty years.

1913—Back from her thirty-third voyage, she was stripped and laid up at Union Wharf in Fairhaven.

1916—She was purchased by Capt. Benjamin Cleveland who outfitted her to hunt sea elephants at Desolation Island. Before leaving, the *Morgan* took part in the movie *Miss Petticoats*.

1918—The vessel was sold to Capt. John A. Cook who changed her port of hail to Provincetown. She left New Bedford in July on her thirty-fifth voyage.

1920 (September)—Set out on her thirty-seventh and last voyage.

1921 (May)—Returned, ending an active whaling career of eighty years.

1922—Took part in the movie *Down to the Sea in Ships*, starring Clara Bow, for which the vessel's rig was changed to that of a ship. Afterwards she sailed to Salem to take part in another movie, *Java Head*, in which she was thinly disguised as a merchant ship.

1924–25—Purchased by artist Harry Neyland and others of a group called Whaling Enshrined. With money given by Col. E. H. R. Greene, she was repaired, repainted, and outfitted and ultimately moved to Greene's estate at South Dartmouth, Mass. where she was placed in a bed of sand and opened to the public.

1935—Col. Greene died, leaving no provision for her future.

1938—Already falling into disrepair, the *Morgan* was jostled and damaged further by the great hurricane.

1941—At the age of one hundred, she was acquired by Mystic Seaport, removed from the sand at South Dartmouth to be placed in a similar berth at Mystic after being towed there less than a month before World War II was declared.

1942—She was opened as an exhibit after being rigged and painted.

1947—Many new spars and much rigging were renewed with all of the masts, including the three lowers, being removed for the purpose.

1955–62—The hull was retopped above the 'tween deck by being given new topsides, bulwarks, and weather deck.

1967—The *Charles W. Morgan* was declared a National Historic Landmark.

1968–72—The entire 'tween deck was rebuilt. New steam-bent boat davits were made up and fitted.

1973–76—The ceiling and standing knees were renewed in the area between the two decks.

1973 (December)—The *Morgan* was

Left: *1925–73,* **Morgan** *was ship rigged, port painted and berthed in sand (Photo: L. D. Martel)* **Right:** *1973, gangway removed and sand dug from her hull, the* **Morgan** *prepares to float (Photo: L. D. Olin)*

refloated after nearly fifty continuous years in the sand.

1974 (January to June)—She was hauled on the new lift dock at the Seaport's Henry B. duPont Preservation Shipyard for an inspection and other work. While at the shipyard she was refastened, recaulked, and resheathed. A new false keel and worm shoe were fitted and her rig was overhauled and converted to that of a double topsail bark. The captain's day cabin was refinished. She was returned to a new berth in the center of the museum, afloat, and open to visitors.

1977—Work began to retop her port topsides. Restoration began on the joinerwork below deck.

STATUS:
Under continuing restoration and maintenance, lower hull original, good condition.

DONOR:
Mystic Seaport Purchase

FURTHER READING:
Ashley, Clifford. *The Yankee Whaler.* Garden City: Halcyon House, 1942.

Bray, Maynard. "The Magnificent *Morgan.*" *The Log of Mystic Seaport,* Spring, 1974.

Church, Albert Cook. *Whaleships and Whaling.* New York: W. W. Norton & Co., 1938.

Dow, George F. *Whale Ships and Whaling.* Salem: Marine Research Society, 1925.

Goode, George Brown. *The Fisheries and Fishing Industries of the United States.* Washington: Government Printing Office, 1887.

Leavitt, John F. *The Charles W. Morgan.* Mystic: The Marine Historical Association, Inc., 1973.

Starbuck, Alexander. *History of the American Whale Fishery.* (Part IV of the Report of the U.S. Commission on Fish and Fisheries) Washington: Government Printing Office, 1878.

ACCESSION NO. 41.761

The **Morgan** *hauled in 1974 (the first time since 1916) on the Seaport's new lift dock (Photo: Thomas Lamb)*

*The whaler **Charles W. Morgan** being warped into her berth in 1974*
(Photo: M. A. Stets)

Furling sail on the **Joseph Conrad** *in 1972*
(Photo: M. A. Stets)

Joseph Conrad (ex-*Georg Stage*)
TRAINING SHIP

111′0″ x 25′2″   1882

"A single topsail full-rigged ship crossing three royals, she was 100 feet on the waterline, 25 feet beam, drew 12 feet, grossed 212 tons. She had been, when I found her, for fifty-two years a schoolship for the Danes. She was built by Burmeister and Wain in Copenhagen in 1882, of Swedish iron; her name was the *Georg Stage,* after the shipowner who financed her building, and she had been training 80 young Danes annually. Built for safety, she was exceptionally strong and as able and seaworthy as a good ship could be made." Alan Villiers in *Cruise of the Conrad.*

Villiers bought her and sailed her around the world during 1934–36. Afterwards, the *Conrad* became millionaire Huntington Hartford's private yacht for a few years; she then served as a training vessel for the U.S. Maritime Commission during World War II.

STATUS:
Lower hull lined with ferro-cement 1969, partly replated around waterline 1977, fair condition, in use for demonstration and as housing for Mariner Training Program.

DONOR:
U.S. Maritime Commission

FURTHER READING AND STUDY:
Underhill, Harold A. *Sail Training and Cadet Ships.* Glasgow: Brown, Son & Ferguson, Ltd., 1956.—*Contains photographs and plans of this vessel as both* Georg Stage *and* Joseph Conrad.

Villiers, Alan. *Cruise of the Conrad.* New York: Charles Scribner's Sons, 1952.

The Log of Mystic Seaport, July, 1978.—*Entire issue devoted to the* Conrad *with special emphasis on the 1977 Shipyard restoration.*

A rigged model, two movies, and a number of historic photographs are in Mystic Seaport's collection.

ACCESSION NO. 47.1948

The **Georg Stage** *off Copenhagen at the turn of the century, with Danish cadets aboard*
(Photo: Source unknown)

The training ship **Joseph Conrad**
in her berth at Mystic Seaport in 1970
(Photo: L. D. Olin)

ROWING CRAFT

Chapter One
FLAT BOTTOM

DUCKING PUNT

8′7″ x 3′6″

Although simplicity and shallow draft are achieved in this punt, she would be hard to conceal when in use because of her high sides. The fact that she has such a small deck makes camouflage with brush difficult.

STATUS:
Original, good condition.

DONOR:
Isaac B. Merriman, Jr.

ACCESSION NO. 61.393

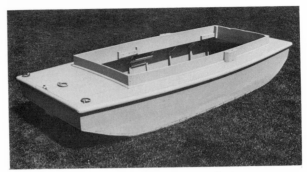

Ducking Punt, 1975 (Photo: Author)

WORK PUNT

10′1″ x 3′11″   ca. 1935

This simple and rather good looking punt was built in Stonington, Connecticut for a yard work boat. Its stability and short length make a punt ideal for this purpose, for oftentimes there is little space around the crowded waterfronts of boatyards. Punts are usually propelled by a sculling oar and this one has a scull hole in either end, giving her a means of quick reverse. Yard punts were more common before the "travel lift." Back when boats were hauled on railways, the yard's docking master usually worked from a punt while positioning the craft being hauled and adjusting her blocking. Fishermen who moor their boats near shore in sheltered harbors often use a punt as a tender to row back and forth.

STATUS:
In use, bottom covered with fiberglass, some repair, good condition.

DONOR:
John B. Bindloss

FURTHER READING:
Gardner, John. *Building Classic Small Craft.* Camden: International Marine Publishing Co., 1977.—*Has chapter on punts.*

ACCESSION NO. 73.719

Work Punt, 1975 (Photo: Author)

The Butthead Skiff, Kathy, *makes an unusual cargo as she is loaded in the* Morgan's *hold.*

While the Morgan's *hold was flooded with water, work beneath her 'tween deck was done from the Butthead Skiff,* Kathy *(Photo: R. A. Fowler)*

Kathy
BUTTHEAD SKIFF
(PUNT), BY CULLER

10'8" x 4'2"   1970

Designed, built, and given the "butt-head skiff" classification by Captain R.D. "Pete" Culler of Concordia Co., Inc., this skiff rows easily in spite of her blunt appearance. She is stable, rugged, and because of her high freeboard can be worked out of without shipping water over her sides. For work around the Seaport waterfront she is ideal. As Captain Pete says, she is ". . . a good beach boat with her long snout, as one can step ashore dry."

STATUS:

In use, excellent condition.

DONOR:

Purchased for Mystic Seaport by John R. Deupree

FURTHER READING:

Culler, R.D. *Skiffs and Schooners.* Camden: International Marine Publishing Co., 1974.—*Contains information on building similar boats by the designer and builder of this one.*

Gardner, John. *Building Classic Small Craft.* Camden: International Marine Publishing Co., 1977.—*Has chapter on building punts.*

ACCESSION NO. 70.647

Skiff in 1976 (Photo: K. Mahler)

SKIFF

10'3" x 3'11"

Flatiron skiff was the common name for these boats because of their resemblance to the housewife's old-fashioned iron. Boats like this, with their two-plank sides and cross-planked bottoms, were not only easy to set up and build, but didn't require hard-to-get material; in fact, scraps from many boat shops oftentimes would do nicely. Thousands of flatiron skiffs have been built; some well constructed and nicely modeled and others quite poorly done. This particular boat was duplicated in 1977 in small numbers by students enrolled in various education programs at the Seaport.

STATUS:
Original, fair condition.

DONOR:
Edward A. Ackerman

FURTHER READING:
Chapelle, Howard I. *American Small Sailing Craft.* New York: W. W. Norton & Co., Inc., 1951.

Culler, R. D. *Skiffs and Schooners.* Camden: International Marine Publishing Co., 1974.

Gardner, John. "The Flatiron Skiff." *National Fisherman*, January–April, 1961.

ACCESSION NO. 76.72

SKIFF FROM SOUTHPORT, MAINE BY BREWER

10'11" x 3'9"

Osborne (Ob) Brewer built this skiff and many like her for lobstermen and summer people. Most were kept and used within sight of Brewer's shop on Cozy Harbor in the village of West Southport. The harbor is small and sheltered so great seaworthiness and speed were not of much concern. Brewer died about 1960 and most of his skiffs were constructed long before then. Nevertheless, quite a few of them are still active.

STATUS:
Original, good condition.

DONOR:
Timothy S. Brewer

FURTHER READING:
Chapelle, Howard I. *American Small Sailing Craft.* New York: W. W. Norton & Co., 1951.

Gardner, John, "The Flatiron Skiff." *National Fisherman*, January and April, 1961.

ACCESSION NO. 70.392

Southport skiff in 1975 (Photo: Author)

Clara
SKIFF FROM NOANK, CONNECTICUT

12′2″ x 4′2″   ca. 1930

Noank fishermen used boats like this to row to their larger vessels from the shore. When not in use the "sharpies," as they were called, were hauled out on wooden ramps or runways at the water's edge, or tied to haulout lines set up between the land and stakes driven into the bottom a short distance offshore.

STATUS:
Paint stripped to bare wood, some repair, approximately 90% original, poor condition.

DONOR:
Maynard E. Bray

FURTHER READING:
(Same as for Brewer skiff 70.392)

ACCESSION NO. 73.87

Clara in 1973 (Photo: M. A. Stets)

Early scene of the Noank waterfront showing skiffs hauled out on ramps (Photo: Source unknown)

SKIFF FROM UNCASVILLE, CONNECTICUT

13′11″ x 3′5″   ca. 1912

Fourteen dollars reputedly was paid for this skiff when she was brand new. Fred Perkins built her part way up the Thames River at Uncasville for use in that area. Although without a centerboard or rudder, she has provision for a mast and probably set a small sail when the wind was fair. Her seats are removable, held in by turnbuttons. Her unusually narrow bottom and the fact that she could be rowed triple banked contributed to her speed, up to a point. But her run is probably too steep and she is too short on the waterline to do much but drag a lot of water when rowed hard.

STATUS:
Original, transom damaged, good condition.

DONOR:
H. Downer Johnson, Jr.

FURTHER READING:
Dolbeare, Harwood B. *A History of Point Breeze on the Thames.* Privately printed.— *Illustration on p. 11 shows a similar boat.*

ACCESSION NO. 74.471

Uncasville skiff in 1975 (Photo: Author)

101

Asa Thomson Skiff, 1978 (Photo: Author)

SKIFF
FROM NEW BEDFORD,
MASSACHUSETTS
BY THOMSON

11'2" x 4'3"   ca. 1925

This unusual model of the skiff, with its high freeboard and kicked up bottom aft, would probably remove her from the flatiron category. For such a basic shape, however, she is rather elegantly constructed with a double-planked bottom, delicate side framing, special brass oarlocks and sockets, and a beautifully worked out stemband and cap having an integral towing eye. She is varnished inside and out and has a built-in bait well under the hinged middle seat. Her large skeg is reinforced by a "sternpost" which runs up the outside of the transom and which has done its intended job well. Strangely enough, she has no seat knees whatsoever; yet she doesn't seem to have suffered because of it.

Her builder, Asa Thomson, was born in 1859 and set up his boatbuilding shop in New Bedford in 1885. By the time this skiff was built, Thomson had nearly a lifetime of experience behind him. Some of those years were spent building delicate and exquisitely finished canoes; thus, it is no wonder that his latter-day skiffs were highly thought of. They were apparently his own design and were particularly sought after as tenders. High sides allowed several persons to be carried in safety; a flat bottom permitted easy landing on a beach; the absence of bottom framing made her quick and simple to clean out; and the turned up run aft kept her bow high when being towed. This latter feature also prevented her stern from dragging water with a load of passengers aboard. When hauled out of the water for a few days, even in the hot summer sun, she could be put overboard without fear of leaking thanks to her double planked bottom. Like all Thomson boats, she is fastened with copper and brass throughout.

STATUS:
Original, good condition.

DONOR:
Richard F. Hunt

ACCESSION NO. 76.148

Asa Thomson takes time out for a smoke while the varnish dries
(Photo: Gift of Mrs. L. Francis Thomson)

Tom Cod
SAILING SKIFF

15'3" x 4'10"   1976

Members of Mystic Seaport, school groups, and the museum staff make use of this simple boat on the Mystic River, either for sailing or rowing. She was designed by Capt. R. D. "Pete" Culler and was built by Willits Ansel of the Seaport staff for ruggedness and easy care. Although a bit larger than the well known Culler-designed "Good Little Skiff," she is of the same easy-to-build construction with lapstrake sides and a cross-planked bottom.

STATUS:

In use, excellent condition.

DONOR:

Mystic Seaport built

FURTHER READING:

Culler, R. D. *Skiffs and Schooners.* Camden: International Marine Publishing Co., 1974.—*The prime source for Culler boats.*

————. "What Makes Classics Real." The *Mariner's Catalog. Vol. 3.* Camden: International Marine Publishing Co., 1975.—*Contains some good details not covered in his* Skiffs and Schooners.

ACCESSION NO. 76.53

Tom Cod *under sail in the Mystic River (Photo: J. Deupree)*

Toad Grunt
SAILING SKIFF

15'8" x 4'8"   1976

This boat is a near sister to *Tom Cod* and was also built by Willits Ansel. For comparison, she was fitted without a headsail while *Tom Cod* is rigged as a sloop. Both carry boomless spritsails, however.

STATUS:

In use, excellent condition.

DONOR:

Mystic Seaport-built

FURTHER READING:

(Same as for *Tom Cod* 76.53)

ACCESSION NO. 76.60

Tom Cod *under construction in the Shipyard's main shop*
(Photo: W. Ansel)

Dory from the **Black Hawk**, *1975 (Photo: Author)*

BANKS DORY FROM SCHOONER *BLACK HAWK*

18'3" x 5'1"   ca. 1940

Of unknown origin, this dory last saw service aboard the 63-foot auxiliary schooner *Black Hawk* which, after conversion from a yacht, fished commercially from New London and Noank during the 1940s and 50s. *Black Hawk* was perhaps the last dory fisherman to sail out of this area. Her plans are shown in the June 1922 issue of *Rudder* magazine.

STATUS:
Restored, mostly original, equipped, exhibited, good condition.

DONOR:
H. H. Kynett

FURTHER READING:
Chapelle, Howard I. *American Small Sailing Craft*. New York: W. W. Norton & Co., Inc., 1951.

———. National Watercraft Collection. Washington: Government Printing Office, 1960.

Gardner, John. *The Dory Book*. Camden: International Marine Publishing Co., 1978.

ACCESSION NO. 55.320

Dory from the **Black Hawk**, *1975 (Photo: Author)*

BANKS DORY FROM SCHOONER *BLACK HAWK*

18'3" x 4'10"   ca. 1940

Also from the schooner *Black Hawk*, this dory appears to be by the same builder as 55.320.

STATUS:
Original, fair condition.

DONOR:
H. H. Kynett

ACCESSION NO. 55.321

Monhegan Island shore scene
(Photo: The Hudson Collection)

Monhegan shore fishermen tending a stop seine from a Banks Dory
(Photo: The Hudson Collection)

From Goode's
Fisheries Report, *1887*

Milton J. Burns (1853–1933) Two Dories and Nets. Watercolor on
paper. (Mystic Seaport Collections 75.32)

Nested Dories (Photo: Author)

Milton J. Burns (1853–1933) Cod Fishing. From **Harper's Weekly,** *October, 1885*

BANKS DORY
FROM LUNENBURG, N.S.
19′8″ x 5′8″   1970

Thousands of simple, seaworthy, inexpensive, and expendible dories have been built over the years. Their first widespread use was by codfishermen around 1860 when fishing from the decks of vessels declined in favor of small fleets of two-man dories. Banks fisherman was the name given to the schooner which carried the dories out to the fishing grounds, or banks, as they were called. The man himself was also called a banks fisherman and his boat a banks dory. Similar dories, usually larger, carried the seine twine (net) of the shore fisherman who fished for herring and mackerel with a seine, while smaller banks dories are the favored lifeboat of the modern fishing draggers. One of the advantages of the dory to the banks fisherman, other than her low cost and seaworthiness, was that she could be stored one inside the other once the seats and other gear had been removed. Customarily, these boats

Allen's Dory Shop, Lunenburg, Nova Scotia. **Left to right:** *planing final bevel, clamping garboard*

would be nested on deck in two stacks of five or six boats each while not in use.

Most old-time dory shops are gone now, but at least two shops still turn out banks dories commercially. At Strawbery Banke in Portsmouth, N.H., the tools, patterns, and expertise acquired from the country's oldest dory shop, Lowell's of Amesbury, Mass., are put to good use as part of that museum's apprentice program; and in Lunenburg, N.S., the Allen dory shop keeps a full-time dory-building crew going.

This dory is really a by-product of a Seaport movie-making project which filmed each step in her construction while she was being built in Capt. Lawrence Allen's shop. The boat and her prefabricated sister are available for study, and viewing the movie serves to visually preserve the way men of long experience go about building a dory.

STATUS:
Unused, excellent condition.

DONOR:
Mystic Seaport purchase

ACCESSION NO. 70.686

Lunenburg Dory in 1975 (Photo: Author)

plank to "tombstone" sternboard, first two strakes of planking in place, and finishing and smoothing before painting (Photos: L. S. Martel)

FURTHER READING:

Atkinson, Bob. "As Old as a Dory." *WoodenBoat*, No. 18, September–October, 1977.

Gardner, John. *The Dory Book.* Camden: International Marine Publishing Co., 1978.

———. "Navy Dory Was Drawn at Height of Type's Use." *National Fisherman*, December, 1977.

Goode, George Brown. *The Fisheries and Fishery Industries of the United States.* Washington: Government Printing Office, 1887.—*Section V, Volume 1 contains a good description of the early use of the banks dory.*

Zimmerman, Jan. "Building the Banks Dory." *WoodenBoat*, No. 19, November–December, 1977.—*A detailed, step-by-step explanation of how the Lowell banks dory is built at Strawbery Banke.*

BANKS DORY (PREFABRICATED) FROM LUNENBURG, N.S.

19′8″ x 5′8″ 1970
(Approximate dimensions of completed boat)

Purchased as separate pieces, this dory has been partially assembled to illustrate the parts that go to make up a dory and the name of each one.

STATUS:
Partly assembled, excellent condition.

DONOR:
Mystic Seaport purchase

ACCESSION NO. 70.687

Prefabricated Dory, 1975 (Photo: Author)

TEN BANKS DORIES, MYSTIC SEAPORT REPRODUCTIONS

18'2" x 4'11"   1976–1978

These boats were built as replacements for the worn out banks dories exhibited aboard the Seaport's fishing schooner, *L. A. Dunton;* the first one was completed in 1976. They are planked with cedar rather than pine and have hackmatack knees for frames instead of iron reinforced oak frames; thus they are expected to far outlast the Nova Scotian dories which preceded them. Will Ansel of the Seaport staff was in charge of the dory-building program and also served as an instructor to students who helped with their building at the museum.

Chapelle's plans for Higgins and Gifford's standard model of the 1880s were used as the representative epitome of banks dory development.

Dory demonstrations are given in the summertime by Seaport staff members so visitors can see just how a dory is hoisted overboard by the schooner's dory tackles, how dories are rigged for fishing, and how they are rowed.

L. A. Dunton *at Chubb's Wharf with Dories (Photo: C. White Peterson)*

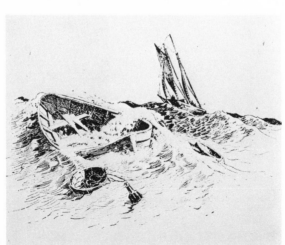

These dynamic drawings by I. W. Taber were illustrations for the first edition of Kipling's wonderful story, **Captains Courageous,** *1897*

108

STATUS:

In use, excellent condition.

DONOR:

Mystic Seaport built reproductions

FURTHER READING:

See also this section under *L. A. Dunton.*

Chapelle, Howard I. *American Small Sailing Craft.* New York: W. W. Norton & Co., Inc., 1951.—*Figure 29 shows the plan from which these boats were built.*

Gardner, John. *The Dory Book.* Camden: International Marine Publishing Co., 1978.

Goode, George Brown. *The Fisheries and Fishery Industries of the United States.* Washington: Government Printing Office, 1887.

ACCESSION NOS. 78.51, 78.52, 78.53, 78.54, 78.55, 78.56, 78.57, 78.58, 78.59, 78.60

A ten-dory-power auxiliary moves this fishing schooner clear of the harbor at St. John's, Newfoundland (Courtesy: Stuart Wilson)

BANKS DORY, MASSACHUSETTS HUMANE SOCIETY

17′4″ x 4′8″   ca. 1900

The crew of the Siasconset, Nantucket, life-saving station used this dory along with the usual double-ended surfboat. Later on it was bought by Jim Coffin and used to gather seaweed for his famous clambakes. It is a slight departure from the usual banks dory in that its bottom is not rockered, and steam-bent, rather than sawn, frames are used.

STATUS:

Paint stripped to bare wood, original, good condition.

DONOR:

Charles F. Sayle

FURTHER READING:

Howe, M. A. DeWolfe. *The Humane Society of the Commonwealth of Massachusetts—An Historical Review 1785–1916.* Boston: The Riverside Press, 1918.

Gardner, John. *The Dory Book.* Camden: International Marine Publishing Co., 1978.

ACCESSION NO. 63.1517

Massachusetts Humane Society Dory in 1975 (Photo: Author)

*Lumberman's Batteau in 1973, with stern
modified for an
outboard motor (Photo: Author)*

MAINE LUMBERMAN'S BATEAU #2556

24'8" x 6'0"

Until recently bateaux were used for
spring log drives on the great rivers of
Canada and Maine. They are crudely
built but of rugged construction to withstand the chafe and pressure from moving logs. Neither select materials nor
exacting fits were necessary to produce
them.

STATUS:

Stern cut off and transom added for outboard power, otherwise mostly original,
fair condition.

DONOR:

Great Northern Paper Co., Inc.

FURTHER READING:

Chapelle, Howard I. *American Small Sailing Craft*. New York: W. W. Norton Inc.,
1951.

Gardner, John. *The Dory Book*. Camden:
International Marine Publishing Co., 1978.

Thoreau, Henry D. *The Maine Woods*. New
York: Thomas Y. Crowell & Co., 1909.

"Tin Boats Take Over for Classic Batteaus
On River Drive." National Fisherman, May,
1971.—*Photo-story of modern Machias
River log drive, photos by Red Boutilier.*

ACCESSION NO. 73.408

*A Batteau in action during the spring pulp
drive for the Great Northern Paper Company
(Courtesy: Great Northern Paper Company)*

PISCATAQUA RIVER WHERRY

16′5″ x 4′1″   ca. 1850

Easy to build, as are most dory types, the long lines of this so-called wherry and her low freeboard make for easy rowing. She needed to row well for the river current is strong near Eliot, Maine, where she was built as a means of basic transportation. A flat bottom protected by a sacrificial "false bottom" of hardwood enables boarding her from the beach without damage. The reproduction of this boat was remarkably easy to build. Only 8-inch boards were needed in her topside planking and these were easily hung without the use of steam or fancy clamping.

She is a handsome boat and would make an ideal craft for an amateur builder, and when complete would row about as well as the more complex Whitehall, peapod, or St. Lawrence River skiff.

STATUS:
Original, very good condition.

DONOR:
David C. Wherren, in exchange for Seaport-built reproduction

FURTHER READING:
Gardner, John. *Building Classic Small Craft.* Camden: International Marine Publishing Co., 1977.

————. *The Dory Book.* Camden: International Marine Publishing Co., 1978.

ACCESSION NO. 73.236

*Piscataqua River Wherry, 1975
(Photo: Author)*

*Piscataqua River Wherry, 1975
(Photo: Author)*

In exchange for the original, Mystic Seaport built this reproduction of the Piscataqua River Wherry (Photo: M. A. Stets)

Gunning dory, 1975 (Photo: Author)

DOUBLE-ENDED GUNNING DORY FROM MARBLEHEAD

16′1″ x 4′6″   ca. 1940

These boats were favored around Marblehead harbor for bird shooting. This one was built over the dory molds of William Chamberlain either by Capt. Gerald Smith or by Albert Cloutman, foreman at Graves Yacht Yard at the time, but who earlier had worked for Chamberlain. Of these boats John Gardner says, "The gunning dory as perfected in Marblehead by William Chamberlain is the queen of all dories, and one of the handsomest double-enders ever built anywhere, not to mention its easy speed under oars and its unexcelled rough-water ability with capable hands at the oars." Quote from *Building Classic Small Craft*, p. 100.

Although the sheer is flatter and less handsome than the larger boat which Gardner concentrates on in his writing, she is nevertheless a good looking boat.

STATUS:
Fiberglass covered outside, otherwise original, good condition.

DONOR:
Richard Parker

FURTHER READING:
Gardner, John. *Building Classic Small Craft*. Camden: International Marine Publishing Co., 1977.—*Has chapter on the Marblehead gunning dory.*

———. *The Dory Book*. Camden: International Marine Publishing Co., 1978.

ACCESSION NO. 69.99

Chaisson double-ended dory, 1975
(Photo: K. Mahler)

Point Sardine Life Boat No. 1
DOUBLE-ENDED DORY BY CHAISSON

14′4″ x 4′6″   ca. 1920

George Chaisson, whose shop in Swampscott, Massachusetts, produced a great many boats large and small, built this handsome variation of the traditional Swampscott round-sided dory. Reportedly she was designed by John G. Alden for use as a tender on one of his well known Malabar schooners.

STATUS:
Original, although modified somewhat with the addition of a steering oar brace, very good condition.

DONOR:
R. Livingston Ireland

FURTHER READING:
Gardner, John. *Building Classic Small Craft*. Camden: International Marine Publishing Co., 1977.

———. *The Dory Book*. Camden: International Marine Publishing Co., 1978.

ACCESSION NO. 75.397

SWAMPSCOTT DORY
BY CHAISSON

15'2" x 4'6"   ca. 1920

This production model called a "clipper dory" (by the well-known Swampscott boatbuilder, George L. Chaisson) was used as a tender for a larger boat and for pleasure rowing.

STATUS:
Restored 1972, approximately 85% original.

DONOR:
Mystic Seaport purchase

FURTHER READING:
Gardner, John. *The Dory Book*. Camden: International Marine Publishing Co., 1978.

Promotional catalog describing and illustrating the standard boats built by Chaisson. Privately printed and undated. Copy of this catalog is in the library at Mystic Seaport.

ACCESSION NO. 71.205

Chaisson Swampscott dory, 1975 (Photo: Author)

DORY-SKIFF
BY CHAMBERLAIN,
MYSTIC SEAPORT
BUILT REPRODUCTION

13'5" x 4'0"   1971

In the early decades of this century boats of this model were built in quantity by William Chamberlain in his shop at Marblehead. Lately, in addition to this boat, there have been others built to this same model using plans published in the *National Fisherman* by John Gardner. Among them is the Parimar dory-skiff built in fiberglass.

STATUS:
In use, excellent condition.

DONOR:
Mystic Seaport built reproduction

FURTHER READING:
Gardner, John. *The Dory Book*. Camden: International Marine Publishing Co., 1978.

ACCESSION NO. 71.238

Seaport built Chamberlain dory-skiff in 1971 with John Gardner at the oars
(Photo: R. A. Fowler)

Amesbury dory-skiff, 1975 (Photo: Author)

AMESBURY DORY-SKIFF

14'0" x 4'0"   ca. 1930

Models such as this were favorites of fishermen and yachtsmen alike as tenders for larger craft. Most were built on the north shore of Massachusetts; this one probably came from the Lowell shop at Amesbury.

STATUS:
Hull stripped of paint and fiberglass 1973, mostly original, fair condition.

DONOR:
Ann W. Kenyon

FURTHER READING:
Gardner, John. *The Dory Book.* Camden: International Marine Publishing Co., 1978.

ACCESSION NO. 57.290

Amesbury dory-skiff as she appeared in her early days at the Seaport with her hull covered with fiberglass (Photo: L. S. Martel)

SWAMPSCOTT SAILING DORY, MYSTIC SEAPORT BUILT

17′3″ x 4′6″   1974

"These Swampscott boats are the aristocrats of the dory clan, and are not to be confused with their clumsier, more crudely built cousins, the heavy slab-sided working dories of the Grand Banks fishermen. . . . The true Swampscott dory . . . is essentially a round-bottom boat, yet with enough flat in its relatively narrow board bottom to sit upright on the beach when it grounds out. For a boat that is to be beached frequently, this is an especially desirable feature, particularly as it permits a double bottom, the outer layer of which is easily renewed when it wears thin from dragging over rocks." This quote is from John Gardner's *Building Classic Small Craft.*

Barry Thomas of the Seaport's Small Craft Lab built this boat and her plans are much like those contained in chapter 11 of *Building Classic Small Craft.* Both boats were modeled by John Gardner after the dories of Massachusetts' north shore.

STATUS:
In use, excellent condition.

DONOR:
Mystic Seaport built

FURTHER READING:
Gardner, John. *Building Classic Small Craft.* Camden: International Marine Publishing Co., 1977.

————. *The Dory Book.* Camden: International Marine Publishing Co., 1978.

ACCESSION NO. 74.1025

December trial of the Swampscott sailing dory. Later a conventional rudder replaced the oar shown here (Photo: K. Mahler)

Swampscott sailing dory on launching day, November, 1974 (Photo: K. Mahler)

Beachcomber dory in 1975 (Photo: Author)

CATALOGUE
...... OF ......

POWER BOATS

Sailing and Clipper Dories

Rowboats and Skiffs

BUILT BY

WILLIAM H. CHAMBERLAIN

14 Orne Street . . . . . Marblehead, Mass.

These boats are all built under my personal supervision, by skilled workmen. They are noted for their stability and seaworthiness and their lines are the result of years of study and practical experience, and are guaranteed second to none.

BEACHCOMBER DORY

These dories have gained a much envied name for themselves, being adopted by the Beachcomber Club of Marblehead and the Alpha Club of Salem. They are well known for their speed, stability and seaworthiness. They are the fastest dories of their size on the market.

15 feet bottom, 21 feet over all, $57.00

Rigged with mast, sails and oars, complete, $90.00.

7

BEACHCOMBER-ALPHA SAILING DORY BY CHAMBERLAIN

20′10″ x 4′11″   ca. 1900

William Chamberlain modeled this boat and built many like her for the Beachcomber and Alpha Dory Clubs of Marblehead and Salem, respectively. These two clubs came into being about 1890 and interest in racing these big dories continued into the 1930s. During that time there were several changes in the rig, the most apparent being the adoption of the cross-cut battened mainsail with its rather extreme roach in place of the original up and down cut sail.

While few boats survive today from the original fleet, a number of reproductions have been built from the very detailed drawings prepared by John Gardner for the *National Fisherman* in 1964. Anyone making a study of these boats would also do well to inspect the rigged model at the Peabody Museum of Salem which was carefully researched then built in 1959 under the direction of a special committee of surviving members of the Beachcomber and Alpha clubs.

STATUS:
Original, fair condition.

DONOR:
Sylvester B. Kelley

FURTHER READING:
Gardner, John. *Building Classic Small Craft.* Camden: International Marine Publishing Co., 1977.

———. *The Dory Book.* Camden: International Marine Publishing Co., 1978.

Promotional catalog describing and illustrating the standard boats built by William Chamberlain. Privately printed and undated. A copy of this catalog is in the library at Mystic Seaport.

ACCESSION NO. 73.386

SAILING DORY BY CHAMBERLAIN

18′5″ x 4′9″ ca. 1930

This is similar to, but smaller than, Chamberlain's standard "Beachcomber" model. Like the "Beachcomber" she steers with a yoke and continuous steering line, led about halfway forward, so the helmsman can get well up to windward and still steer.

STATUS:

Some repair, split in garboard planks has been reinforced with blocking, mostly original, good condition.

DONOR:

Estate of Welles V. Moot

FURTHER READING:

(Same as for dory 73.386)

ACCESSION NO. 77.256

Chamberlain sailing dory in 1978
(Photo: Author)

SAILING DORY BY CHAISSON

16′5″ x 5′3″ ca. 1930

"This is the only boat of its type to survive, so far as I know. Once in common use on Fisherman's Beach (Swampscott, Mass.) but for a rowing work boat, not fitted for sail. This boat is in practically new condition and was stored in a barn unused for something like 40 years until found and sailed for two summers by John M. Chaisson, the designer's grandson, and Paul Sherry, husband of Joan C. Sherry, Joe Chaisson's granddaughter . . ." John Gardner.

STATUS:

Original, excellent condition.

DONOR:

John M. Chaisson, William J. Chaisson, Joan C. Sherry

FURTHER READING:

Gardner, John. *The Dory Book*. Camden: International Marine Publishing Co., 1978.

————. *Building Classic Small Craft*. Camden: International Marine Publishing Co., 1977.

Promotional catalog describing and illustrating the standard boats built by Chaisson. Privately printed and undated. A copy is in the library at Mystic Seaport.

ACCESSION NO. 77.262

Chaisson sailing dory in 1978 (Photo: Author)

117

Chapter Two
ROUND BOTTOM

Bailey Whitehall on exhibit, 1978 (Photo: Author)

BAILEY WHITEHALL

16′9″ x 3′7″   1879

Whitehalls, most experts agree, originated about 1820 as runners' boats around the New York waterfront, taking their name from nearby Whitehall Street. As a deepwater sailing vessel made her way up the bay after months at sea, her crew was accosted by runners who came aboard huckstering for local brothels, ship chandlers and the like, hot on the trail of whatever money the poor sailors had managed to earn during their passage. Runners from the ships' owners or agents might be rowed out as well in a working Whitehall boat with a couple of "Battery boatmen" at the oars.

As the years went by the boatmen of other seaports, notably Boston, adopted Whitehalls, perhaps modified, which were described by Capt. Charlton Smith as being "not under seventeen nor over twenty feet in length. The breadth not less than four feet. The depth not less than nineteen inches. They were rowed on the gunwales and had to weigh at least 265 pounds. So read the rules of the boat clubs."

Within the past thirty-five years there has been a renewed interest in Whitehall boats, their history, and their characteristics—an understandable feeling because of their grace and beauty. W. P. Stephens, Capt. Charlton Smith, and Howard Chapelle have been leaders in Whitehall re-

search, but it has been John Gardner who, quite recently, has fitted all the pieces together and must be recognized as Dean of the Whitehalls.

Of this boat, John Gardner says in his book, *Building Classic Small Craft* that she is "a fancy pleasure Whitehall apparently built at Boston, Massachusetts, in 1879. A sliding seat for the oarsman on runners extending over the top of the daggerboard case is a refinement not to be found in the runner's workboat. Yet in essentials the boat conforms to standard Boston Whitehall construction, although its scantlings are reduced to an absolute minimum, and its hull lines are drawn extra lean and fine. The peerless workmanship found in this boat, its exquisite lines, and delicate yet sturdy construction which has lasted so well after so many years, bespeak the hand of a master craftsman. Although we do not know the name of the builder, there is good reason to conclude that this boat came out of one of the leading Boston boatshops of the era, when the boatbuilding craft was practiced on a level which we do not begin to approach in this country today."

As far as is known, this boat is the only surviving contemporary Whitehall from either New York or Boston. The Baileys, father and son, owned her from 1881 until she was given to Mystic Seaport seventy-two years later.

STATUS:
Some repair but mostly original, fair condition.

DONOR:
Edwin M. and David C. Bailey

FURTHER READING:
Chapelle, Howard I. *American Small Sailing Craft.* New York: W. W. Norton & Co., Inc., 1951.

Gardner, John. *Building Classic Small Craft.* Camden: International Marine Publishing Co., 1977.

Smith, Charlton L. "The Whitehall Boat." *Rudder*, August, 1943.

ACCESSION NO. 54.211

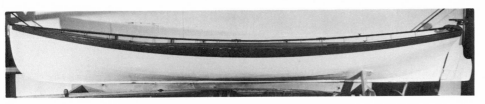

Bailey Whitehall in storage, 1975 (Photo: Author)

BOSTON WHITEHALL

13′2″ x 4′0″   ca. 1900–1920

Although this boat is smaller than the old working Whitehalls and was built later, probably in Maine rather than Boston, Charles Lawton called her a good representative of the nineteenth-century Boston Whitehall. Lawton, as a young man, had built boats for the H. V. Partelow Co., a firm noted for its superior Whitehalls and its improved ways of building them. This particular boat was first pointed out to John Gardner in the early 1940s when he and Lawton, who was then an old man, worked together at Graves' Yacht Yard in Marblehead. After studying the boat and learning all he could about Whitehall construction from Lawton, Gardner lost track of her until a few years ago when she turned up again, dried out and paint sick, and was given to Mystic Seaport.

To be classed as a Whitehall type, a boat must have not only the right shape but certain other features as well. Her frames must lay square to the keel and be bevelled to fit the planking which is hung later; her frames also must be tapered so they are deeper at their heels than at their heads. Whitehalls always had an oak sheer strake, bevelled on its lower edge to fit against, and stand out slightly beyond, a matching bevel on the top edge of the binding strake as the second plank down was called. The rest of the planking was smooth-seamed. An inwale always covered the heads of the frames and a horseshoe-shaped stern seat with a backrest was standard on Whitehall boats.

STATUS:
Restored 1970, mostly original, good condition.

DONOR:
William F. Peach

FURTHER READING:
(Same as for 54.211)

ACCESSION NO. 69.584

Boston Whitehall on exhibit, 1978 (Photo: Author)

Seaport built Whitehall tender in 1974 (Photo: T. J. Baker)

WHITEHALL TENDER,
MYSTIC SEAPORT BUILT REPRODUCTION

14′10″ x 4′2″   1974

Barry Thomas, of the Seaport's Small Craft Lab, built this lovely boat to lines taken from an old (ca. 1910) tender by Rice Bros., East Boothbay, Maine, now in the Bath Marine Museum. But the new boat's construction was altered to that of a classic working Whitehall and building her this way yielded the first-hand experience and photos needed to produce an authoritative book on the subject. The Whitehall has always been a favorite of amateur builders and many plans of this boat have been sold. Her plans are used as well by the first-year students at the state-sponsored boat-building school in Lubec, Maine, who complete several boats each year.

STATUS:
In use, excellent condition.

DONOR:
Mystic Seaport built reproduction

FURTHER READING:
(Same as for 52.211 and 69.584)

ACCESSION NO. 74.94

121

General Lafayette *on exhibit, 1978 (Photo: Author)*

The **American Star** *was taken to Lafayette's estate outside Paris in the 1820s and has*

General Lafayette
EARLY NINETEENTH-CENTURY PULLING BOAT, MYSTIC SEAPORT BUILT REPRODUCTION

27′4″ x 3′10″   1975

John Gardner built this near replica of the New York Harbor race-boat *American Star* (ca. 1820). The original, which defeated the British boat *Dart* in a now-famous race during the winter of 1824, was presented to General Lafayette who visited the United States a short time later. Lafayette prized the gift; he took her to his chateau just outside Paris and placed her inside out of the weather, where she has since remained. Realizing her importance as the oldest American small boat known to exist, Gardner seized the first opportunity to view, study, and record her lines, and structural details with the idea of duplicating her at the Seaport.

Compared with small boat construction as most of us know it, these boats were very differently put together, being planked with thin ¼-inch cedar over an alternating structure of substantial floor timbers and very light steam-bent frames. For her great length she is quite light; yet, due largely to her gunwales and seats, she is stiff and strong. Fun to row, fast and responsive, but not the boat to use if the course isn't straight, or nearly so.

STATUS:
In use, excellent condition.

DONOR:
Mystic Seaport built reproduction sponsored by John R. Deupree

FURTHER READING:
Gardner, John. *Building Classic Small Craft.* Camden: International Marine Publishing Co., 1977.

————. "Early Days of Rowing Sport." *The Log of Mystic Seaport*, Winter, 1971.

————. "The American Star." *The Log of Mystic Seaport*, Fall, 1972.

ACCESSION NO. 74.1026

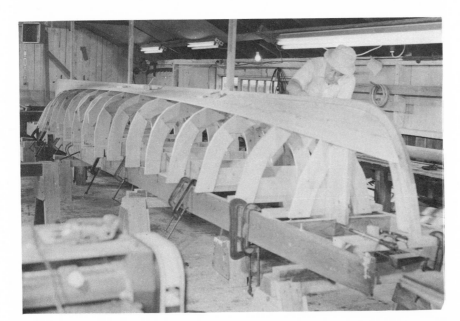

John Gardner planking up the **General Lafayette** *in 1974 (Photo: K. Mahler)*

been preserved there ever since. This photo taken about 1971 (Photo: H. Grey)

General Lafayette *underway on the Mystic River (Photo: K. Mahler)*

Mary A. *in 1975 (Photo: Author)*

Mary A.
PULLING BOAT FROM SOUTHPORT, MAINE

12′6″ x 3′10″   ca. 1910

Rowing for pleasure was what "rusticators" who came to their cottages each summer from the cities did in boats like this. Most were owned by the summer people themselves and were kept at their floats or at the yacht club. It is true, however, that such craft were sometimes rented by summer hotels to their guests. This particular boat is believed to have been built by one of the McFarlands and was last used at Southport, Maine.

STATUS:

Some repair, approximately 85% original, fair condition.

DONOR:

Maynard E. Bray

FURTHER READING:

Clifford, Harold B. *The Boothbay Region, 1906 to 1960.* Freeport: Bond Wheelwright Co., 1961.

Gardner, John. *Building Classic Small Craft.* Camden: International Marine Publishing Co., 1977.

ACCESSION NO. 73.88

123

PULLING BOAT FROM SOUTHPORT, MAINE

11′11″ x 3′10″   ca. 1920

This boat was also found in Southport, Maine, and is quite similar to the *Mary A.* above. Known simply as round bottom rowboats along the Maine coast, they descend directly from the Whitehall boats of New York and Boston.

STATUS:
Restored by donor in 1973, approximately 80% original, good condition.

DONOR:
Richard W. Conant

FURTHER READING:
(Same as for pulling boat 73.88)

ACCESSION NO. 74.472

Pulling boat from Southport, 1975 (Photo: Author)

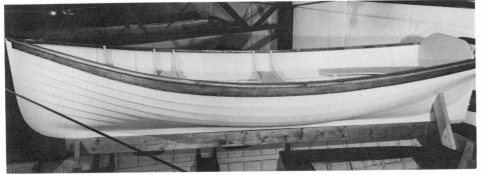

Wardwell pulling boat in 1975 (Photo: Author)

PULLING BOAT BY WARDWELL

14′0″ x 4′6″   ca. 1930–40

For an amateur, Dr. I. F. Wardwell did a commendable job building this boat to modified Whitehall lines. Both frames and floors are joggled to fay tight against the planking between laps, a good idea to back up and help strengthen the unusually thin planking. However, her garboards are too wide, even for thicker planking, and in spite of the little use this boat has seen, they have already started to buckle.

STATUS:
Refinished 1973, original, good condition.

DONOR:
Charles A. Betts, Jr.

FURTHER READING:
Gardner, John. *Building Classic Small Craft*. Camden: International Marine Publishing Co., 1977.

ACCESSION NO. 49.323

GIG, PROBABLY FROM SCHOONER *DAUNTLESS*

16'2" x 4'3" ca. 1870

The famous schooner-yacht *Dauntless* was built as *L'Hirondelle* at Mystic, Connecticut, in 1866. Three years later, under the ownership of James Gordon Bennett and with the name *Dauntless*, she raced across the Atlantic against the America's Cup challenger *Cambria*, losing by only one hour. Unfortunately there is some doubt as to whether this gig belonged to *Dauntless* although photos do show a similar craft on her davits. In any event, *Dauntless* ended her days on the Connecticut River at Essex as the *Dauntless* Club headquarters and was an inspiration for the name of the Dauntless Shipyard there.

The Seaport has in its collection two rigged models and a very fine series of photographs of the *Dauntless*.

STATUS:
Some repair, mostly original, fair condition.

DONOR:
Dr. C. K. Stillman

FURTHER READING:
Bunting, W. H. *Steamers, Schooners, Cutters and Sloops.* Boston: Houghton Mifflin Co., for the Society for the Preservation of New England Antiquities, 1974.—*A photograph and good writeup of* Dauntless *appear on p. 29.*

Perry, Lawrence. *"Dauntless—A Boat With a Great Heart." Yachting,* December, 1911.—*A good biography of the schooner* Dauntless *which covers her racing career.*

ACCESSION NO. 38.570

Dauntless at the start of her 1887 race to Ireland against Coronet (Photo: N. L. Stebbins; Courtesy: The Society for the Preservation of New England Antiquities)

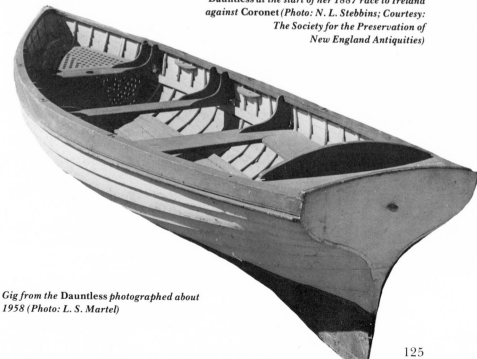

Gig from the Dauntless photographed about 1958 (Photo: L. S. Martel)

Gig from the **Noma,** *1975 (Photo: Author)*

GIG FROM
STEAM YACHT *NOMA*

24'10" x 5'1"   ca. 1890

The 263-foot *Noma* came out in 1892 from the Staten Island yard of Burlee Shipbuilding & Dry Dock Co. Clinton Crane designed her for railroad mogul W. B. Leeds who used her a few years, after which she belonged to the Astors, then the Wanamakers, finally going to foreign registry as *Vega* in the early 1930s. Her gig was but an insignificant part of her outfit, for also on davits were a couple of naphtha launches, a racing sailboat of about 25-feet, and another gig. Each of this gig's four-man crew pulled one oar. A splendid model of *Noma* is in Mystic Seaport's collection.

STATUS:

Mostly original, good condition.

DONOR:

Bard College

FURTHER READING AND STUDY:

Crane, Clinton H. *Clinton Crane's Yachting Memories.* New York: D. Van Nostrand Co., Inc., 1952.

Hofman, Erik. *The Steam Yachts.* Tuckahoe: John De Graff, Inc. 1970.

ACCESSION NO. 59.967

Helen N. *about 1972 (Photo: M. A. Stets)*

Helen N.
PULLING BOAT

16'9" x 3'10"

Similar in shape to a Whitehall but of different and lighter construction, *Helen N.* was found by the donor in a Gloucester, Massachusetts, boatyard in 1961. He bought her on the spot and afterwards tried unsuccessfully to track down her history.

STATUS:

Original, fair condition.

DONOR:

Michael D. Sturges

ACCESSION NO. 72.930

Whitehalls in front of a Lake George summer hotel
(Photo: Source unknown)

Pulling boats for hire at Castine, Maine
(Courtesy: Joel White)

Livery Boat in 1975 (Photo: Author)

PULLING BOAT, PROBABLY FOR LIVERY USE

13'7" x 3'8"

Quite probably this is a livery boat which, along with others like her, might have been kept by a lakeside summer hotel for use by its guests. Or it might have belonged to a boat livery to be rented out for public use. It is apparent that short cuts were taken by whomever built her, for she was not produced with a discriminating buyer in mind. For example, her garboards, when fitted to the keel batten, were allowed to run out past it to be cut off flush later after fastening, so that what appears to be the keel is in reality only a chafing strip to protect the garboards from damage. Thus built, the garboard seam is hidden and cannot be caulked later. Yet, in spite of the quick and dirty way she is built, there is nothing at all second rate about her shape; she is one of the nicest modeled pulling boats in the entire collection.

STATUS:
Original, fair condition.

DONOR:
John S. Van Etten

ACCESSION NO. 73.728

Favorite in 1975 (Photo: Author)

Favorite
PULLING BOAT

11'9" x 4'0"   ca. 1900

Favorite is smooth inside as well as out because she has no frames. Her hull is strip-planked and held in shape with extra large seat knees which extend below as well as above the seats. Her lines are much like those of a Whitehall even though her construction is far removed from one.

STATUS:

Refinished 1969, original, good condition.

DONOR:

Elwell B. Thomas

FURTHER READING:

Gardner, John. *Building Classic Small Craft.* Camden: International Marine Publishing Co., 1977.

ACCESSION NO. 40.504

Punch
PULLING BOAT
BY CULLER

17'8" x 4'1"   1970

A modified Whitehall model designed and built by Captain R. D. Culler of Concordia Co., Inc., who says: ". . . it is not a boat suited to beach work as a steady thing, it is quite slow in turning, and on account of this sculls very well. The charm of these boats seems never to die out, even in a modern age—if one wants the best, along with the cost of it and the few drawbacks, the Whitehall is it."

STATUS:

In use, excellent condition.

DONOR:

B. Glenn MacNary

FURTHER READING:

Culler, R. D. *Skiffs and Schooners.* Camden: International Marine Publishing Co., 1974.

ACCESSION NO. 74.1011

Punch in 1975 (Photo: Author)

Lawton in 1975 (Photo: Author)

Lawton
PULLING BOAT
BY GARDNER

14′8″ x 3′11″   1970

John Gardner modeled this boat with the entrance of a St. Lawrence skiff and an especially buoyant afterbody inspired by lifesaving requirements of the Red Cross. She was beautifully built by Gardner, who used Whitehall construction features such as bevelled frames and a closed gunwale. He named her after Marblehead's one-time sage of small craft, Charles A. Lawton, one of his mentors—"Somehow in talking with Charlie, I became enamored of the Whitehall."

STATUS:
In use, excellent condition.

DONOR:
Mystic Seaport built

FURTHER READING:
Gardner, John. *Building Classic Small Craft.* Camden: International Marine Publishing Co., 1977.—*Source of above quote by John Gardner.*

————. "Toward a Better Rowboat." *National Fisherman,* January, 1971.

ACCESSION NO. 71.236

PULLING BOAT RELICS

Partelow built pulling boat in 1975

Lenox model pulling boat in 1975

Lake boat in 1975

These boats were brought to Mystic Seaport for study. Measured drawings have already been made of some of them. It is doubtful if any restoration work will be done; however, such relics are often more valuable if simply preserved for future reference.

Accession No.	Dimensions	Donor	Remarks
73.39	14′0″ x 3′10″	Dwight P. Quigley	Partelow-built, ca. 1890
73.235	15′6″ x 3′10″	Matthew Griswold, Jr.	Lenox model
73.25	15′8″ x 3′6″	Thomas R. Wilcox	Lake boat
74.1065	15′0″ x 4′0″	Robert Worsley	Rabbeted bottom board, planked down like wherry
73.489	15′10″ x 3′8″	E. Zell Steever V	Sheet metal hull

Lapstrake pulling boat in 1975

Metal pulling boat in 1975

(Photos: Author)

129

Rangeley Lake boat in 1975 (Photo: Author)

FURTHER READING, RELICS:

Gardner, John. "Whitehall and Canoe—An Era Ends," The *Log of Mystic Seaport*, Summer, 1973.

————. *Building Classic Small Craft*. Camden: International Marine Publishing Co., Inc., 1977.

Illustrated catalog of W. H. Mullins Co. entitled *Pressed Steel Boats, Catalog No. 13*. Salem, Ohio: The W. H. Mullins Co. ca. 1915–20.

Illustrated catalog of Partelow Co. Privately printed and undated. A copy is in the library at Mystic Seaport.

RANGELEY LAKE BOAT

14'7" x 3'3"   ca. 1915

Less delicate than the Adirondack guide boat or the St. Lawrence skiff, Rangeley boats were mostly used for the same purpose: taking city sportsmen out fishing. It is possible that a St. Lawrence skiff inspired the Rangeley. Regardless of origin, it became popular in the 1870s and remained so for the next fifty-odd years. This boat was probably built by C. W. Barrett. Since she was laid out for single person use, she is smaller than the usual two-person, 17-footer.

STATUS:
Original, good condition.

DONOR:
Godfrey W. Kauffmann

FURTHER READING:
Gardner, John. *Building Classic Small Craft*. Camden: International Marine Publishing Co., 1977.

————. "Rangeley Boat." *National Fisherman*, January–April, 1968, September–October, 1969.

————. "The Rangeley Boat." *The Log of Mystic Seaport*, Winter, 1973.

ACCESSION NO. 74.1007

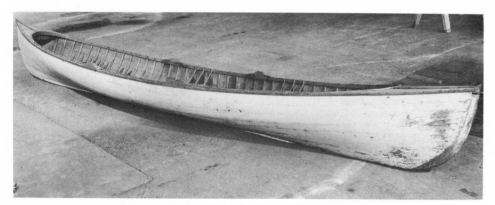

Lake type double-ended pulling boat, 1978 (Photo: Author)

PULLING BOAT, LAKE TYPE

18'6" x 3'6"

While the designer and builder of this sleek craft are not known, they must have been inspired somewhat by the Rangeley Lake boat and perhaps even the St. Lawrence skiff. Her planking method derives from yet a third well-known boat type, the Adirondack guide boat. The planks form a smooth skin inside and out; yet their edges are bevelled and fastened along the laps making what is commonly called a guide boat seam. There is no indication of her ever having had a centerboard, but she was rigged for sailing at one time. Her mast partner is a rather fancy affair made of bronze and pivoted to open so the mast can be more easily stepped.

STATUS:
Original, frames broken and rotted in many places, poor condition.

DONOR:
Joel M. White

ACCESSION NO. 77.257

A. L. Rotch
PULLING BOAT

14′1″ x 3′0″   ca. 1888

This boat was fresh from the Rushton Shop when the Rotch family bought her. We believe she is a standard version (Rushton called it his Grade B construction) of the boat (75.440) described on page 132. Not only is her shape (except for a minor variation in beam) the same as 75.440, but her oarlock sockets, gudgeons, and bow eyes match perfectly to those shown in Rushton's illustrated catalog.

Although she lay idle for about fifty years before coming to the Seaport in 1960, she was carefully kept in covered storage by the family who had always owned her.

STATUS:
Mostly original, good condition.

DONOR:
Arthur Rotch.

ACCESSION NO. 60.261

A. L. Rotch *in 1975 (Photo: Author)*

PULLING BOAT WITH CANOE-LIKE ENDS

15′0″ x 3′5″

Nothing is known about the origin or history of this canoe-like rowing boat except that she was last used in Maine. Certainly the quick sheer at her ends along with the profiles of her bow and stern show that she descended from the open Indian canoe. Perhaps another feature of the Indian canoe, its flat frames, should have been used in this boat as well, because the small square frames with which she was built have nearly all broken.

STATUS:
Original, fair condition.

DONOR:
William C. Page

ACCESSION NO. 76.65

Pulling boat, 1976 (Photo: J. Deupree)

Rushton pulling boat in 1978 (Photo: K. Mahler)

PULLING BOAT BY RUSHTON

14′1″ x 3′2″   1888

J. Henry Rushton's boatshop in Canton, New York, produced this boat and she was purchased as a birthday gift for the donor's great aunt, Miss Catherine Kitchell, when she turned ten. The boat first used at the family summer place on Lake George, New York, eventually went to Lake Memphremagog, Vermont. The Rushton catalog of 1887 shows a similar boat as No. 109. There is no doubt that Rushton built wonderful boats; yet he did his share of "puffing up" his products. His catalog claims that by 1887 he had received more than 75,000 letters, apparently most of them from satisfied customers. These letters were the basis for his statement that 99⅓% of his customers "expressed unqualified approval of our work."

STATUS:
Refinished by donor, mostly original, good condition.

DONOR:
Gordon K. Douglass

FURTHER READING:
Manley, Atwood. *Rushton and His Times in American Canoeing.* Syracuse: Syracuse University Press for Adirondack Museum, 1968.

Promotional catalog describing and illustrating the boats by Rushton. Privately printed, dated 1887. A copy is in the library at Mystic Seaport.

ACCESSION NO. 75.440

PULLING BOAT BY JOYNER

·14′0″ x 3′1″   ca. 1890

The Schenectady, New York, shop of Fletcher Joyner and Sons built this boat and advertised it as a standard model called a "cedar hunting and ladies boat." Joyner was a well known competitor of J. Henry Rushton in that wonderful era of high-quality lightweight wooden small craft production. She is smooth-planked over closely spaced frames and has outrigger type oarlocks to permit the use of longer oars. The design of her hinged backrest is particularly neat and could be adapted to fit the thwart of most any small boat.

STATUS:
Original, good condition.

DONOR:
John C. Gehrig

FURTHER READING:
F. Joyner & Son's Photographic Catalog and Price List for 1884, Glens Falls, N.Y.—*A copy is in the library at Mystic Seaport.*

ACCESSION NO. 75.459

Joyner built pulling boat, 1978 (Photo: Author)

Comet
YACHT TENDER
BY NEVINS

10'0" x 4'0"   ca. 1920

Her overall length was probably dictated by the stowage space on board one of the many yachts built by the Nevins yard at City Island, New York. She is too short for good rowing and really a bit small to carry more than three persons. But being able to take the tender or dinghy aboard is a distinct advantage, and the sacrifice in performance was oftentimes a worthwhile compromise.

STATUS:
Some repair, mostly original, fair condition.

DONOR:
Isaac B. Merriman, Jr.

ACCESSION NO. 64.632

Comet in 1975 (Photo: Author)

Madelon in 1978 (Photo: Author)

Madelon
YACHT TENDER BY LAWLEY,

HULL # 1571

9'3" x 3'8"   ca. 1920

The donor used *Madelon* until a few years ago as the tender for his 31-foot Victory class sloop of the same name. Lawley's, as the yard of George F. Lawley & Sons, Neponset, Massachusetts, was called, built numbers of yacht tenders each year to have them on hand for outfitting its large yachts and to sell individually. John Harvey ruled the boatshop and demanded perfection from his men; his small boats were put together with the same exacting fits, superior woods, and fine finish for which the Lawley yard was famous in its elegant large yachts. Everyday use is hard on these delicate little shells and in time, even with reasonable care, which this one probably had, weaknesses begin to show up. For example, the screw fastenings holding her lower planking against the stem have pulled out and in the process have caused the planks themselves to split. Perhaps a heavier stem of oak rather than hackmatack would have served better.

STATUS:
Damaged as noted above, finish in poor shape, original, good condition.

DONOR:
Francis H. Chafee, M.D.

FURTHER READING:
Gardner, John. "Small Craft Wizardry at Lawley's." *National Fisherman*, September, 1977.

ACCESSION NO. 77.254

133

Lawley tender #1710 in 1978 (Photo: Author)

YACHT TENDER BY LAWLEY,
HULL #1710
12′2″ x 4′3″   ca. 1920

Following the custom of Lawley's, this larger tender is carvel planked rather than being lapstraked like *Madelon*.

Her teak trim was probably special, since mahogany was usually used to enhance the basic cedar-on-oak hull. There is no record of her early history, although chances are she was part of some elegant Lawley-built teak-trimmed yacht's outfit. Bronze lifting eyes fore and aft enabled her to be hoisted aboard on the larger yacht's davits when not being used. Special bronze castings also form the seat knees, quarter knees, and the breasthook. A few years ago, this tender was used as a plug from which the fiberglass-hulled "Harbormaster" dinghies were molded.

STATUS:
Outside of hull covered with fiberglass, finish is quite weathered, original, good condition.

DONOR:
James F. Steele

FURTHER READING:
Gardner, John. "Small Craft Wizardry at Lawley's." *National Fisherman*, September, 1977.

ACCESSION NO. 77.253

YACHT TENDER,
PROBABLY BY LAWLEY
12′1″ x 4′5″   ca. 1932

The donor ordered her with a specific purpose in mind: he wanted a lifeboat to tow behind his New York 50, *Midnight Sun*. Although she was never needed as a rescue craft, she was certainly modeled with that in mind, for she is very burdensome and has unusually high freeboard. Construction features indicate she was probably built by the Lawley yard at Neponset, Massachusetts.

STATUS:
Refinished 1974, original, excellent condition.

DONOR:
Warner Eustis

FURTHER READING:
Gardner, John. "Small Craft Wizardry at Lawley's." *National Fisherman*, September, 1977.

ACCESSION NO. 72.929

Eustis tender in 1974 (Photo: K. Mahler)

Seafarer *in 1974 (Photo: K. Mahler)*

Seafarer
YACHT TENDER
BY HERRESHOFF,
HULL #1–485

10'3" x 4'3"   1926

Charlie Sylvester built this tender and figures that, with few exceptions, all the dinghies and tenders from the Herreshoff yard between 1920 and when he left its employ in 1942 were personally built by him. Such experience together with a keen memory for detail made Charlie the prime information source for Barry Thomas' monograph on building a similar boat. She is a bit more burdensome than the Herreshoff *Columbia* lifeboat model and was developed in 1915 for the new Herreshoff 40-foot (WL) one-design sloops of the New York Yacht Club. Records show these boats were built as late as 1927,

some lengthened by as much as 2-feet. Origin of the name *Seafarer* is uncertain; it was on her stern when she came to Mystic and was probably the name of the yacht she last served.

STATUS:
Restored 1970, mostly original, good condition.

DONOR:
Roberts Parsons

FURTHER READING:
Herreshoff, L. Francis. *The Common Sense of Yacht Design.* New York: The Rudder Publishing Co., 1948.—*Chapter XIX entitled "Small Craft" gives the background of the* Columbia *model tender.*

Thomas, Barry. *Building the Herreshoff Dinghy.* Mystic: Mystic Seaport, Inc., 1977.—*Gives a detailed description of building a similar boat.*

ACCESSION NO. 65.389

Yacht tenders abuilding at the Herreshoff shop at Bristol, R.I. in 1926 (Courtesy: A. Sidney DeWolf Herreshoff)

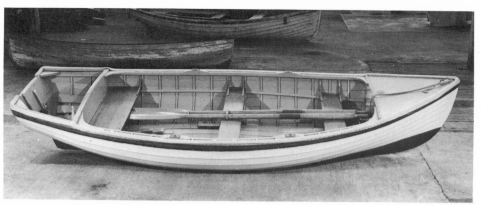

Columbia lifeboat yacht tender in 1978. Her aft deck, missing here, gave her a watertight compartment at either end, hence the name lifeboat (Photo: Author)

YACHT TENDER BY HERRESHOFF, *COLUMBIA* LIFEBOAT MODEL

12′5″ x 4′10″   1929

"... soon after 1900 he (Nathanael Herreshoff) brought out a model which we in the rowboat shop used to call the *Columbia* lifeboat model. The first of these was the racing boat on the deck of the cup boat *Columbia*, ... and a very great many similar ones were built. Perhaps my father modeled ten rowboats of varying proportions after the *Columbia* lifeboat model, but he never departed radically from this shape. This is the best model for a tender I have ever seen. They row well, sail well, and are good dry sea boats, and will tow through anything ... a short deck over the stern very much increases their value as a lifeboat, as they can be easily and quickly launched stern first from the yacht without being partially swamped. In the case of a man overboard or a fire, the delay in bailing out a partly swamped tender may be most serious ..." L. Francis Herreshoff, *The Common Sense of Yacht Design.*

To add even more to her ability as a lifeboat, she has a watertight compartment under her foredeck. According to the donor, who at the time was president of the Herreshoff Manufacturing Co., this boat was used on the America's Cup defender *Enterprise* or the cup contender *Weetamoe.*

STATUS:

Fiberglass covered outside, stern compartment cover missing, original, good condition.

DONOR:

R. F. Haffenreffer 3rd

FURTHER READING:

Herreshoff, L. Francis. *The Common Sense of Yacht Design.* New York: The Rudder Publishing Co., 1948.

Thomas, Barry. *Building the Herreshoff Dinghy.* Mystic: Mystic Seaport, Inc., 1977.—*Gives detailed description of building a similar boat.*

ACCESSION NO. 75.454

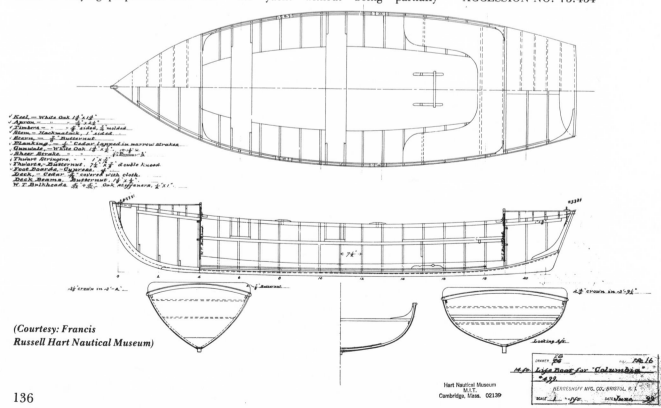

(Courtesy: Francis Russell Hart Nautical Museum)

Dixie
YACHT TENDER
BY HERRESHOFF

18'7" x 5'6"   ca. 1910–20

When Commodore George P. P. Bonnell bought the 89-foot Herreshoff power yacht *Comfort* in the middle of the depression, he told me once there were two boats aboard. Since then both have become part of the Seaport's watercraft collection by different paths. (The other is *Cormorant Rose*, a 17-foot power launch.) *Comfort*, which had been built in 1909 as *Enaj*, perished in the 1938 hurricane but her boats were both rescued. For awhile, until old age got the best of her and she was returned to him, this boat was loaned by Bonnell to the Seaport as a tender for the schooner *Brilliant*. To my knowledge three others have been built recently using this hull for measurements and details, but all three were smooth-planked rather than lapstraked. Joel White's yard in Brooklin, Maine, produced two, one for *Brilliant* and one for the Hudson River Sloop, *Clearwater*.

Herreshoff yacht tender (Photo: Author)

When the first of these was lost at sea from *Brilliant* a few years ago, Barry Thomas built the third boat, *Afterglow*, to replace her.

Herreshoff referred to this model and even to her smaller sisters as lifeboats, which for that time was surely true. But today, considering how boats of this type are most often used and to avoid any confusion with the standard ship's lifeboat, I feel it is more appropriate to use the term tender.

STATUS:
Fiberglass tape on plank laps, original, fair condition.
DONOR:
Robert Florin
FURTHER READING:
(Same as for *Columbia* lifeboat, 75.454)
ACCESSION NO. 74.995

Cleopatra's Barge
YACHT TENDER

16'6" x 5'0"   ca. 1930

Thomas Davidson of New Castle, New Hampshire, built this boat for the Warren family to go with the 60-foot sloop *Valiant*. Both boats were designed by Charles Drowne, also of New Castle. A small outboard was sometimes used on the tender and with her rather large stern, it appears that she was modeled with that idea in mind.
STATUS:
Original, good condition.
DONOR:
Mrs. Richard F. Warren
ACCESSION NO. 75.432

Cleopatra's Barge *in 1975*.
She was tender for the yacht Valiant *whose name appears on her backrest (Photo: Author)*

Bradshaw tender in 1978 (Photo: Author)

YACHT TENDER

12′9″ x 4′5″   ca. 1925

The delicate, high quality construction of this boat and the lifting eyes which are fitted fore and aft indicate that she was once a tender for a larger yacht. She came upon hard times afterwards, though, and one of her later owners fitted her out with heavy and rather crude guard rails, seats and seat knees. She has been abused and certainly has seen more rugged service than originally intended. She has a natural-crook hackmatack stem and oak frames which run from rail to rail across a plank-type keel.

STATUS:

Repaired and modified, approximately 80% original, poor condition.

DONOR:

Forrest and Katherine Bradshaw

ACCESSION NO. 75.456

Arbutus in 1971
(Photo: Mystic Seaport)

Arbutus
ADIRONDACK
GUIDE BOAT

16′0″ x 3′2″   ca. 1900

Once the common means of transportation in the Adirondack region of New York State, these exquisite craft were regularly used by guides taking sportsmen on camping and fishing trips. Rivalry—keen among the guides—produced a highly refined boat, ideal for its intended use. The boats were carried upside down on the guides' shoulders when portaging to the next lake; a contoured carrying yoke made the operation comfortable. Adirondack Museum at Blue Mountain Lake, New York, which specializes in collecting, exhibiting, and studying guide boats, should be visited by anyone wishing to know more about them. *Arbutus*, built for Anna Hyatt Huntington, the sculptress and daughter-in-law of railroad mogul Collis P. Huntington, was used at the family "summer camp" in the Adirondacks, also named *Arbutus*.

STATUS:
Original including the painted finish, good condition.

DONOR:
Thomas L. Cheney

FURTHER READING:
Durant, Kenneth. *Guide-boat Days and Ways*. Blue Mountain Lake: Adirondack Museum, 1963.

Evans, Cerinda W. *Anna Hyatt Huntington*. Newport News: The Mariners Museum, 1965.

Ford, Howard. "Building the Adirondack Guide Boat." *WoodenBoat*, No. 18, September–October, 1977.

Gardner, John. "Adirondack Guide Boat." *National Fisherman*, April, 1963.

———. "Adirondack Guide Boat." *Outdoor Maine*, August–September, 1959.

Manley, Atwood. *Rushton and His Times in American Canoeing*. Syracuse: Syracuse University Press for Adirondack Museum, 1968.

ACCESSION NO. 75.429

With its yoke in place, one man could carry a guide boat between lakes as shown here
(Courtesy: Adirondack Museum)

Native guides and vacationing city sportsmen with their combined skill, good taste, and money brought these craft to a high degree of refinement
(Courtesy: Adirondack Museum)

Guide boats served the lake region of New York State in a number of ways
(Courtesy: Adirondack Museum)

Adirondack guide boat, probably by Austin or Cole, 1975 (Photo: Author)

ADIRONDACK GUIDE BOAT, PROBABLY BY AUSTIN OR COLE

13′4″ x 3′2″   ca. 1890

One of the reasons this boat is still in existence is that she has been in storage since 1907 after being slightly damaged. The donor states that she was never actually used by a guide, but rather for family recreation.

STATUS:
Original, good condition.

DONOR:
Given in memory of Bertram A. Redington by Elizabeth Webster, Nancy Webster, and Caroline W. Corwin.

FURTHER READING:
(Same as other Adirondack guide boats)

ACCESSION NO. 75.377

Adirondack guide boat variants by Salisbury, 1975 (Photo: Author)

ADIRONDACK GUIDE BOAT VARIANTS BY SALISBURY

14′4″ x 3′0″ and 14′4″ x 3′3″

The same man appears to have built both of these boats, although only one (74.460) carries a builder's nameplate: H. L. Salisbury & Bro., Long Lake, N.Y. They differ from the true guide boat in that they have keels rather than bottom boards. Number 74.461 is fitted for rowing.

STATUS:
Some repair, mostly original, good condition.

DONOR:
Mr. and Mrs. James C. Smith

FURTHER READING:
(Same as other Adirondack guide boats)

ACCESSION NOS. 74.460 and 74.461

140

St. Lawrence River skiff by Spaulding, 1975 (Photo: Author)

ST. LAWRENCE RIVER SKIFF BY SPAULDING

17′1″ x 3′6″   ca. 1890

"The St. Lawrence River Skiff, so highly praised by all who have used it, is the outgrowth of certain conditions and local surroundings and . . . is specially good for its destined use.

"The boats are used everywhere about the Thousand Islands (upstate New York) for fishing, rowing and sailing, to the exclusion of all other small boats. They are handled by professional boatmen who show the greatest skill in their handling." *Forest and Stream,* April 25, 1889.

This boat was built by the Spaulding St. Lawrence Boat Company of Ogdensburg, New York. Her construction is lapstrake with white cedar planking fastened with copper rivets and clinch nails.

The Hudson River near Rhinebeck rather than the St. Lawrence was her home, perhaps explaining why a rudder and regular oarlocks were fitted. These skiffs usually had their oars mounted on fixed pins, a convenience when landing a fish as the oars could simply be dropped without fear of their slipping overboard, but frustrating indeed to the pleasure rower accustomed to feathering his oars.

STATUS:
Restored 1972, original, excellent condition.

DONOR:
Mrs. Frank B. Washburn

FURTHER READING:
(Same as for skiff 73.31)

ACCESSION NO. 71.382

Barkis in 1975 (Photo: Author)

Barkis
ST. LAWRENCE RIVER SKIFF

16′1″ x 3′5″   ca. 1894

Like many St. Lawrence skiffs, this one is fitted for a mast enabling her to sail downwind. Some were fitted with "radix" fan-type centerboards as well, but rarely with rudders: they would spoil the excitement of rudderless sailing, a skiff owner's refined but sometimes wet sport.

STATUS:
Rig missing, original, good condition.

DONOR:
Edward L. Crabbe

FURTHER READING:
(Same as for skiff 73.31)

ACCESSION NO. 72.570

141

ST. LAWRENCE RIVER SKIFF BY SHELDON

14′0″ x 3′2″   ca. 1900

The nameplate on this skiff reads "O. Sheldon & Co., Boat Builders, Boston, Mass." Although smaller than the usual St. Lawrence skiff this boat is a beautiful model and exhibits some first class workmanship.

STATUS:
Some fittings missing, hull has been stripped to bare wood, original, fair condition.

DONOR:
William B. Dodge

FURTHER READING:
(Same as for 73.31)

ACCESSION NO. 75.177

St. Lawrence River skiff by Sheldon, 1975 (Photo: Author)

St. Lawrence River skiff for hunting
(Photo: Author)

ST. LAWRENCE RIVER SKIFF FOR HUNTING

18′0″ x 4′9″

Obtained for study only, John Gardner acquired this boat at Clayton, New York, home of the Thousand Island Museum. Here several examples of preserved skiffs have promoted a revival of local historic boat types through the annual Antique Boat Show. Chances are this boat was originally a practical hunting craft used where a fancy finish wasn't needed, and where her owner made his living directly from nature instead of as a guide.

STATUS:
Relic, poor condition.

DONOR:
John Gardner

FURTHER READING:
Gardner, John. *Building Classic Small Craft.* Camden: International Marine Publishing Co., 1977.

Haxall, Boling W. "St. Lawrence Skiffs." *WoodenBoat*, No. 11, July–August, 1976.

Simpson, Dwight S. "The St. Lawrence River Skiff." *Forest and Stream* (93:248).

Steever, Andrew. "Native to the Thousand Islands." *WoodenBoat*, Nos. 20, 21, January–April, 1978.

Additional information on these boats is contained in *Rudder*, July and September, 1890 and March and April, 1891. There is more in *Yachting*, November, 1969.

ACCESSION NO. 73.31

A mid-day picnic must be in the wind for the
passengers in these guide boats and St. Lawrence River skiffs
(Courtesy: Adirondack Museum)

(Courtesy: Thousand Islands Museum)

The St. Lawrence type of oarlock
keeps the oars from sliding overboard when
dropped to land a fish. Their disadvantage
is that the oars cannot be feathered
(Courtesy: Thousand Islands Museum)

Peapods at Deer Isle, Maine in 1882 (Photo: The Hudson Collection)

PEAPOD, PROBABLY FROM DEER ISLE, MAINE

16'0" x 4'5"   ca. 1900

Peapods are believed to have originated in "lobster country" Penobscot Bay, Maine, and most were used for just that purpose. Standing up and facing forward, his oars in "raised up" oarlocks, the lobsterman rows from trap to trap, each being marked by a cedar buoy of his own particular color scheme. Planking was either lap or smooth and centerboards were fitted in many pods to make long passages easier by sailing.

STATUS:
Restored, approximately 75% original, good condition.

DONOR:
Robert S. Douglas (by exchange)

FURTHER READING:
(Same as for boat 71.237)

ACCESSION NO. 59.1472

Peapod in 1975 (Photo: Author)

144

Red Star as she appeared in 1975 (Photo: Author)

Red Star under sail a few years ago in Eggemoggin Reach (Courtesy: Mrs. Albert Hunt)

Red Star
SAILING PEAPOD FROM DEER ISLE, MAINE

14′11″ x 4′5″   ca. 1920

Sheldon Torrey, *Red Star*'s original owner, used to sail her from his home waters of the Benjamin River in Sedgwick mostly for pleasure, although she was used by a later owner for clamming in the same part of the coast. She was built in the Mountainville region of Deer Isle by Nate Eaton and in later years was used as a yacht tender by the donor. A spritsail, rather than the leg-o-mutton sail, was fitted originally.

STATUS:
Mostly original, good condition.

DONOR:
Mrs. Albert B. Hunt

FURTHER READING:
(Same as for boat 71.237)

ACCESSION NO. 70.638

PEAPOD FROM CAPE SPLIT, MAINE

16′2″ x 4′2″   ca. 1880

Crudely built at or near Harrington, Maine, this peapod is finer-lined than most. She was used for lobstering until the end of her career when the donor experimented with her, writing up his results in the February 1962 issue of *National Fisherman.*

STATUS:
Relic, some repair, poor condition.

DONOR:
Benjamin B. Drisko

FURTHER READING:
(Same as for boat 71.237)

ACCESSION NO. 67.302

Peapod from Cape Split, Maine, taken when she arrived at the Seaport in 1967 (Photo: L. S. Martel)

Sailing peapod in 1975 (Photo: Author)

SAILING PEAPOD

12′0″ x 4′1″   ca. 1945

Little is known about this pod, other than she was reportedly built somewhere in Maine. She is on the small side for a peapod and is quite heavily built. With some changes to reduce her weight, she would make a fine little tender for a larger boat. An unusual feature is the way in which her seat knees fay against the edges instead of the tops of her seats.

STATUS:
Original, poor condition.

DONOR:
John A. Knauth

FURTHER READING:
(Same as for boat 71.237)

ACCESSION NO. 75.457

PEAPOD, MYSTIC SEAPORT BUILT

14′2″ x 4′5″ 1971

With more deadrise and easier bilges than most working pods, this one was modeled to row easily, rather than to be stiff while lobster traps are hauled over her rail. She was designed by John Gardner and built by Sylvester Costelloe of the Seaport's Small Craft Lab. Her plans appear in Gardner's *Building Classic Small Craft.*

In their shape, peapods are a lot like St. Lawrence skiffs and these two types of small craft are compared by John Gardner in his *Building Classic Small Craft*, pages 161–164. Although unheralded as a rudderless sailboat, peapods probably perform as well as their fresh-water cousins. In Brooklin, Maine, where Jim Steele's shop turns out a standard traditionally-built pod, peapods rigged with boomless spritsails have been sailed with great success in recent years, sans both rudders and centerboards.

STATUS:
In use, excellent condition.

DONOR:
Mystic Seaport built reproduction

FURTHER READING:
Brooks, Alfred A. "The Boats of Ash Point, Maine." *The American Neptune,* October, 1942.

Chapelle, Howard I. *American Small Sailing Craft.* New York: W. W. Norton & Co., Inc., 1951.

Gardner, John. *Building Classic Small Craft.* Camden: International Marine Publishing Co., 1977.

———. "Maine Peapods." *Maine Coast Fisherman,* September and October, 1951.

———. Various articles contained in *Building Small Boats for Oar and Sail,* a 1971 reprint of earlier pieces appearing in *National Fisherman.*

Goode, George Brown. *The Fisheries and Fishery Industries of the United States.* Washington: Government Printing Office, 1887.

Van Ness, C. W. "A Maine Peapod." *Yachting,* February, 1932.

ACCESSION NO. 71.237

Seaport peapod, 1975 (Photo: Author)

Horse drawn carriages got surf boats to the beach where stranded vessels' crews could be rescued (Photo: Source unknown)

Massachusetts Humane Society surf boat with crew at practice (Courtesy: Marblehead Historical Commission)

*Massachusetts Humane Society surf boat in
1973, after restoration (Photo: M. A. Stets)*

SURF BOAT
FROM MASSACHUSETTS HUMANE SOCIETY

28′8″ x 6′8″   ca. 1900

Starting with the country's first coastal life-saving station (Cohasset, 1807) the Massachusetts Humane Society continued as a volunteer organization throughout the more than one-hundred years of its existence. But with the expansion of the U.S. Life-Saving Service around the turn of the century, the need for such an organization began to diminish and by the time the U.S. Coast Guard was formed in 1915 (by combining the Life-Saving Service with the U.S. Revenue Cutter Service) only a few of the old Humane Society Stations were still active.

This boat was built for the Society's Marblehead station by Graves boatyard also of Marblehead. She was used in the twilight years of the society's existence mostly for boat-handling practice and competitive rowing against the boats of other stations. She was modeled after the previous boat, which was damaged beyond repair in a rescue the year before, and was commanded by James

Frost, father and son, until she was given up sometime before World War II. Later on, under a subsequent owner, she was fitted with an inboard engine and still later was abandoned ashore. A complete restoration was in order when the Seaport acquired her. Some of the details and thinking that went into her restoration are reported in the Preservation Press publication listed below.

STATUS:
Restored 1975, approximately 80% original, excellent condition.

DONOR:
Mystic Seaport purchase

FURTHER READING:
Howe, M. A. DeWolfe. *The Humane Society of the Commonwealth of Massachusetts—An Historical Review 1785–1916.* Boston: The Riverside Press, 1918.

MacArthur, Keith R. "The Research Behind the Restoration: Mystic's Life Saving Craft." *Wooden Shipbuilding & Small Craft Preservation,* Washington: The Preservation Press, 1976.

ACCESSION NO. 72.901

*Massachusetts Humane Society surf boat just
prior to coming to Seaport (Photo: Author)*

Race Point surf boat, 1975 (Photo: Author)

Plans of the Race Point surf boat by Ralph E. Winslow were published in Rudder *magazine August, 1926 (Courtesy:* Rudder *magazine)*

RACE POINT SURF BOAT,
USCG HULL #24311

24'7" x 6'1"   ca. 1940

Although most Race Point surf boats were built before the turn of the century for the old U.S. Life-Saving Service and came out of private boatshops on Cape Cod, this boat and some others like her were produced much later by the Coast Guard's Curtis Bay, Maryland, shipyard. In 1930, when the Coast Guard started building them, the Race Point model was only in limited use, having been replaced in most stations by the self-bailing "standard service" surf boat (see 63.1516). Nevertheless, before the end of World War II Curtis Bay had turned out sixty-two of them, mostly for use along the coasts of New England and Long Island. Only three more were built after the war and they came out in 1958.

For a light boat that would hold together in spite of rough use, yet was a match for whatever screeching gale came along, the Race Point boat was hard to beat. Coastal stations of the U.S. Life-Saving Service began using them back in 1894, mostly along the outer shore of Cape Cod. It is likely that the inspiration for their design came from the surf boats of the privately-run Massachusetts Humane Society. They take their name from the headland at the tip end of Cape Cod, near Provincetown.

STATUS:

Restored 1975, approximately 90% original, good condition.

DONOR:

Anonymous

FURTHER READING:

MacArthur, Keith R. "The Research Behind the Restoration: Mystic's Life Saving Craft." *Wooden Shipbuilding & Small Craft Preservation.* Washington: The Preservation Press, 1976.

Wilkinson, William D. "Surfboat Authority Sheds Light on Race Point Type." *National Fisherman,* November, 1972.

ACCESSION NO. 47.1982

A surf boat from the station at Orleans pushing off the beach (Photo: Source unknown)

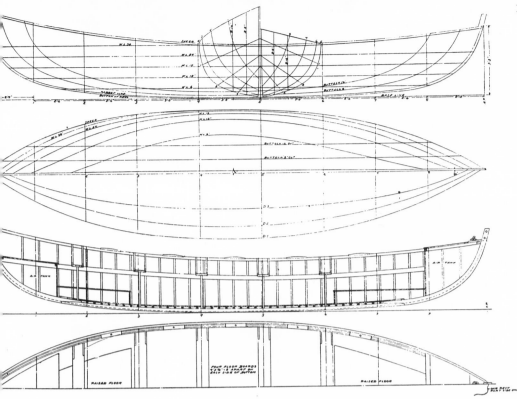

SELF-BAILING
SURF BOAT

25'7" x 7'5"

A watertight platform running the length of a surf boat with several scuppers along each side open to the sea makes pumping or bailing by hand unnecessary—certainly a convenience for her crew and a feature which also makes her safer, perhaps. At least that's what surf boat builder Fred Beebe and Lt. Charles McLellan of the U.S. Life-Saving Service thought when they developed the first self-bailing boat in 1886. But her unique feature, her platform, made her weigh more and the lightweight open surfboats with bow and stern air cases for flotation were often

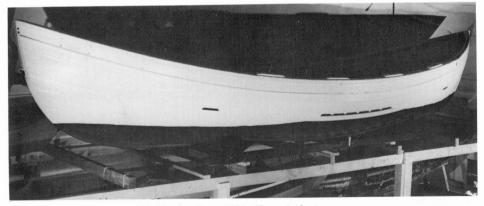

Self-bailing surf boat, 1975 (Photo: Author)

preferred. However, there were a great many self-bailing surf boats built and for a time Beebe's Greenport, Long Island shop was one of that town's most important businesses. Since then, particularly after the Coast Guard was created from a merger of the Life-Saving Service and Revenue Cutter Service in 1915, there have been modifications to the Beebe-McLellan self-bailing design. As a later boat, perhaps

from the Coast Guard's shop at Curtis Bay, Maryland, about the time of World War II, this one reflects some of those changes.

STATUS:
Extensively and somewhat crudely repaired, fair condition.

DONOR:
James Mayo

ACCESSION NO. 63.1516

Surf Boat in 1959 (Photo: Mystic Seaport)

Surf Boat as she looked when owned by Major William Smyth. Called **Dawn**, *she was fitted out for pleasure fishing (Courtesy: William Smyth)*

SURF BOAT

25′1″ x 6′9″

The early history of this boat is uncertain, but chances are she belonged to some coastal life-saving station and was built before the Coast Guard standardized its designs and began building its own boats.

About 1924, while he was Superintendent of the New England Oil Company fleet in Fall River, Mass., Major William Smyth acquired this boat. She was in Westport, Mass., at the time, fitted with a crude cabin, a self-bailing cockpit, and a small sailing rig.

He used her for pleasure fishing in nearby waters and took *Dawn*, as he named her, to Essex, Conn., a few years later when he moved there to manage the Dauntless Shipyard. She was transferred to his brother, Hugh, about 1935 and a short time later was bought by the donor who, like the Smyths, used her for pleasure fishing in adjacent Long Island Sound waters. Major Smyth is a long time member of Mystic Seaport's Ship's Committee and his advice offered after a lifetime of building, caring for, and operating wooden boats of all kinds, has been sought and heeded many times.

The cabin was still with her when she arrived at the Seaport in 1941. Around 1953, through the efforts of the men at the Coast Guard Station in nearby Groton, it was stripped off and the boat was restored somewhere near her original appearance.

STATUS:
Partly restored, fair condition.
DONOR:
Thomas Willets, Jr.
ACCESSION NO. 41.65

Four-Oared Racing Shell (Photo: L. S. Martel)

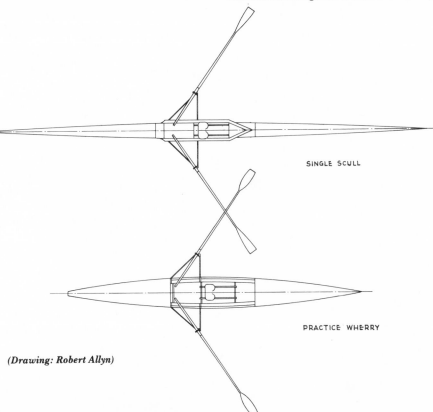

SINGLE SCULL

PRACTICE WHERRY

(Drawing: Robert Allyn)

FOUR-OARED RACING SHELL

43′9″ x 1′11″

While not as spectacular as the very large eight-oared shells used in Ivy League competition, the proportions of this craft are nevertheless impressive.

STATUS:
Original, good condition.

DONOR:
Riverside Boat Club

FURTHER READING:
Gardner, John. "Early Days of Rowing Sport." *The Log of Mystic Seaport*, Winter, 1971.

Kellet, Robert F. *American Rowing: Its Background and Traditions*. New York: G. P. Putnam's Sons, 1932.

ACCESSION NO. 63.27

SINGLE SCULL SHELL BY DAVY

30′0″ x 1′0″   ca. 1890

Boston's Charles River would be where one might expect to use a shell, particularly one built in nearby Cambridge by W. H. Davy. Yet Dr. Charles Weld took this one to his beloved North Haven, Maine, where the Fox Island Thoroughfare's shelter was nearly as good as the Charles' and the scenery breathtaking. At least Dr. Weld thought so, for he was one of that Maine island's first summer settlers and had a big hand in convincing other well-heeled Bostonians to build there. This shell, obvi-

ously cherished and carefully taken care of over the years, was passed down through the family for awhile, but eventually became the possession of Charles P. Williamson, a summertime neighbor, who continued to use and enjoy her in the same waters.

STATUS:
Minor repair, mostly original, very good condition.

DONOR:
Given in memory of Charles P. Williamson by Mrs. Charles P. Williamson

FURTHER READING:
(Same as for shell 63.27)

ACCESSION NO. 74.450

PRACTICE WHERRY

22′2″ x 2′3″

Primarily an exercise boat for competing collegiate rowers, the greater beam of a practice wherry makes her more stable than a shell, and being shorter she is more easily transported and stored.

STATUS:
Relic, poor condition.

DONOR:
Martha Fuller

FURTHER READING:
(Same as for shell 63.27)

ACCESSION NO. 72.1112

(Photo: K. Mahler)

PRACTICE WHERRY BY WILLIAMS

20'0″ x 2'0″   ca. 1934

The term wherry used out of context can be misleading, as may be seen by contrasting this lightweight exercise boat with the wherry which follows, a boat used for salmon fishing on the coast of Maine. To be understood, one must specify exactly what kind of a wherry he is talking about as there are even others besides these two; for example, the big freight-carrying Norfolk wherries of England.

The Williams Racing Shell Boat Yard, Foxboro, Massachusetts, built this wherry, according to her nameplate. She has had little use and arrived at Mystic in like-new condition, crated, and completely equipped.

DONOR:
Harry D. Deutschbein
FURTHER READING:
(Same as for shell 63.27)
ACCESSION NO. 75.313

Lincolnville Salmon Wherry in 1975 (Photo: Author)

FURTHER READING:
Brooks, Alfred A. "The Boats of Ash Point, Maine." *The American Neptune*, October, 1942.

Gardner, John. *Building Classic Small Craft*. Camden: International Marine Publishing Co., 1977.—*Contains the plans of this boat as well as much other information about wherries. A prime source.*

Gardner, John. "14' 'Reach Boat' is Obvious Maine Wherry Kin." *National Fisherman*, July, 1974.—*Good comparison of*

SALMON WHERRY FROM LINCOLNVILLE, MAINE

13'4″ x 4'4″   1892

The Maine salmon wherry, the New Jersey Sea Bright skiff (pages following) the Adirondack guide boat, some dories, and probably the early peapods, were structurally alike though different in outward appearance. They were lap-fastened bottom-board boats with softwood frames sawn from natural crooks. This was an old-time way of boatbuilding that had a lot going for it, although today getting good framing stock might be a problem. Boats so built sit upright while on land and if the bottom board is of hardwood, as it is in the wherries, the heels of the frames have a secure landing and good fastening into it. Installing a strong center-board trunk is easy and if the bottom board is protected on its outside with a sacrificial false bottom, beaching out in a hard chance landing place like Lincolnville is no problem.

Afloat and in use the salmon fisherman knelt in the bow while tending his weir, taking aboard whatever fish were caught up in it. Thus the wherries were full forward and, being launched stern first off the beach, were fine-lined aft. This is the boat of Robie Ames, a Lincolnville fisherman, whose fish house, its entire contents, and his wherry are in the Seaport's collection.

STATUS:
Original, fair condition.

DONOR:
The Adirondack Historical Association in exchange for a Seaport built reproduction
ACCESSION NO. 71.239

Left: *three generations of the Wade family, shore fishermen at Lincolnville Beach, Maine about fifty years ago.* Right: *the reason for the* salmon wherry's *full and buoyant bow is shown as Osborne Wade brings aboard a 12 pounder (Courtesy: Osborne Wade)*

wherry and Reach boat characteristics, including the known history of each.

————. "The New England Wherry." *The Log of Mystic Seaport*, Winter, 1970.

Goode, George Brown. *The Fisheries and Fishery Industries of the United States.* Washington: Government Printing Office, 1887.—*Gives good description of the salmon weir-fishing process.*

Simmons, Walter. "The Lincolnville Wherry." *WoodenBoat*, No. 2, November–December, 1974.

Seaport built salmon wherry reproduction in 1975 (Photo: Author)

SALMON WHERRY, MYSTIC SEAPORT BUILT REPRODUCTION

13′6″ x 4′3″   1975

Two of these wherries were built at the Seaport in recent years; one remains, the other is now at the Adirondack Museum, exchanged for the original Robie Ames boat (71.239). Will Ansel built this one in more or less the old-time way; that is, he first set up the backbone (stem, stern, and bottom board) then planked her up over a few molds set in place to give the right shape and finally scribed in the frames and fastened them into position. Being

familiar with the shape the planks had to be to give him the boat he wanted, the old-time builder would doubtless have gotten by with fewer molds, perhaps only one at the mid point would have sufficed. This wherry, like the other Seaport reproductions, was built to be put overboard each year and used. I have rowed her often and find that although she moves along easily under oars, she is tiddlish when light (much like a banks dory) while at the same time her high freeboard makes rowing in a breeze a bit of a chore. I'd say that

for recreational rowing there are better boats than this one, and unless one plans on going salmon fishing in the traditional way, he'd do well to choose another model. Tied off along the Seaport's waterfront near the Robie Ames fish shack is where she spends most of her time afloat.

STATUS:
In use, excellent condition.

DONOR:
Mystic Seaport built reproduction
ACCESSION NO. 75.438

St. John Wherry in 1971 (Photo: R. A. Fowler)

WHERRY FROM ST. JOHN, NEW BRUNSWICK

21'9" x 5'10"

A boat of unknown origin, it has many of the same features as the smaller salmon wherry on page 154 including the fully planked skeg area where no deadwood is used. A gasoline engine was installed at one time.

STATUS:
Pieces missing, mostly original, fair condition.

DONOR:
Mystic Seaport purchase

FURTHER READING:
(Same as for wherry 71.239)

ACCESSION NO. 71.246

Lavallette Beach Patrol
SEA BRIGHT SKIFF BY HANKINS

16'3" x 5'0"   **1964**

Waves, sometimes born of a savage Atlantic storm, sometimes kicked up by a summer sea breeze, pound north Jersey's exposed coast—relentlessly. Penetrating these breakers by boat in either direction calls for balance, strength, and a feel for the task; one also needs a good boat under him. Shore fishermen, back in the 1850s had to conquer the same surf as New Jersey lifeguards do today. Both used the Sea Bright skiff or "dory surf boat" in her builder's parlance. That builder was Charles Hankins & Son whose Lavallette shop has been in the business since 1906 and is still at it. According to Peter Guthorn in his book *Sea Bright Skiffs and Other Jersey Shore Boats:* "(Their) design and scantlings are almost identical to those built more than a century ago, except that they are no longer equipped with a centerboard or sails." Demand for their new boats certainly hasn't been hurt by the state law requiring an available surf

Sea Bright Skiff (Photo: Author)

boat at all recreational beaches or by the spirited surf boat competition among lifeguards each year. Although New Jersey sand is easier on a sea skiff's bottom than Maine rocks are on a wherry's, the surf is much worse and requires a bow-first launching.

Structurally a sea skiff is a lot like a wherry. Both are lapstraked and have planked-down skegs. They are both bottom-board-boats and even look a little alike. Sea skiffs, at least most of them, have steam-bent frames rather

than sawn ones which in the skeg area pass over and are fastened to "cod-wads," or floor timbers connecting them to the bottom board.

STATUS:
Original, very good condition.

DONOR:
Charles E. Hankins

FURTHER READING:
(Same as for skiff 72.572)

ACCESSION NO. 72.571

 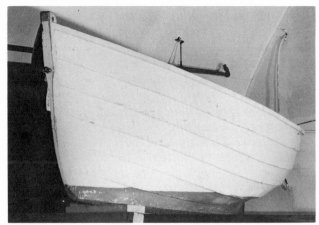

Sea Bright Skiff (Photo: Author)

SEA BRIGHT SKIFF, PROBABLY BY HANKINS

16'0" x 4'11"   ca. 1922

Except for her rail, which is open, and her Davis-pattern oarlocks, this skiff is much like the other one (72.571) and was probably another of Hankins' standard models.

STATUS:
Original, good condition.

DONOR:
George E. Horr, Jr.

FURTHER READING:
Bouchal, Gerald. "Surfing Sea Bright Style." *WoodenBoat*, No. 17, July–August, 1977.—*First-hand account of handling these boats in the surf by a New Jersey lifeguard.*

Chapelle, Howard I. *American Small Sailing Craft.* New York: W. W. Norton & Co., Inc., 1951.

Gardner, John. *Building Classic Small Craft.* Camden: International Marine Publishing Co., 1977.

Goode, George Brown. *The Fisheries and Fishery Industries of the United States.* Washington: Government Printing Office, 1887.

Guthorn, Peter J. *The Sea Bright Skiff and Other Jersey Shore Boats.* New Brunswick: Rutgers University Press, 1971.

ACCESSION NO. 72.572

*New Jersey Pound Boat,
an outgrowth of the Sea Bright Skiff and is sometimes referred to as one
(Photo: L. S. Martel)*

NEW JERSEY POUND BOAT

20'4" x 6'10"   ca. 1913

"We have reports of 21 footers landing over 5,600 pounds of fish through the surf and 20,000 pounds is not exceptional for the 32 footers. These boats are pulled out of the surf on rollers with their load and stand up under this treatment year after year." "The landing of a loaded boat through a heavy surf was an exciting experience which never failed to attract many onlookers." (Both quotes are from the *Sea Bright Skiff and other Jersey Shore Boats* pages 22 and 18 respectively.)

Fish pounds, supported by poles and projecting out from shore a half mile or more into coastal New Jersey's shallow waters, used enlarged Sea Bright skiffs called pound boats in their operation. The skiffs were used at first back in 1875 or '80, but as pounds became bigger and moved offshore, and as the crews and catches increased in size, more burdensome boats like this one were built. Pound fishing peaked out in the 1920s with about a hundred operating pounds, and by then pound boats,

fitted with engines, had reached lengths of more than 40-feet. This boat was built earlier during the transition to power and in size and shape is more like the turn-of-the-century six-man, one-coxswain rowing pound boats, a grown-up sea skiff, its engine an after-thought.

Pound fishing in New Jersey waters ceased in 1961, and as of 1977 the only pound still working on the Atlantic

coast was off the back side of Long Island, New York. Ray Hendrickson describes its operation in the *National Fisherman* for November, 1977.

STATUS:
Original, fair condition.

DONOR:
Jersey Coast Boat Show, Inc.

FURTHER READING:
(Same as skiff 72.572)

ACCESSION NO. 63.248

Yankee Skiff in 1978 (Photo: Author)

YANKEE SKIFF

22'8" x 6'2"

For tonging oysters in the bays and inlets of Staten Island and northern New Jersey, skiffs built like the Maine salmon wherries and Sea Bright skiffs (but far prettier than either) were used. As far as can be determined not one of these so-called Staten Island or Raritan Bay oyster skiffs survived, but thanks to Martin Erissmann who carefully measured a boat and drew up her plans in 1909, we do have a good record of what one looks like. Remarkably she is about the same as the Yankee skiff of Chesapeake Bay, a boat also nearly extinct, and like the New Haven sharpie, a migrant from New England. These boats were ceiled inside over their frames for ease in shoveling out the oysters and when in use were fitted with

culling boards astride their gunwales. Another of the Yankee skiffs is on exhibit at Mariners Museum, Newport News, Virginia.

STATUS:
Modified for inboard engine, relic, poor condition.

DONOR:
Mystic Seaport purchase through Mariners Museum

FURTHER READING:
Guthorn, Peter J. *The Sea Bright Skiff and Other Jersey Shore Boats.* New Brunswick: Rutgers University Press, 1971.—*The chapter on the Raritan Bay oyster skiffs is good and includes Erissmann's plans.*

Kochiss, John M. *Oystering from New York to Boston.* Middletown: Wesleyan University Press for Mystic Seaport, Inc., 1974.—*Good information on Staten Island oystering including material quoted from contemporary sources.*

ACCESSION NO. 76.4

Brant in 1975 (Photo: Author)

Brant
DUCK BOAT

10′3″ x 4′7″   1894

The *Brant* was owned by Charles Ferguson of Groton, Connecticut, a boatbuilder by trade, who probably built her as well. She has a low profile and could be made quite inconspicuous, but it is doubtful if she ever ventured far from shore. She was built neither for seaworthiness nor ease of rowing, truly a special purpose boat. Her construction is of unusually high quality.

STATUS:
Mostly original, good condition.

DONOR:
The family of Charles F. Ferguson

ACCESSION NO. 57.917

DUCK BOAT FROM
THE ILLINOIS RIVER

15′10″ x 4′0″   ca. 1900

A sheet-metal bottom prevented her from drying out while on land where she probably sat most of the time. When used in the marshes bordering the Illinois River, she was rowed or poled in shallow water with a "push paddle." Wooden sides raise her freeboard to a safe height. Metal boats were quite common at the turn of the century, but offsetting their obvious advantages was a propensity to rust out and dent.

STATUS:
Original, fair condition.

DONOR:
William S. Faurot

ACCESSION NO. 64.33

Illinois River Duck Boat about 1965 (Photo: L. S. Martel)

DUCK BOAT
FROM GREAT BAY, NEW HAMPSHIRE

14'8" x 3'4"

Without fuss, duck hunters' boats like this could sneak within range of their prey. The duckboat would be covered with brush nearly concealing the hunters as well as the craft. Hidden also was the upper part of the sculling oar contained within an open-ended well aft of the transom. Scull float was an alternate name because of her propulsion.

STATUS:

Original, good condition.

DONOR:

Philip S. Drake

FURTHER READING:

Ansel, Willets, "Duckboat Job Has Builder a Bit Skeptical." *National Fisherman*, December, 1975.—*Brief writeup about the building and trials of a reproduction of this boat.*

Chapelle, Howard I. *American Small Sailing Craft.* New York: W. W. Norton & Co., Inc., 1951.

ACCESSION NO. 61.559

Duck Boat from Great Bay, New Hampshire in 1975 (Photo: Author)

DUCK BOAT FROM GREAT SOUTH BAY, NEW YORK

Duck Boat from Great South Bay, Long Island (Photo: Author)

16'3" x 3'9"   ca. 1900

If a low profile was the builder's objective he certainly succeeded. She is almost like a surfboard as her deck is joined directly to her bottom. The open rail which completely encircles the deck is interesting and must have been a big help in securing the brush used to help hide her from suspecting ducks. Of interest also is her fan-tail stern which, although quite handsome, does not permit the convenient use of a sculling oar. For watertightness, her bottom has been covered with fabric.

STATUS:

Some repair, mostly original, poor condition.

DONOR:

R. Nelson Rose

FURTHER READING:

Chapelle, Howard I. *American Small Sailing Craft.* New York: W. W. Norton & Co., Inc., 1951.

ACCESSION NO. 76.79

Bartlett Duck Boat in 1975 (Photo: Author)

DUCK BOAT BY BARTLETT

14'2" x 3'1"   1959

Before starting work on this boat, at age ninety-two, Capt. Howard Bartlett had the experience of building about forty-five others like her. This was to be his last boat as sickness forced him to turn her over to a friend, Myron Cowden, for finishing. The Warrens of York Harbor, Maine, for whom Capt. Bartlett had been a long-time professional yacht skipper, commissioned her building.

She is planked with mahogany and covered on the outside with fiberglass.

STATUS:

Original, excellent condition.

DONOR:

Mrs. Richard F. Warren

FURTHER READING:

Chapelle, Howard I. *American Small Sailing Craft.* New York: W. W. Norton & Co., Inc., 1951.

ACCESSION NO. 75.431

Chiquita and *Pedro*
SEINE BOATS, MYSTIC SEAPORT BUILT REPRODUCTIONS

36′4″ x 8′1″ & 36′0″ x 8′6″   1975

Encircling a school of mackerel by rowing around them while heaving out a purse seine called not only for an experienced crew, but also for a fast and maneuverable boat, one large enough to hold the 200-fathoms or so of seine twine. Our boats were reproduced from photos, descriptions, and sketches, since no originals survive today. Seine boats were once built in large numbers (mostly between 1870 and 1920) and were towed by schooners like the *L. A. Dunton* to the fishing grounds or occasionally taken aboard if the weather was bad. Seine boats and whaleboats have much in common and were often produced by the same boatshop. Both of these boats are used in the Seaport's youth training program for rowing instruction.

STATUS: In use, excellent condition.

DONOR: Mystic Seaport built reproductions

FURTHER READING:

Ansel, W. D. "A Seine Boat to Save and Study." *National Fisherman*, September, 1975.

Church, Albert Cook. *American Fisherman*. Text by James B. Connolly. New York: W. W. Norton & Co., 1940.

———. "The Catching of Mackerel." *Yachting*, October, 1911.

Goode, George Brown. *Fisheries and Fishery Industries of the United States*. Washington: Government Printing Office, 1887.

Smith, Edward W., Jr. *Workaday Schooners*. Camden: International Marine Publishing Co., 1975.—*Wonderful photographs of seine boats and fishing schooners coming and going from Newport, Rhode Island, at the nineteenth century's end.*

ACCESSION NOS. 74.1028 and 75.453

Chiquita in 1975 (Photo: K. Mahler)

From Goode's Fisheries Report, *1887*

Pedro in 1975 (Photo: Author)

Striker Boat in 1970 (Photo: L. S. Martel)

MENHADEN STRIKER BOAT

11'11 x 4'8"

A lead boat, manned by the "striker" who rowed her, proceeded two larger net-carrying purse boats to the school of menhaden and helped them encircle it without the fish getting away. Uncommonly heavy she was built to hold her own with the operation's larger boats at sea, where flat calms don't last long. Ringbolts fore and aft enable hoisting her aboard the big fishboat which is home to all hands while on a trip. This boat was last used in Gardiners Bay at the east end of Long Island.

STATUS:

Original, poor condition.

DONOR:

The Smith Meal Co., Inc.

FURTHER READING:

Frye, John. "The Smell of Money—A History of Virginia's Menhaden Industry." *National Fisherman* Yearbook, 1973.

Goode, George Brown. *The Fisheries and Fishery Industries of the United States.* Washington: Government Printing Office, 1887.

Greer, Rob Leon. "The Menhaden Industry of the Atlantic Coast." *Report of the Commissioner of Fisheries,* 1914. Washington: Government Printing Office, 1915.

ACCESSION NO. 70.390

John Leavitt drawing showing push-pull rowing technique used by the two man crew of a Rhode Island hook boat 75.88

Hook Boat in 1975 (Photo: Author)

RHODE ISLAND HOOK BOAT

15'9" x 5'6"   ca. 1910

Putting to sea through the shallow inlets on Rhode Island's south coast often compelled fishermen to row through several steep breaking waves before reaching the open water fishing grounds. And on the return, if it had "come on to blow," one might find matters fearfully worse. A double-ended boat invariably has proved best for such service since, with equal buoyancy at each end, its actions are more predictable than a transom-sterned craft. Two men, facing each other with one pushing on his oars and the other pulling, rowed this boat. Although the man who push-rowed could not reach full effectiveness in that position, his value as a lookout more than made up for it. Steve Peckham built this boat and several others like her. Used at Quonachontaug inlet, she is a typical shore boat having lapstrake planking and stem-bent frames which notch or "joggle" over the laps.

STATUS:

Restored 1969, approximately 90% original, good condition.

DONOR:

George W. King

FURTHER READING:

Goode, George Brown. *The Fisheries and Fishery Industries of the United States.* Washington: Government Printing Office, 1887.

ACCESSION NO. 67.201

Newport Shore Boat in 1975 (Photo: Author)

NEWPORT SHORE BOAT

11′4″ x 4′8″   ca. 1860

With one man to a boat, these craft fished along the rocky shores of Newport and could be rowed, sailed, or sculled. Setting out in the early morning calm, under oars, the fisherman doubtless planned his route to return under sail before the afternoon sou'west breeze, thus not needing windward ability and the complications of a centerboard. He operated from aft with his catch contained amidships by parting boards under the seats. The anchor could be let go and hauled up from aft with the rode running over a sheave at the stemhead.

STATUS:
Restored 1972, approximately 80% original, good condition.

DONOR:
Robert H. Baker

FURTHER READING:
LaFarge, C. Grant. "Button Swan." *Scribner's Magazine*, Oct. 1921, Vol. LXX–29. Reprinted in *The Catboat Association Bulletin*, No. 46, March 1975.

Leavens, John M. "Unusual Boat Type (Newport Beach) Confined to a Single Rhode Island Cove." *National Fisherman*, June, 1975.

ACCESSION NO. 54.1482

Shore fishermen and boats in front of the old stone boathouse, Newport, Rhode Island, about 1860 (Courtesy: Robert H. Baker)

Westport Smack in 1974 (Photo: K. Mahler)

WESTPORT SMACK

12'4" x 5'0"   ca. 1880

Damaged in the 1954 hurricane, this so-called smack was repaired and used for awhile by the donor who purchased her from Howland Ballard for whose uncle she was built. Used originally as a one-man shore fishing boat, like the Newport Shore Boat above, she is unusually well modeled and when new was exquisitely constructed.

STATUS:
Relic, mostly original, poor condition.
DONOR:
Robert H. Baker
ACCESSION NO. 74.312

DOUBLE-ENDED PULLING BOAT FROM FISHERS ISLAND, N.Y.

12'4" x 3'10"   ca. 1880–1900

Reputedly built by Ebenezer Morgan Stoddard, she is unfamiliar as a type and quite possibly one of a kind.
STATUS:
Mostly original, fair condition.
DONOR:
Mrs. H. Lee Ferguson, Jr.
ACCESSION NO. 72.300

Double-ended boat from Fishers Island (Photo: Author)

Moosabec Reach Boat in 1975
(Photo: Author)

MOOSABEC REACH BOAT

12′8″ x 4′4″

"The Maine Reach boats, which are extensively used in the coast fisheries of Maine, are also, to some extent, employed in lobstering. They range in length from 10 to 18-feet, but the most common length is about 14-feet. They are sharp in the bow, round bilged, keeled, clinker or lap-strake, and have a square, heart, or V-shaped stern, with two or three thwarts, according to their size; they are as a rule entirely open, fore and aft, rarely having washboard. They are well adapted both for rowing and sailing and all but the smallest usually carry one or more sprit sails." (Quote from *The Fisheries and Fishery Industries of the United States* pages 670–671.) Apparently Reach boats used to be common back in 1887 but as far as can be determined this is the only one that survived. John Gardner says it is the only Reach boat he knows of— anywhere—that is responsive to Goode's description above. But as he points out in the August, 1974 *National Fisherman*, there is conflicting information as to what a Reach boat looks like and how she was built. Lawrence Crowley of Addison, Maine, owned this boat; thus it is assumed she took her name from nearby Moosabec Reach.

STATUS:

Relic, mostly original, poor condition.

DONOR:

Mystic Seaport purchase

FURTHER READING:

Chapelle, Howard I. *American Small Sailing Craft.* New York: W. W. Norton & Co., 1951.

Gardner, John. "14′ Reach Boat is Obvious Maine Wherry Kin." *National Fisherman,* August, 1974.

Goode, George Brown. *The Fisheries and Fishery Industries of the United States.* Washington: Government Printing Office, 1887.

Mitman, Carl W. *Catalog of the Watercraft Collection, U.S. National Museum No. 127.* Washington: Government Printing Office, 1923.

ACCESSION NO. 74.978

© Lois Darling

POWER CRAFT

Chapter One
INBOARD-POWERED

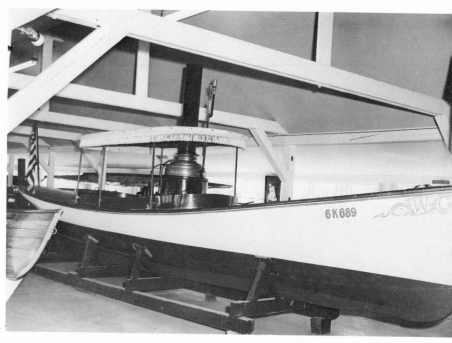
Nellie *on exhibit (Photo: L. S. Martel)*

Nellie *underway (Courtesy: Robert Holbrook)*

Nellie (ex-*Glory B., Old River, -Clermont*) STEAM LAUNCH

30'10" x 5'1"   1872

Nellie (her original name) is believed to have been the first propeller-driven boat on New Hampshire's Lake Winnipesaukee. The Atlantic Works built her at East Boston and she was used at Portsmouth, New Hampshire, before going to the lake. Sheltered waters must have been favored, for in a seaway she probably was quite cranky and certainly very wet.

A passing glance shows that most all of the best space is taken up by her boiler and engine, explaining why so few of these small steam-powered launches were built. It wasn't until the compact naphtha and gasoline engines were on the market that the small power launch came into common use.

STATUS:
Mostly original, good condition.
DONOR:
George Lauder, Jr.
ACCESSION NO. 56.1085

Lillian Russell (ex-*Helen G.*) NAPHTHA LAUNCH

21'3" x 5'1"   ca. 1904

The engine of the *Lillian Russell* makes her unique. Frank Ofeldt of Newark, New Jersey, patented the naphtha engine in 1883 in which naphtha serves not only as fuel but recirculates as a heat transfer fluid through the engine, condenser, retort (boiler) and other parts of the power system; much the same as steam does in a steam plant. Its operation was simple compared to steam, and no license was needed to run it. Compared to contemporary gasoline engines, it was trouble-free and quiet. Naphtha launches proliferated in sizes up to 50-feet during the years 1885 (when the first one was built) to around 1903 when there were over three thousand in use. Production dropped off with the coming refinements in gasoline engines, but it is notable that one company, The Gas Engine and Power Company of Morris Heights, New York, held the patent rights to the naphtha engine and was the exclusive builder of naphtha launches and engines. It is also interesting that this company, under its later name of Consolidated, went on to design and build some of the finest stock power yachts ever produced in the country.

Lillian Russell is one of the standard naphtha launches and had spent much of her life in storage before being reactivated by John Haln, who also gave her the present name. The lifting shackles fore and aft would lead one to believe she was a tender to a larger yacht early in her career and was hoisted out on davits when not in use.

STATUS:
Mostly original, engine restored 1973, good condition.

DONOR:
Purchased for Mystic Seaport by P. R. Mallory

FURTHER READING:

Chapman, Wilbur R. "Early American Launches." *Steamboat Bill*, Spring, 1959.

Durant, Kenneth. *The Naphtha Launch.* Blue Mountain Lake: Adirondack Museum, 1976.

Hiscox, Gardner D. *Gas, Gasoline and Oil Vapor Engines.* New York: Munn & Co., 1901.

Kunhardt, C. P. *Steam Yachts and Launches.* New York: Forest and Stream Publishing Co., 1887.

MacDuffie, Malcolm, "Naphtha Launch . . . The Missing Link." *National Fisherman.* May, 1971.

McConnell, Chrystie. "The Redoubtable Naphtha Launch." *The Ensign*, 1967.

"New American Industry." *Forest and Stream*, December 8, 1887.

"The Naphtha Launch." *Rudder*, July, 1890.

"Where Naphtha Launches Grow." *Rudder*, December, 1898.

Promotional catalog describing and illustrating its boats entitled *Yachts, Launches and Their Propellers.* Privately printed by Gas Engine and Power Company, Chas. L. Seabury & Company, Consolidated and dated 1909. A copy is in the library at Mystic Seaport.

ACCESSION NO. 53.3071

Lillian Russell
on exhibit, 1975
(Photo: Author)

THE NAPHTHA ENGINE IN THE LAUNCH.

HOW TO START ENGINE.

TURN Air Valve (*B*) from left to right ; give Air Pump (*E*) sufficient number of strokes (2 to 5) to force gas from tank, through outlet pipe to burner, and ignite by match introduced through hole in base (*A*), and so heat retort by means of the flame, which is kept up by using the Air Pump. Use air pump one to two minutes in warm weather ; but in cold weather much longer, as gas then generates very slowly in the tank. Open wide Naphtha Valve (*D*) and give 10 to 20 quick strokes with Naphtha Pump (*F*), which pumps Naphtha from tank in bow to Retort on top of Engine, and if Retort has been sufficiently heated, the pressure will at once be indicated on gauge. Then open Injector Valve (*C*) which supplies fuel to burner, and keeping the Damper (*I*) partially closed, especially if there be much wind blowing ; after which, by the Handwheel (*G*), which is the starting and reverse wheel combined, turn the Engine over several times, both forward and back, by turning the wheel from right to left, and from left to right, during which operation the fire will go down, unless prevented by four or five strokes of the Naphtha Pump (*F*), as often as necessary to keep the fire going and the pressure at about 20 pounds, until the Engine starts itself. Should fire go out, it is important to shut off Injector Valve and light by using Air Pump, as before, opening Injector immediately thereafter. If Engine starts or turns over hard, block open Safety Valve, and keep using Naphtha Pump ; this allows the pressure to go through the Engine, and blows out condensed Naphtha that is on top of piston To go ahead, turn Wheel (*G*) to the left ; to back, turn to the right.

Now the Engine takes care of itself.

Use 76° Deodorized Naphtha.

(3)

Naphtha Engine operating instructions from a manufacturer's catalog of 1909

Panhard I
GASOLINE
RACING LAUNCH

31'2" x 4'7"   ca. 1904

Built by the Electric Launch Co., Bayonne, New Jersey, this torpedo-boat-like craft was exhibited at the 1905 New York boat show to promote the Panhard & Levassor automobile engine, which powered her, for marine use. Her photograph appears on the cover of *Rudder* for February, 1905.

The early gasoline engines were hard to start and quite unreliable compared to either naphtha or steam, and they were noisy as well. But they were cheap, attainable by persons of moderate means, and quickly surpassed all other forms of small craft propulsion, even traditional working sail. The first decade or two of the twentieth century was overrun with small gasoline engine builders as a look at any contemporary boating magazine will confirm, each one claiming that his model was the best, when in fact there were few engineering differences among any of them.

STATUS:
Loose diagonal planking, mostly original, engineless, fair condition.
DONOR:
D. Cameron Peck
ACCESSION NO. 53.3072

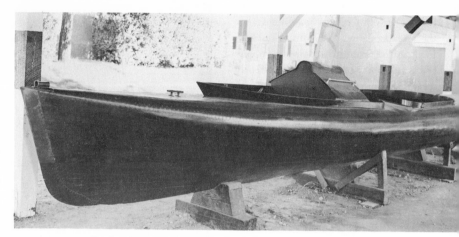

Panhard I *on exhibit in the mid-1950s (Photo: L. S. Martel)*

Panhard I *underway in 1904 (Courtesy:* **Rudder** *magazine)*

Yankee
GASOLINE LAUNCH
BY LOZIER

21'11" x 5'6"   ca. 1904

During his ten year association with the Lozier Motor Co., Frederick Miller designed boats of all types and sizes and it is quite safe to say that he designed *Yankee*. The boat was no doubt built in Plattsburgh, New York, or in Bascom, Ohio, where Lozier had its boatbuilding factories. As its name implies, the Lozier organization built engines (and automobiles as well) one of which was installed in *Yankee* when she left the plant. Unfortunately, it is no longer with her. The Lozier catalog for 1901, and presumably for other years also, lists models from 12½ to 36-feet and gives a very detailed description of how the launches are put

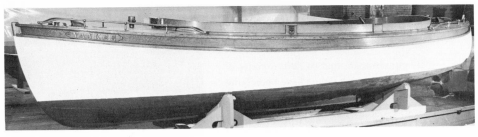

Yankee *in 1978 (Photo: Author)*

together. There is little doubt, after reading it, and after examining *Yankee*, that there was truth in the Lozier statement that "they are built in one grade, which is the best, and no expense is spared to render them durable, safe and speedy."

There are Lozier launches in the collections at the Adirondack and the Thousand Islands Museums and as these boats are more indigenous to New York State, both of these organizations are better prepared for research by those interested in Lozier boats and engines than is Mystic Seaport.

STATUS:
Original, some equipment missing, good condition.

DONOR:
Herbert R. and Harold O. Reif

ACCESSION NO. 61.1167

Papoose
AUTOBOAT

14'9" x 3'1"   1908

Papoose was built in Kennebunkport, Maine, by Clement Clark to the specifications of Atwater Kent, Sr., the radio pioneer. Her hull is canvas-covered and she is powered by a Roberts one-cylinder "make and break" engine. Not surprisingly, her ignition coil is manufactured by Atwater Kent.

STATUS:
Restored 1972, mostly original, excellent condition.

DONOR:
A. Atwater Kent, Jr.

ACCESSION NO. 63.879

Papoose *on exhibit, 1975*
(Photos: Author)

Posse
LAUNCH BY FERGUSON
18'4" x 5'7"   ca. 1910

It is unfortunate that so little remains of *Posse* because she must have been quite good-looking with her strong sheer and oval coaming. The shop of Charles Ferguson, where she was built, was on the Groton side of the Thames River, not more than seven miles from Mystic Seaport. The museum is fortunate in having a number of Mr. Ferguson's half models in its collection as well, since he was a well-known and prolific builder in the early years of this century.

STATUS:
Relic, poor condition.
DONOR:
Paul V. Donahue
ACCESSION NO. 65.803

Posse *about 1965 (Photo: L. S. Martel)*

POWER DORY
BY TOPPAN
21'0" x 5'6"   ca. 1910

Of all the many companies in the power dory business from 1905 until the fad died out around the time of World War I, Toppan Boat Mfg. Co. of Boston was most prolific. "The best boat for the price in the world," they said and perhaps for its type it was; made so by combining the newly-perfected small gasoline engine (Toppan made their own) with an already popular hull which lent itself to the economies of mass-production. Hundreds of these "tomboy sorts of boats," as Malcolm MacDuffie calls them, were bought by middle-class people caught up in the power craze. Only a handful of power dories survive today. Nearly all were built in Massachusetts, with Boston's Haverhill Street being the center of things.

STATUS:
Apparently original, no engine, relic.
DONOR:
Ralph E. Fisher

FURTHER READING:
MacDuffie, Malcolm. "A Special Feeling For Power Dories." *National Fisherman,* March, 1971.—*Delightful account of power dory history by a man who remembers it.*

ACCESSION NO. 76.74

Toppan Power Dory (Photo: Author)

Toppan Power Dory (Photo: Author)

POWER DORY BY TOPPAN

21'2" x 6'8"   ca. 1912

During its heyday, the power dory was widely promoted. Anyone having more interest in them would do well to look through contemporary copies of boating magazines such as *Rudder* and *Yachting*. Sales circulars were printed by major builders which, if they can be located, yield additional information.

This dory had her engine aft in a separate compartment which was the standard arrangement for her type.

STATUS:
Considerable repair, no engine, poor condition.

DONOR:
Michael McDonnell

FURTHER READING:
(Same as dory 76.74)

ACCESSION NO. 76.57

POWER TENDER FROM YACHT *QUILL II*

12'2" x 3'10"   ca. 1905

On a different scale and in a more elegant way, this boat served the same purpose as the yawlboat from the *Mertie B. Crowley*, for the 38-foot yawl *Quill II* had no power for most of her life. Little is known about this nicely built boat except that she was towed rather than hoisted aboard when not in use, hence her big towing eye low on the stem and her somewhat cut away forefoot. *Quill II* was a cruising yawl designed by B. B. Crowninshield and built by Hodgdon Bros. in East Boothbay, Maine. Most of her life was spent in Maine but she is now sailing in Massachusetts waters since the death of her long-time owners. She was built in 1905 and her power tender appears to be of that same vintage. She carries a single cylinder "make and break" engine.

STATUS:
Restored 1975, approximately 75% original, excellent condition.

DONOR:
Robert Eaton

FURTHER READING:
The plans and a commentary for *Quill II* are contained in *Rudder*, November 1905, pp. 615–617.

ACCESSION NO. 70.802

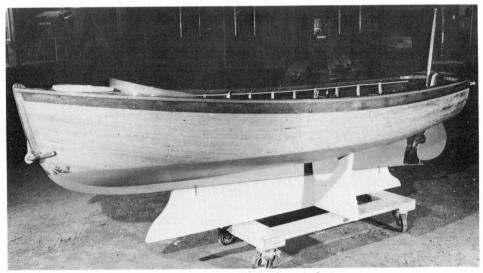

Power Tender from Yacht Quill II *(Photo: Author)*

173

Mertie B. Crowley Yawlboat on exhibit about 1960 (Photo: L. S. Martel)

The yawlboat was probably on deck for repairs when this photograph was taken in 1907 of the **Mertie B. Crowley.** *Usually it would have been hoisted across the schooner's stern on the davits which are clearly visible in this photograph (Photo: N. L. Stebbins; Courtesy: The Society for the Preservation of New England Antiquities)*

YAWLBOAT
FROM SCHOONER
MERTIE B. CROWLEY

25′7″ x 7′11″   ca. 1907

Cargo schooners, such as the six-masted *Mertie B. Crowley*, almost never had auxiliary power and depended upon their yawlboats to push them around in crowded berths and keep them going in calm weather. During an offshore passage, the yawlboats were hoisted on davits, well clear of the water. The *Crowley* was one of several giant schooners launched after 1900 to carry coal to New England from ports further south, such as Newport News and Philadelphia. In January 1910, less than three years after leaving her builder's yard in Rockland, Maine, she came to grief on Wasque Shoal, near Martha's Vineyard, Massachusetts. Her yawlboat was rescued and eventually purchased by the Cromwell family who swordfished with her for many years. The donor took her over in 1954 and gave her to the Seaport shortly thereafter. The museum also has the nameboard and a masthead pennant from the *Crowley* in its collection.

STATUS:

Restored 1961, approximately 60% original, fair condition.

DONOR:

Robert S. Douglas

FURTHER READING:

Bunting, W. H. *Portrait of a Port: Boston 1852–1914*. Cambridge: The Belknap Press of Harvard University Press, 1971.

―――. *Steamers, Schooners, Cutters, and Sloops*. Boston: Houghton Mifflin Co., 1974.

Leavitt, John F. *Wake of the Coasters*. Middletown: Wesleyan University Press, 1970.

Parker, J. W. Lewis. *The Great Coal Schooners of New England, 1870–1909*. Mystic: The Marine Historical Association, Inc., 1948.

Tod, Giles M. S. *Last Sail Down East*. Barre: Barre Publishers, 1965.

ACCESSION NO. 56.1137

Chapter Two
OUTBOARD-POWERED

Sea Sleds underway. The 13' outboard model in the foreground is similar to the Seaport's boat (Courtesy: J. R. Hellier)

HICKMAN SEA SLED FOR OUTBOARD MOTOR

13'2" x 4'1"   ca. 1925

"Sea sleds" were the invention of Albert Hickman and with their boxlike planing hulls were not unlike the "Boston Whalers" of today. They were mass-produced in sizes ranging from this 13-foot boat to high-powered inboards of 32-feet. Nevertheless, they were well made and beautifully finished, becoming one of the many coveted "toys" of the wealthy in those halcyon days before the Great Depression. At one time there were two large production plants nearby, one in Groton and one in West Mystic at the present site of Mystic Shipyard, Inc.

Although the company "failed up" not too long after the crash of 1929, it is surprising that there are not more survivors from the many, many boats it sold. A number of pieces of hardware, some photos, and salesmens' brochures were left behind: most of this material has been donated to the museum. The sales literature makes much of Hickman's "surface propellors," which at rest were partly above the water, but when underway were supposed to do a superior job of driving the hull at high speeds. The theory may be questionable, but there is no doubt that these boats were fast; a 26-footer, powered with two 400 HP Hall-Scott engines was guaranteed to do 45 mph and had an advertised top speed of 50 mph. Early in their development, the sea sled people furnished a 50-footer with four engines to the Navy which used it as a take-off platform, as it ran along at something over 50 mph, for its fighter planes.

STATUS:
Original, poor condition.

DONOR:
Edwin Pugsley

FURTHER READING:
"Launching Airplanes From Motor Craft." *Motor Boating,* July, 1919.

Feature article, *The* (New London) *Day,* September 16, 1972.

"The Wonderful Development of Sea Sleds." *Motor Boating,* July, 1919.

ACCESSION NO. 65.393

Ram
WORK SKIFF FOR
OUTBOARD MOTOR

14'2" x 5'2"   ca. 1950

Ram was probably built in Noank, Connecticut, and descends from earlier flat bottom rowboats (locally termed "sharpies" or sometimes sharpie-skiffs) of the eastern Connecticut coast. Equipped with a small outboard motor, she is used for working around the Seaport waterfront.

STATUS:

New bottom 1972, other repairs from time to time, in use, good condition.

DONOR:

Anonymous

ACCESSION NO. 72.326

*Work Skiff **Ram** (Photo: K. Mahler)*

Maynard Bray
WORK GARVEY FOR
OUTBOARD MOTOR

19'0" x 6'4"   1976

Tending out on the larger vessels at the Seaport is best done from the water and this garvey was built with that specific purpose in mind. Weather permitting, she sets out each day to wash down, pump out, and clean the other floating watercraft at the museum. A gasoline driven pump is part of her outfit. She is equipped with a towing bit, has hefty fenders for coming alongside other boats without damaging them, and is heavily built for her own well-being.

STATUS:

In use, excellent condition.

DONOR:

Mystic Seaport built by Willits Ansel and Keith MacArthur

ACCESSION NO. 76.92

*The Work Garvey **Maynard Bray** shown here equipped with brine barrel and gasoline-driven water pump, provides the means for washing down decks of floating exhibit vessels. Here the **Emma C. Berry** gets her twice-daily washing down (Photo: K. Mahler)*

Chapter Three

LARGER BOATS

Several passenger-carrying trips are made each day by the **Sabino** *from Mystic Seaport Museum during the summer months (Photo: K. Mahler)*

Sabino (ex-*Tourist*)
PASSENGER STEAMBOAT
Official No. 205213

57′1″ x 23′0″   1908

When Irving Adams launched her from his East Boothbay, Maine, yard, *Tourist* was one of countless coastal steamers; today she is one of the last coal-fired passenger steamers in operation in the U.S. Each summer Seaport visitors may ride her, see her compound steam engine work (still the original) watch her engineer fire the boiler and respond to bell signals from the captain who has neither throttle nor shift lever in his pilot house. Over the years her appearance has changed due mainly to a larger upper deck and canopy, sponsons (watertight chambers on each side of her hull to make it more stable) and a wider deckhouse. *Sabino*, as she was renamed about 1920, spent most of her

life in Maine running on the Damariscotta and Kennebec Rivers and later in Casco Bay. When sold by Casco Bay Lines for $500 in 1961, she was quite run down and her new owners worked six years refurbishing her for operation on the Merrimac River. That was still her route when the Seaport acquired her in 1973.

STATUS:

In use, considerable alteration and rebuilding, including new bottom planking in 1976 and a new deck and hull framing in 1978, original Paine engine, good condition.

DONOR:

Purchased for Mystic Seaport by John R. Deupree

FURTHER READING:

Dunn, William W. *Casco Bay Steamboat Album.* Camden: Down East Enterprise, Inc., 1969.

Lang, Constance Rowe. *Kennebec— Boothbay Harbor Steamboat Album.* Camden: Down East Enterprise, 1971.

Steamboat Sabino. Mystic: Mystic Seaport, Inc., 1974.

Perkins, James E. and Jane Stevens. *One Man's World, Popham Beach, Maine.* Freeport: The Bond Wheelwright Company, 1974.

Richardson, John M. *Steamboat Lore of the Penobscot.* Augusta: Kennebec Journal Print Shop, 1941.

Ryan, Allie. *Penobscot, Mount Desert and Eastport Steamboat Album.* Camden: Down East Enterprise, Inc., 1972.

ACCESSION NO. 73.187

Tourist *laid up for the winter (Courtesy: Allie Ryan)*

Sabino *on the Kennebec River in 1924 (Photo: W. H. Ballard)*

On her way into the main shop of the Henry B. duPont Preservation Shipyard for a new deck (Photo: M. A. Stets)

Sabino *during the winter of 1977–78, deck house suspended as her deck is replaced (Photo: M. A. Stets)*

Noank Fish and Lobster Boat **Star**
(Photo: K. Mahler)

*Star on the Seaport's lift dock for annual bottom
painting (Photo: K. Mahler)*

Star
NOANK FISH AND LOBSTER BOAT

Official No. 260030

34'0" x 10'8"   1950

Star was built as a swordfish and tuna
boat by Webster Eldridge and Robert
Whitaker in Eldridge's shop in Noank,
Connecticut. She was modeled by Eldridge to be like most of the contemporary boats from that area, many of which
fished from Block Island, Point Judith,
Greenport, Fishers Island, and other
ports near to Noank. *Star* was Capt.
Jack Wilbur's boat from when new until
he sold her to Jim Giblin in 1969. She
still has her original wet well and Lath-
rop LH-6 engine and is now used as a

workboat around the Seaport waterfront. The building molds for *Star*
and several similar Webb Eldridge
boats are in the Seaport's collection.

STATUS:
The basic boat is original, but there
have been changes to her top-hamper;
for example, her swordfishing pul-
pit and lookout mast have been removed. Good condition.

DONOR:
Mystic Seaport purchase

FURTHER READING:
Thompson, Ellery. *Draggerman's Haul.*
New York: Viking Press, 1950.

ACCESSION NO. 76.231

Both **Star** *and*
Two Brothers *take part
in moving
the* **Joseph Conrad**
(Photo: K. Mahler)

Two Brothers
BEALS ISLAND
LOBSTER TYPE

30'11" x 9'9"   1965

Modeled and beautifully built by Alvin Beal of Beal's Island, Maine, on his standard lobster boat molds, *Two Brothers* was specially fitted out with a toilet, stove, water-cooled exhaust line, and semi-enclosed shelter for the donor's pleasure use on Long Island Sound. Since 1969 she has served as a utility-patrol-tow boat for Mystic Seaport. She is powered by a 150 HP Palmer engine.

STATUS:

In use, some minor alteration and repair, mostly original, excellent condition.

DONOR:

Arthur L. Francisco, Jr.

Two Brothers *in 1970*
(Photo: R. A. Fowler)

FURTHER READING:

Bolger, Philip C. "Successors to the Friendship Sloop." *Yachting*, June, 1953.— *Discussion of Maine lobster boats.*

Coffey, Burton T. "The Beals Island Lobsterboats." *National Fisherman Yearbook, 1971.—Story of Alvin Beal, builder of* Two Brothers.

Franklin, Lynn. "The Building of a Lobster Boat." *Down East*, March, 1974.

Gardner, John. "Joint Program Proposed to Improve Fishing Launch Design." *National Fisherman*, April, 1958.

————. "Lobsterboat Tank Tests at Annapolis." *National Fisherman*, November 1958.

————. "Maine, Mass., and Maryland Small Boat Models in Unique U.S. Testing Program." *National Fisherman*, February, 1959.

Lowell, Royal. *Boatbuilding Downeast.* Camden: International Marine Publishing Co., 1977.—*A prime source for those interested in construction.*

Lunt, Richard. *Lobsterboat Building on the Eastern Coast of Maine.—Comparative Study.* Ph.D. thesis, Indiana University, December, 1975.

Traung, Jan-Olaf, *Fishing Boats of the World: 2.* London: Fishing News (Books) Ltd., 1960.

ACCESSION NO. 70.648

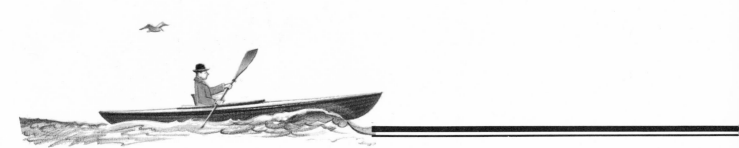

© Lois Darling

CANOES & SPECIALIZED CRAFT

Chapter One

CANOES

Canoeing on the Hudson River, from **Harpers Weekly**

CANOES
FOR
PLEASURE

"Summer vacations, the privilege of the few in 1870, had reached the clerks by 1900."—Samuel Eliot Morison in *The Oxford History of the American People.*

With many more people having much more leisure time on their hands than ever before, it didn't take long for journalists, advertisers, professional sportsmen, and manufacturers to come up with ways to use it. A whole new proliferation of books and magazines announced their ideas far and wide. Canoeing was bound to catch on in such a climate; in fact, it took off like wildfire fanned by the writings of John MacGregor who told wonderful tales of cruising inland Europe in his lightweight decked Rob Roy traveling canoes.

The competitive American spirit, coupled with the era's propensity for "joining," soon saw widespread formal canoe racing under sail and paddle sponsored by newly organized clubs like the American Canoe Association. Racing and cruising paralleled each other in refinement of boats and gear with sliding seats, "radix" centerboards, cam cleats, cockpit tents, and Nautilus canoes all being meat for the canoe chroniclers who expounded at length in magazines such as *Forest and Stream* and in books like W. P. Stephens' *Canoe and Boat Building.*

While the canoe fad lasted, that is, up through the early years of the twentieth century, hundreds of skilled builders in shops like J. Henry Rushton's in Canton, New York, were at work fashioning these delicate little craft. But a short time later, between a subsequent craze for bicycling and competition from less expensive canvas-covered Indian-type canoes, the age of exquisitely-crafted, cedar-planked decked canoes with their piano-like finishes came to a close.

Although subdued, canoeing as a sport was far from dead. Single paddle Indian type open canoes made of canvas-covered wood and, later on, of fiberglass and aluminum, gained ground each year. The near indestructibility of these last-named materials has made widespread white-water canoeing possible in recent years. Sailing canoes continued to be refined with the sport becoming highly organized and international in scope. Equipped with sliding seats and other specialized gear, the sailing canoe is considered one of the fastest single-hulled craft in the world.

"A Clipping Breeze" from Baden-Powell's **Canoe Traveling**

Left to right: *"The False Stroke," "Göta" and "Dame Cyclops" from MacGregor's* **The Rob Roy on the Baltic**

"Night Visitor on Crocodile Lake"
from MacGregor's **The Rob Roy on the Jordan**

"Morning visitors"
from MacGregor's **A Thousand Miles in a Rob Roy Canoe**

Rob Roy type in 1975
(Photo: Author)

DECKED CANOE, ROB ROY TYPE

12'0" x 2'4"   ca. 1880

In 1865, with a canoe much like this, John MacGregor began traveling the lakes, rivers, and canals of Europe. Since this was the first voyage of its kind, MacGregor had to develop a special boat: one that could be either paddled or sailed, would survive rough seas, and yet be light and rugged enough for dragging overland. The skin-covered kayak of the North American Eskimo was probably his inspiration; yet he took a giant step forward from the original.

The success of his creation may be measured by the great many Rob Roys built following the publication of his first book, *A Thousand Miles in a Rob Roy Canoe*. For cruising, as MacGregor did it, his Rob Roy was hard to beat. Her oak bottom planks could withstand being dragged over beaches and hedges, being short kept her weight down and also allowed her to fit railroad cars and wagons for shoreside traveling. And she sailed reasonably well, her paddle being used in lieu of a rudder and her full length keel timber resisting leeway so that a centerboard wasn't needed. MacGregor planned the sailing rig to be way forward so as not to interfere with the pleasure of the man in the cockpit, and he made this rig small enough so it would store underneath the forward deck when not being used.

From her build, it is probable the Seaport's Rob Roy originated in England and one uncorroborated story has her as the boat MacGregor used for a Shetland Island cruise. Unlike the early Rob Roys she carries two masts and a rudder and her cockpit is longer than the 32-inches MacGregor considered ideal in his early writings. In rough weather protective aprons of cloth or India rubber covered the cockpit and were snugged around the torso of the paddler. This canoe's coaming has a provision for such an apron.

STATUS:

Refinished 1972, no paddle, seat, or rig, original, excellent condition.

DONOR:

New York Canoe Club and North Shore Yacht Club

FURTHER READING:

Baden-Powell, Warrington. *Canoe Traveling*. London: Smith, Elder & Co., 1871.

Gardner, John. "Sailing Canoes Once Held Brief Place in Sun." *National Fisherman*, June, 1977.

Hoffman, Ronald C. *The History of the American Canoe Association 1880–1960*. Dissertation, Springfield College, 1967.

Kemp, Dixon. *A Manual of Yacht and Boat Sailing*. 6th ed. London: Horace Cox, 1888.

MacGregor, John. *A Thousand Miles in the Rob Roy Canoe*. London: Low, Marston and Co., 1866.

————. *The Rob Roy on the Baltic*. London: Low, Son and Marston, 1867.

————. *The Rob Roy on the Jordan*. London: John Murray, 1904.

Manley, Atwood. *Rushton and his Times in American Canoeing*. Syracuse: Syracuse University Press for Adirondack Museum, 1968.

Nessmuk [pseud.] *Woodcraft*. New York: Dover Publications, Inc., 1963. Reprint of book first published in 1920 by Forest and Stream Publishing Co.

Schoettle, Edwin J., ed. *Sailing Craft*. New York: The MacMillan Company, 1928.— *Has good chapter on history of sailing canoes, by Maurice Witt*.

Stansfield-Hicks, C. *Yachts, Boats, and Canoes*. New York: Forest and Stream Publishing Co., 1888.

Stephens, W. P. *Canoe and Boat Building*. Forest and Stream Publishing Co.—*This book together with its pack of fifty separate plans went through several editions after first being published in the early 1880s*.

————. *Traditions and Memories of American Yachting*. New York: Hearst Magazines, 1945.

Waters, Balch & Co. *The Annual Illustrated Catalogue and Oarsman's Manual for 1871*. Troy: Waters, Balch & Co., 1871.—*Extensive catalog which, among much other comprehensive data, deals at length with the Rob Roy canoe as first conceived by MacGregor. This company laid up its boats out of laminations of thin paper, much the way fiberglass boats are built nowadays, and their catalog gives some interesting information about the process*.

ACCESSION NO. 58.1286

Chic in 1972 (Photo: R. A. Fowler)

Chic
DECKED CANOE

16′10″ x 2′5″ ca. 1900

Once the sport of canoeing gained momentum, many variations of Mac-Gregor's Rob Roys came into being and some confusion reigned as just how to classify them all. In the United States, about 1880, a special classification committee, which included leading builders J. Henry Rushton and W. P. Stephens, broke them into five classes: Class I—Paddling canoes, Class II—Sailable paddling canoes, Class III—Sailing and Paddling canoes, Class IV—Paddleable sailing canoes, Class V—Sailing canoes.

Chic, since she is not fitted to sail, would belong in class I. Further classification beyond this into an easily recognizable type is nearly impossible. Some would call *Chic* a latter-day Rob Roy, a name which hung around for a long time and was pinned on a number of canoes. Rushton built a model almost like *Chic* which he called an American Traveling Canoe; perhaps *Chic*'s unknown builder would have had his own names for her.

In any event, *Chic* was almost certainly built in America rather than in England since she is longer than most of the English craft and has cedar planking and is of lightweight, simple construction.

STATUS:
Refinished 1971, seat missing, original, excellent condition.

DONOR:
James P. Stow

FURTHER READING:
(Same as for canoe 58.1286)

ACCESSION NO. 61.262

DECKED CANOE BY L. FRANCIS HERRESHOFF

16'4" x 2'6"   ca. 1930

Marblehead saw a brief revival of the double-paddle canoe in the early 1930s when Francis Herreshoff, Norman Skene, Starling Burgess, and some others became interested in the sport. Herreshoff was very high on them and produced a number of different designs. His plan for this canoe shows a two-man 18-footer and a few boats were so built; however, this craft and one other, although using the same plan, were shortened when they were built by Henry Vincent of Warren, Rhode Island. Vincent had worked for the Herreshoff Manufacturing Co. in Bristol and the high standards of that yard were carried over into her construction; she is exquisitely built of cedar and oak and has teak trim. Mr. Herreshoff used this canoe for a number of years (his story of spending a night on the dry breakers ledge originated from one of his trips in her) after which she came to be owned by his long-time friend, W. Starling Burgess. Herreshoff in Chapter I of his

Decked Canoe by L. Francis Herreshoff in 1973 (Photo: M. A. Stets)

Common Sense of Yacht Design, claims this canoe was the most seaworthy craft for her freeboard with which he had ever had personal experience.

STATUS:
Refinished 1972, original, excellent condition.

DONOR:
Dr. Frederic Tudor

FURTHER READING:
(See also further reading list for canoe 58.1286.)

Herreshoff, L. Francis. *The Compleat Cruiser.* New York: Sheridan House, 1956.

———. "The Dry Breakers." *Rudder*, April, 1948 and reprinted in *The Log of Mystic Seaport*, Fall, 1974.

———. *Sensible Cruising Designs.* Camden: International Marine Publishing Co., 1973.—*Chapter 1, which gives instructions and plans for building another canoe of his design, contains valuable data on paddles, backrests, and footbraces as well as some information on the sport of paddling.*

ACCESSION NO. 71.245

Decked canoes in Marblehead Harbor in the early 1930s. An 18 footer is in the foreground while two shorter versions of the same design are in the background. One of these may be the boat now at Mystic Seaport (Courtesy: Mrs. Muriel Vaughn)

Decked canoe by L. Francis Herreshoff about 1931 (Courtesy Mrs. Muriel Vaughn)

Herreshoff dugout canoe in 1973 (Photo: M. A. Stets)

DUGOUT CANOE
BY L. FRANCIS
HERRESHOFF

17'1" x 2'4"   ca. 1930

The swelling and shrinking of wood was a fascination of Mr. Herreshoff's. This canoe, glued up of 1½-inch cedar "lifts" without frames, has the wood grain running all one way; thus it can shrink and swell without opening seams or straining fastenings. Her shell thickness averages about ½-inch, being thicker on the bottom and thinner at the deck. Great care was taken in lofting her and in gluing her up, both operations being done at the Geo. F. Lawley Yard by Herreshoff's good friend, Bror Tamm. It was then up to Herreshoff himself to smooth her up and finish her. Although the process of building a boat in this way takes longer, the result in some cases may be worth it—at least in terms of durability and adaptability to unusual shapes. Copies of this boat, in fiberglass, have been built commercially in recent years by Graves Yacht Yard of Marblehead.

STATUS:
Original, excellent condition.

DONOR:
Mrs. Muriel Vaughn

FURTHER READING:
(See also further reading list for canoe 58.1286.)

Herreshoff, L. Francis. *The Common Sense of Yacht Design.* New York: The Rudder Publishing Co., 1946.—*Chapter III on cabin arrangement says of this boat: "A cuddy only eighteen inches high under a tight deck is nice to crawl into under some circumstances. Figure 59 (which shows this canoe) shows a cabin cruiser I own at the present time with a deck designed to sleep under."*

Bray, Maynard. "The Incredible Herreshoff Dugout." *WoodenBoat,* No. 14, January–February, 1977.—*Contains a first-hand account of how this boat was built by Bror Tamm as well as a more complete history of her.*

ACCESSION NO. 73.100

Outside of a half hull before final gluing
(Courtesy: Mrs. Muriel Vaughn)

Inside half hull of the Herreshoff dugout before final gluing
(Courtesy: Mrs. Muriel Vaughn)

Iola
OPEN CANOE
BY RUSHTON

15′8″ x 2′1″   ca. 1880–1900

Iola is a lightweight smooth-skin racing canoe produced in quantity by J. Henry Rushton, Canton, New York, and known as his Arkansas Traveler model. Unlike most adaptations of the Indian canoe, she is not covered with canvas, but finish-planked with ¼-inch cedar using the guide boat lap.

STATUS:

Refinished and minor repairs made 1971, mostly original, excellent condition.

DONOR:

Edward J. Ludwig III

FURTHER READING:

Manley, Atwood. *Rushton and His Times in American Canoeing.* Syracuse: Syracuse University Press for Adirondack Museum, 1968.

ACCESSION NO. 63.1514

Iola *in 1975 (Photo: Author)*

Sebal *about 1958 (Photo: L. S. Martel)*

Sebal
OPEN CANOE OF BIRCH BARK

16′10″ x 3′0″

Sebal is much like the Maine and New Brunswick Indian canoe of early times but chances are she was built later for pleasure. Later still, Indian-type canoes in this form were mass-produced in canvas-covered wood and after World War II in aluminum and fiberglass.

STATUS:

Original except that stem has been externally strengthened.

DONOR:

E. G. Rogers

FURTHER READING:

Adney, Edwin Tappan and Howard I. Chapelle. *The Bark and Skin Boats of North America.* Washington: Government Printing Office, 1964.

Hofeman, William. "Birch Bark Canoe Builder." *Minnesota History,* Winter 1972.—*Good information on the construction of birch bark canoes.*

McPhee, John. *The Survival of the Bark Canoe.* New York: Farrar, Straus and Giroux, 1975.—*First published as a two-part article in the* New Yorker. *This is the story of a young builder of traditional birch bark canoes. It tells of how he repairs and uses them, and how he feels about his work.*

ACCESSION NO. 50.2848

Kestrel showing detail of hinged deck flap
(Photo: C. White Peterson)

Kestrel
SAILING CANOE

15'0" x 2'8"   ca. 1890

Canoe development for the next two decades after the first Rob Roy was introduced in 1865 is well told in Maurice Wilt's "Canoeing Under Sail" published as a chapter in Schoettle's *Sailing Craft* and from which the following lines are directly taken.

"These early decked canoes, Rob Roys, were not much as sailing craft. They were too low in the water, had too little bearings, and were altogether too wet for anything but pretty fairly smooth water. Also they were steered by paddle alone, a very ineffective method.

"About 1868, several Englishmen, among them Messrs. W. Baden-Powell, Walter Stewart, and E. B. Tredwen, became interested in the possibility of developing better sailing qualities in the decked canoes. Baden-Powell's Nautilus No. 2 was the first model designed mainly for sailing. She had good beam, considerable sheer, a well-crowned deck, and carried two sails, the larger, a standing luff, being forward. The paddle was still the means of steering. The rudder was introduced soon afterward, with lines and attached to a yoke, or to pedals in the fore part of the cockpit, the actual steering being done with the feet. The sailing was done

with the crew sitting or lying on the floor-boards. The lines of Nautilus No. 4 were brought to America by a member of the New York Canoe Club, and in 1870 the first canoes of this sailing type were built by James Everson of Williamsburg, N.Y.

"Very soon after the sailing canoe was introduced into the United States, its type began to diverge from that of the English canoes. The English designs became deeper and somewhat wider, with fuller bodies and deep ballasted keels or heavy centerboards. As they were almost always sailed with the crew in a reclining position, the decks at the location of the crew's shoulders were often fitted with hinged flaps, so that the sailor could lean further to windward, when reaching or on the wind.

"Some of these features were found in the early American sailing canoes, as long as the American canoe sailors remained below deck in the English fashion. It was not very long, however, until the American sailors were sitting on the windward deck, at first during reaching and windward work only, but finally at all times. Almost immediately the necessity for the big-bodied heavy canoes, with heavy centerboards and inside ballast disappeared. The crew was his own ballast, carried in the most advantageous position, well out on the windward side. The canoe could be built lighter with finer lines, and it was easier to handle both afloat and ashore, because of its lessened weight, and much safer in case of a capsize."

Deck flaps and foot-yoke steering indicate that *Kestrel* was normally sailed from inside the cockpit. Yet in size and general shape she is much like *Vesper*, the boat that proved the superiority of sailing from the windward deck to the English challengers and thereby winning the New York Canoe Club's first International Challenge Cup in 1886. *Kestrel* was built for the donor's father, Rev. Francis Goodwin, and is believed to have been designed by W. P. Stephens. She is unballasted and is fitted with a "radix" folding fan centerboard which allows her to perform well when close hauled. With her deck-mounted tiller, it would have been possible at times to have sailed her while sitting on the deck. After 1886 canoes were almost always sailed from this position and the need for deck flaps vanished.

STATUS:
Restored 1971, original, excellent condition.

DONOR:
Charles A. Goodwin

FURTHER READING:
Baden-Powell, Warrington. *Canoe Traveling*. London: Smith, Elder & Co., 1871.

Bishop, Nathaniel H. *The Voyage of the Paper Canoe*. Boston: Lee and Shepard, 1878.

Gardner, John. "Sailing Canoes." *The Log of Mystic Seaport*, Summer, 1971.

———. "Sailing Canoes Once Held Brief Place in the Sun." *National Fisherman*, June, 1977.

Hoffman, Ronald C. *The History of the American Canoe Association 1880–1960*. Dissertation, Springfield College, 1967.

Kemp, Dixon. *A Manual of Yacht and Boat Sailing*. 6th ed. London: Horace Cox, 1886.

Manley, Atwood. *Rushton and His Times in American Canoeing*. Syracuse: Syracuse University Press for Adirondack Museum, 1968.—*Good description of the development of* Vesper *and of the 1886 meet at Grindstone Island.*

Schoettle, Edwin J., ed. *Sailing Craft*. New York: The MacMillan Company, 1928.—*Has good chapter by Maurice Wilt on the history of sailing canoes.*

Stephens, W. P. *Canoe and Boat Building*. Forest and Stream Publishing Co.—*This book together with its pack of fifty separate plans went through several editions after first being published in the early 1880s. One of its plans is for the original* Vesper *canoe.*

ACCESSION NO. 47.1508

Kestrel *in 1971 (Photo: C. White Peterson)*

Argonaut being refinished in 1971 (Photo: L. D. Olin)

Argonaut
VESPER-TYPE SAILING CANOE

16′0″ x 2′7″   ca. 1910

Rushton's Vesper canoes sold like hot-cakes right after the original Vesper, designed and sailed by Robert H. Gibson and built by J. Henry Rushton, won the International Challenge Cup at the Grindstone Island meet of 1886. J. Henry wasn't at all bashful about puffing up his boats and made much of *Vesper*'s success, paying little heed that a competitor's boat, Fletcher Joyner's *Pecowsic*, was favored by some as the faster boat at the same event. In spite of being born from a racing environment and of being altered a bit from the original *Vesper*, Rushton's model was considered the ultimate in cruising canoes from which one could explore America's vanishing wilderness. It was classed as a "paddleable" sailing canoe and had refinements such as easily reefed bat-wing sails, a swing-up rud-der, a small sliding seat, a smooth skin (made possible by flush lapping the planking in guide boat fashion) and the

wonderful "radix" centerboard. This last item was in the form of a telescoping fan, each leaf of which was of hollow sheet brass. So conceived, the whole affair was housed inside a small box whose top came about flush with the floorboards and left the cockpit free for comfortable sleeping. It was operated by a folding rod having a handle on its upper end and working through a stuffing tube in the top of the centerboard box.

The Rushton shop continued building its standard Vesper canoes, of which *Argonaut* is one, until shortly before its closing in the winter of 1916–17, although other models had long before surpassed it in popularity.

STATUS:
Restored 1971, original, excellent condition.

DONOR:
William R. Wilson, M.D.

FURTHER READING:
(Same as for *Kestrel*, 47.1508)

ACCESSION NO. 69.207

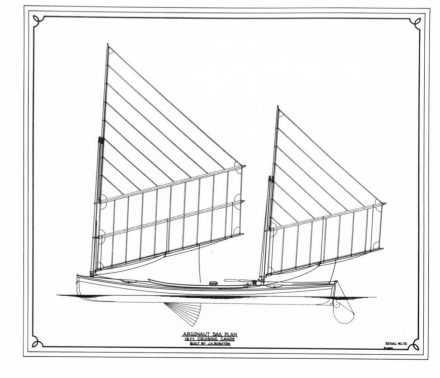

Sail Plan of the **Argonaut** *drawn by Robert C. Allyn*

Bee
DECKED SAILING
CANOE
BY BUTLER & STEVENS
16'0" x 2'6"   ca. 1890

The great American Canoe Association meet of 1886 with its emphasis on racing under sail spurred Paul Butler, who had joined only a year earlier, into developing such a number of advanced features for these boats that he later became known as the father of the modern sailing canoe. In eulogizing Butler, his friend H. Dudley Murphy says: "Few in this generation realize to what extent the sport of decked canoe sailing is indebted to Paul Butler. In the early days the canoe had no bulkheads, nor self-draining cockpit; it was unmanageable after an upset, could carry only some fifty or sixty square feet of sail, with the sailor sitting on deck, and was steered by means of rudder chains and a short fore and aft tiller. Butler, weighing only one hundred and ten pounds, invented the cross sliding deck seat, added bulkheads, self-draining cockpit, and the Norwegian tiller (a thwartship tiller with a rod to the rudder head) and invented the most wonderful hollow spars ever made. He invented the clutch cleats for the sheet lines, reefing gears, and many appliances used with the enormous sails carried before sail-area was limited. From a craft little better or more seaworthy than our present open cruising canoe, he developed by his inventive genius the fastest sailing craft for its displacement the world has ever seen, a seaworthy, unsinkable boat capable of a speed of fifteen miles an hour. He designed his own boats, and started W. F. Stevens, a shell builder, to building canoes that after thirty-five years are still in fine condition and among our fastest. Every man who has sailed on a sliding seat in a good breeze of wind and experienced the thrill of the speed owes a debt of gratitude for the

Bee **with altered rig in 1975 (Photo: Author)**

invention and development of the finest of all water sports to the memory of Paul Butler." The foregoing is quoted as it appears in Schoettle's *Sailing Craft*, pages 118 and 119.

Bee was one of Paul Butler's boats and reflects many of the above-mentioned inventions including featherlight hollow masts laid up of spirally wrapped veneer. She was built by W. F. Stevens who did all of Butler's canoe building; *Wasp*, now at the Adirondack Museum, is another of his Butler commissions.

STATUS:
Fiberglass-covered hull, mostly original, fair condition.
DONOR:
William L. Saltonstall
FURTHER READING:
(Same as for *Kestrel*, 47.1508)
ACCESSION NO. 70.639

Mermaid in 1975 (Photo: Author)

Mermaid
DECKED SAILING CANOE BY STEVENS AND GILBERT
16'0" x 2'7"   1923

When the first *Mermaid* came out in 1913 to defend the New York Canoe Club's International Challenge Cup (the same trophy *Vesper* captured at the 1886 A.C.A. meet) she embodied the sliding seat, self-bailing cockpit, cam cleats, and Norwegian tiller developed earlier by Paul Butler; and carried the restricted sail area then imposed by Association rules. Indeed she was an out-and-out 16 x 30 (length and beam measurements) racer, probably W. F. Stevens' most famous one and he not only built her, but designed her as well. The combination of Leo Friede, *Mermaid*'s owner and skipper, and Stevens was practically unbeatable. Sailing the first *Mermaid* again the following year, Friede won the International Challenge Cup from the Canadians as well as the A.C.A. National Sailing Trophy for that year. He continued to win with that boat until she was destroyed by fire in 1923. Stevens was dead by then so Fred Gilbert, a boatbuilder from Brockville, Ontario, was given the contract to duplicate *Mermaid* and build several others like her. The second *Mermaid* proved just as fast, and Friede continued as undisputed champion having won more important sailing canoe races by 1927 than anyone, ever. The 16 x 30 *Mermaid* type of canoe was brought up short, however, in 1933 when Uffa Fox and Roger deQuincy challenged the New York Canoe Club for its coveted International Challenge Cup. They won, beating Friede in his *Mermaid* and Walter Busch in *Loon*, another 16 x 30, in their wider, heavier, longer, sloop-rigged canoes of Fox's design. The two English boats, *East Anglian* and *Valiant*, cleaned up in American waters that year also winning the A.C.A. Na-

tional Sailing Trophy, the National Paddling and Sailing Combined Championship, and the Paul Butler Trophy. Since then canoe racing has become more of an international sport, and several cooperating countries have worked out similar rules and standards for boats; thus winning depends more on the man than his craft.

STATUS:
Refinished 1972, original, excellent condition.

DONOR:
Leo Friede

FURTHER READING:
(See also further reading list for canoe *Kestrel*, 47.1508)

Fenger, Frederic A. *Alone in the Caribbean.* Belmont: Wellington Books, 1958.—*A first hand account of adventures in* Yakaboo, *a 17-foot rudderless canoe of Stevens' design and build.*

Fox, Uffa. *Sailing, Seamanship and Yacht Construction.* New York: Charles Scribners' Sons, 1934.—*First hand account of the international canoe races of 1933.*

Schoettle, Edwin J., ed. *Sailing Craft.* New York: The MacMillan Company, 1928.—*The chapter by Maurice Wilt entitled, "Canoeing Under Sail," shows plans and photographs of* Mermaid *and contains a comprehensive history of the sport by one who participated in it.*

Stephens, W. P. "The International Canoe Matches." *Yachting,* October, 1933.

ACCESSION NO. 59.1373

Mermaid *with Leo Friede at her helm (Courtesy: Walter Schalle)*

Doris
DECKED SAILING CANOE BY FROHLING & PETERBOROUGH

17′1″ x 3′3″   ca. 1930

"Imagine if you can, a 17′ boat that will sail at 16 knots—and one that you can watch from a distance of five feet while you sail her. Imagine yourself taking a full capsize, getting your boat up again and under full way in just 30 seconds without a drop of water in her bilge. And, if you are interested in design, imagine a boat of 450 pounds displacement putting a 900-pound stress on her weather shroud—a boat whose center of gravity may sometimes be a good two feet outboard of her weather rail."—(From Irwin W. Tyson's article

published in the July, 1949, issue of *Yachting*.)

Doris was designed by Hilding Frohling of Lubec, Maine, and built by the Peterborough Canoe Co. of Ontario. It is believed she came out originally as a two-masted cat ketch, with a rig and cockpit layout much like *Mermaid*, and that later on she was altered to compete against the more modern boats. *Rudder* May, 1918, shows plans for another 17-foot canoe by Frohling.

STATUS:
Modified, excellent condition.

DONOR:
John S. Parsons

FURTHER READING:
(See also further reading lists for canoes *Kestrel*, 47.1508, and *Mermaid*, 59.1373.)

Doris becalmed (Photo: K. Mahler)

Blanchard, Fessenden S. *The Sailboat Classes of North America.* New York: Doubleday & Co., Inc., 1968.

Tyson, Irwin W. "The Modern Sailing Canoe." *Yachting*, July, 1949.

ACCESSION NO. 74.996

Teal II
DECKED SAILING CANOE BY WHITMAN, ANDERSEN & FISHMAN

Far from becalmed, a canoe similar to **Teal II**
(Courtesy: Walter Schalle)

17′0″ x 3′4″   1953

Teal II was designed by Louis Whitman and is built to the same plans as *Manana II* with which Whitman won back the International Challenge Cup in 1952. She is of molded plywood construction and her hull was built by Max

Teal II *in 1975 (Photo: K. Mahler)*

Andersen of Vasteras, Sweden, who manufactured these Whitman hulls on special order. *Teal II* was completed and rigged by her donor in this country, after which she was raced near his home on Great South Bay and occasionally took part in the A.C.A. races at Sugar Island. The most recent chapter in the story of the sailing canoe is represented by *Teal II*.

STATUS:

Original, excellent condition.

DONOR:

David S. Fishman

FURTHER READING:

(See also further reading lists for canoes *Kestrel*, 47.1508, *Mermaid*, 59.1373, and *Doris*, 74.996)

Wascheck, George. "The International Decked Sailing Canoe." *American Canoeist*, July, 1962.—*Brief history of the sport and a good description of the Whitman canoe and its accessories. Also contains the lines of the Whitman canoe and some good instructions on how to sail one of these craft.*

ACCESSION NO. 74.1059

Open sailing canoe in 1975
(Photo: Author)

OPEN SAILING CANOE
BY
CANADIAN CANOE CO.
15′11″ x 2′7″

After being refinished and used recently at a Seaport-sponsored Small Craft Workshop, her owner turned this lovely and complete canoe over to the museum for its collection. She carries the nameplate of her builder, the Canadian Canoe Co. of Peterborough, Ontario. Because she'll paddle as well as she'll sail, one could enjoy quite unrestricted use of her in sheltered waters.

STATUS:

Nearly original, fully equipped, refinished, very good condition.

DONOR:

William B. Coolidge

ACCESSION NO. 75.47

Blackbird
OPEN SAILING CANOE
20′0″ x 3′3″

Blackbird is an extra wide, heavy canoe designed primarily for use with leeboards and a sailing rig. Fleets of canvas-covered canoes such as *Blackbird* were raced before World War II, although they were never as popular for sailing as the decked canoes were. Rigged as a ketch, *Blackbird* came from the Sheepshead Bay fleet in Brooklyn, New York.

STATUS:

Original, good condition.

DONOR:

Arnold Rupp

ACCESSION NO. 57.842

Blackbird *in 1975 (Photo: Author)*

Chapter Two
DUGOUTS & KAYAKS

Oyster Tonging Dugout in 1975 (Photo: Author)

Oyster Tonging Dugout on exhibit, 1975 (Photo: Author)

OYSTER TONGING DUGOUT FROM FAIR HAVEN, CONNECTICUT

27′1″ x 3′2″   ca. 1824

The records say that this dugout was built at Cayuga Lake, New York, by John Smith about 1824 and if that information is correct this craft and the one following are the oldest in the Seaport's entire collection. There is little reason to doubt that these go back that far since the new Erie Canal (completed 1825) opened vast areas of wilderness to timber harvesting. The big white pine trees needed for these dugouts had become scarce even at the head of the long Connecticut River and according to historian W. P. Stephens the local builder went up the Hudson to the inland lakes, bringing down a fleet of twenty to thirty canoes every spring.

These are primitive craft, their only refinement being a small sail and leeboard and a long sculling oar over the stern; yet they served the oyster tongers a good long time. Older boats were often given cross-planked bottoms when the original wore through and this particular one has been so repaired.

Scarcity of big trees, convenient access to sawmills, availability of metal fastenings, and a need to go further off shore for oysters all contributed to the dugout's replacement by the sailing sharpie. (See 47.597 and 74.1031)

STATUS:
Restored 1968, bottom replanked, approximately 50% original, good condition.

DONOR:
F. Mansfield & Son

FURTHER READING:
(Same as for dugout 46.644)

ACCESSION NO. 46.643

OYSTER TONGING DUGOUT FROM FAIR HAVEN, CONNECTICUT

30′8″ x 3′7″   ca. 1824

Much like the restored dugout (46.643 above) and having the same history, this one still has her original bottom, a part of the log itself. The length of all oyster dugouts probably varied some, being whatever the tree would make. Their long life was made possible, at least in part, by having the wood grain running all in the same direction so it could shrink and swell without damage and by having no metal fastenings to rust or corrode. Radial checking around the heart of the tree at the bow and stern was probably troublesome, particularly if the craft were allowed to dry out in the hot summer sun, but the tongers no doubt had some effective way of minimizing this.

STATUS:

Original, poor condition.

DONOR:

Ernest E. Ball

FURTHER READING:

Gardner, John. "Native Dugout Canoes." *The Log of Mystic Seaport*, June, 1969.

Hall, Henry. *Report on Shipbuilding Industry in the United States*. Washington: Government Printing Office, 1884.

Kochiss, John. *Oystering from New York to Boston*. Middletown: Wesleyan University Press for Mystic Seaport, 1974.

Morris, E. P. *The Fore and Aft Rig in America*. New Haven: Yale University Press, 1927.

ACCESSION NO. 46.644

Four Dugouts and a Sharpie on the Quinnipiac River about 1890
(Courtesy: Eric Ball)

DUGOUT CANOE FROM THE MIRAMICHI RIVER

28′1″ × 2′3″   ca. 1930

Indians from the New Brunswick region of Canada built this canoe from a single pine log for fishing on the Miramichi River. Several natural crook hackmatack frames reinforce the hull.

STATUS:

Original, good condition

DONOR:

Henry Bradford

ACCESSION NO. 75.245

Miramichi River Dugout in 1975 (Photo: Author)

203

Eskimo Kayaks in 1975 (Photo: Author)

ESKIMO KAYAK, ONE HOLE

15′1″ x 2′4″

Dr. David W. Zimmerly, an arctic ethnologist and probably North America's leading authority on kayaks, has identified this craft as being the classic type of the King Island Eskimo. King Island is in the Bering Strait.

Animal skin sewn over a wooden frame forms the hull of these craft. Decks are also skin-covered with only small one-man cockpits; so that the paddler, fitted with a waterproof jacket drawn tight over the cockpit rim, becomes almost part of his kayak. So outfitted, it is perhaps the most seaworthy boat of its size anywhere, and with a properly manipulated double paddle, can be righted after a capsize. Seal skin, waterproofed with animal oil and fat, is usually used for the covering be-cause of its resilience. This, along with the resilience of the framework itself, makes it quite resistant to ice damage. The kayak is the hunting craft of the Eskimo and like the dugout canoe was a product of a people who, using only hand tools, made the best use of their native materials.

STATUS:
Extensive repairs have been made to frame, good condition.

DONOR:
Estate of Dr. Alexander Forbes

ACCESSION NO. 65.903

ESKIMO KAYAK, TWO-HOLE

18′0″ x 2′5″   ca. 1920

Although two-hole kayaks were more common in waters farther south, the King Islanders of the Bering Strait are believed to have built only four of these so-called *baidarkas*, encouraged to do so by the Russians who wanted help in hunting sea otters. Remarkably, three of these Bering Strait two-hole kayaks are still around. Besides this one there is a similar boat in the Southwest Museum of Canada and one in the Mariners Museum at Newport News, Virginia. Plans of the latter are included in Dr. Zimmerly's paper entitled "Kayaks: Their Design and Use" which is referenced below.

The skin coverings of these boats were removed each winter and their bare frames were stored outside but up high to be safe from damage by prowling animals. The coverings were usually renewed completely each year.

Mystic Seaport has a number of kayak models in its collection, some of them very well built.

STATUS:
Very good condition.

DONOR:
Old Town Canoe Co.

ACCESSION NO. 38.312

FURTHER READING:
(Same for all kayaks)

Adney, Edwin Tappan, and Howard I. Chapelle. *The Bark Canoes and Skin Boats of North America.* Washington: Government Printing Office, 1964.

Zimmerly, David W. "Kayaks: Their Design and Use." Washington: The Preservation Press, 1976.—*This paper is a chapter in a publication entitled* Wooden Shipbuilding & Small Craft Preservation.

————. *Preliminary Kayak Bibliography No. 2* (unpublished) dated Sept., 1975. A copy of this comprehensive work is on file in the Seaport's library. Others may be obtained from the Canadian Ethnology Service, National Museum of Man, Ottawa, Canada.

Whaling scenes from
Goode's **Fisheries Report**, *1887*

ESKIMO KAYAK FRAME

19'0" × 1'10"

Much of the strength of a kayak was in its gunwales, as is indicated by this frame which was once the property of Admiral Byrd.

STATUS:
Bottom has been reinforced by a mounting board, mostly original, good condition.

DONOR:
Mystic Seaport purchase
ACCESSION NO. 64.1562

Kayak frame (Photo: Author)

Chapter Three
SPECIALIZED CRAFT

Left: Box in background holds the boat when folded. The stretcher platform in foreground serves to keep the boat open when in use
Right: Boat in open position, 1975 (Photo: Mystic Seaport)
(Photo: J. Deupree)

FOLDING BOAT BY OSGOOD

15'0" x 3'0"   ca. 1890
Its portability was its virtue, but it was also quite light in weight as indicated by the following quote from an advertisement in an 1891 *Rudder* magazine for a 12-foot model. "Weight, for trout fishing, and paddling, 25 lbs. With stretcher, sideboards, gunwale and paddle, 32 lbs. With stretcher, side-boards, gunwale, stools and oars, 40 lbs. With bottom board, sideboards, gunwale, stools and oars, 50 lbs."

Invented and manufactured by N. A. Osgood, Battle Creek, Michigan, these folding boats were also advertised as being "The best! The safest! The lightest! The steadiest! The staunchest and most durable! Impossible to tip over by rocking! Easy to row! Safest and best hunting and fishing boat made."

STATUS:
Original, excellent condition.

DONOR:
Given in the name of Kenneth Osgood Huff by Mrs. Richard Siller

ACCESSION NO. 75.455

PORTABLE EXTENSION BOAT BY FENNER

9'6" x 2'9" (extended), 23" x 33" x 22" (closed)   ca. 1875
Many kinds of folding devices were manufactured by the C. A. Fenner Company of Mystic River, Connecticut, from 1869 until Charles Fenner sold the business in 1883. Fenner's catalog describes this boat as follows:

"(Folded up), a strong trunk is thus formed which contains the canvas cover of the boat, with room enough left for tent or clothing. It may be enclosed in a box, trunk, or canvas trunk-cover, or may be carried without any protection as the case may require. The largest size occupies a space only one foot wide, two feet high, and three-and-a-half feet long, the smaller sizes proportionally less.

"This frame (can be) drawn out in an instant to eleven times (its folded) length. In order to obtain this sudden extension, the frame is made in the form of lattice-work with a rivet at each intersection upon which the joints move easily and accurately. Great strength also is secured, as may be seen in the ordinary railway bridge built upon the same general principle. Longitudinal pieces lock the whole firmly and stiffly in place. No tools nor ingenuity are required to set it up, nor even the assistance of a second person.

"The cover is made of heavy seamless duck, stouter than the usual thickness of birch bark or cedar in canoes. The value of this material for boat coverings has been too well proven to need defense. These are woven to order for this special use, and are waterproof. They are then treated by a special process which preserves the fibre, prevents mildew, and renders every part impervious to water. The cover is quickly and easily attached to the frame in a way to secure the least delay and the greatest strength. The boat can, without difficulty, be made ready for the water in five minutes. The best materials are used throughout, selected ash and hickory for the frame, with brass joinings and fastenings, making a thoroughly safe and reliable boat. A pair of jointed paddles, with rowlocks, are packed inside each boat, with extra seats according to its carrying capacity. A sail, with jointed mast, can also be used. Air-tight compartments can be furnished to place under the end seats, thus making a life-preserving boat, which can be carried in the form of a serviceable trunk by travelers upon the water. For yachts it saves taking a boat in tow, and for steamers and sailing vessels it is the best of life-boats, as it occupies little room, and is set up in a few minutes.

"The inventors of this boat offer it with the confidence which comes from a practical knowledge of watercraft, and of the needs of sportsmen and travelers for a boat which can be carried and checked as an ordinary trunk, and therefore occupying no space, at the same time capable of being made ready for the water in a few minutes, and as quickly put up compactly for conveyance again. When not in use it can be stored in the house. To sportsmen going from our cities and towns by rail or stage into the wilderness, or by wagon over the game regions of the West and South with their frequent lakes, and to tourists in general, it will be found to be a convenient and available companion in many ways."

Mystic's noted photographer, E. A. Scholfield, owned this boat and doubtless found her convenient for his business. He was the donor's father.

STATUS:
Original, complete with all pieces, excellent condition.

DONOR:
Everett E. Scholfield

FURTHER READING:
Promotional catalog describing and illustrating the Fenner Portable Extension Boat. Privately printed, 1876.

ACCESSION NO. 72.279 (Separate pieces numbered 72.279.1 through .7)

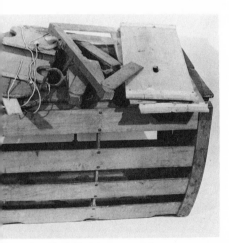

Boat in folded position, with components
(Photo: C. White Peterson)

E. A. Scholfield photo of this boat
on the Mystic River, circa 1875
(Photo: E. C. Scholfield Collection)

GREAT SOUTH BAY
ICE SCOOTER

16′10″ x 6′0″

At home on both "hard" and "soft" water, scooters were developed for sailing on the salt water ice of Great South Bay on the back side of Long Island. They were steered by shifting one's weight and by hauling or slacking the jib sheet (the main sheet remains cleated most of the time). The name came from "scooting" over holes in the ice after hitting them at high speed, slacking the sheets to keep from capsizing, and letting the momentum carry the craft to the firm ice on the other side. A "pike pole" was standard equipment, taking the place of oars or a paddle on the bay's shallow waters. The skipper of a scooter sits forward to tend the sheet of the balanced jib, while his crew is aft awaiting orders to trim or slack the main sheet. The sport of scooting was first organized in 1904 and was at one time very active, indeed.

Ice Scooter in 1963 (Photo: L. S. Martel)

STATUS:

Some equipment missing, mostly original, fair condition.

DONOR:

W. Dorsey Smith

FURTHER READING:

Dodge, Henry Irving. "A Day's Scooting on Great South Bay." *Yachting*, March, 1910.

————. "Dimensions and Specifications for Building a Scooter." *Yachting*, January, 1919.

————. "The Scooter." *Yachting*, December, 1918.

Harless, William H. "The Great South Bay Scooter." *Long Island Forum*, June, 1970.

Underhill, Andrew M. and Harvey Garrett Smith. "What! No Rudder?" *Yachting*, January–February, 1963.

ACCESSION NO. 63.249

Similar Ice Scooter "Eagle" in action as she appeared in **Rudder**, *January 1909. (Courtesy:* **Rudder** *magazine)*

METAL LIFE SAVING CAR

Getting the crew and passengers safely ashore from stranded vessels was once a job for the men of coastal life saving stations. While most rescues could be accomplished with a surfboat, extreme conditions forced the life savers to rig a high line from the shore to the ship. Some sort of rescue vehicle was then suspended to shuttle back and forth from the ship to shore. The metal life saving car was one such vehicle, making its appearance about 1849, and was essentially a covered, double-ended lifeboat. Later on, the better known breeches buoy came into widespread use, although chances are it did not give such a dry ride.

The builder's plate indicates that this car was built by T. F. Rowland, Continental Works, Brooklyn, New York. It was last in service at the Watch Hill, Rhode Island, Coast Guard Station.

DONOR:
U.S. Coast Guard

FURTHER READING:
Bennett, Robert F., Cmdr., USCG. *Surfboats, Rockets, and Carronades*. Washington: Department of Transportation, U.S. Coast Guard, 1976.

ACCESSION NO. 50.3086

Life Saving Car in 1975 (Photo: Author)

Appendix

Included here are reduced samples of plans for a number of craft in the Seaport collection. They have been drawn by Robert C. Allyn, Robert H. Baker, Edward F. McClave, Robert A. Pittaway, and Alison Pyott. Plans for these craft and some others in the collection can be obtained from Mystic Seaport Museum. For an up-to-date list and prices, write:

Curatorial Department
Mystic Seaport Museum, Inc.
Mystic
Connecticut 06355

PLANS

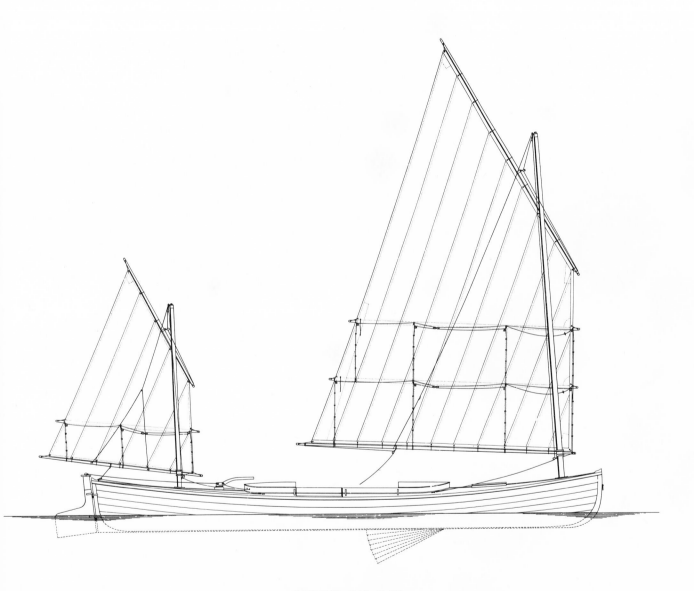

<u>KESTREL SAIL PLAN</u>
<u>15 FT. CRUISING CANOE</u>

SERIAL NO. 132

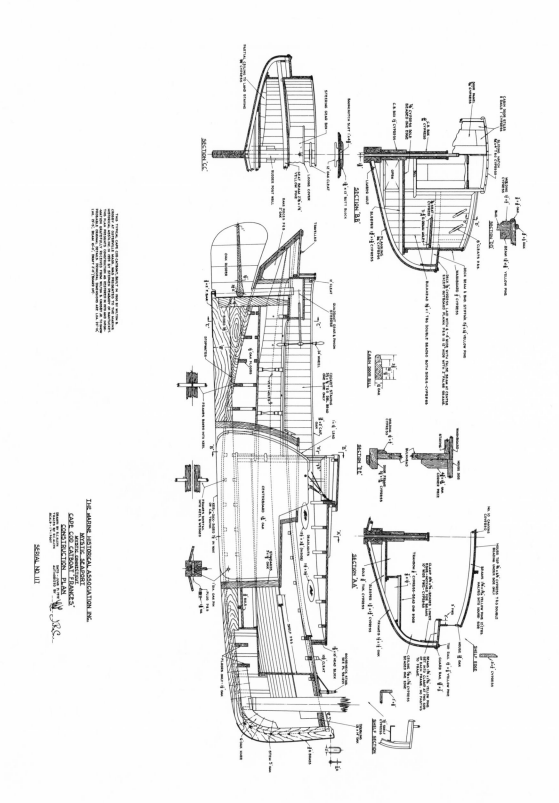

THE MARINE HISTORICAL ASSOCIATION, INC.
MYSTIC SEAPORT
CAPE COD CATBOAT "FRANCES"
CONSTRUCTION PLAN

SERIAL NO. 117

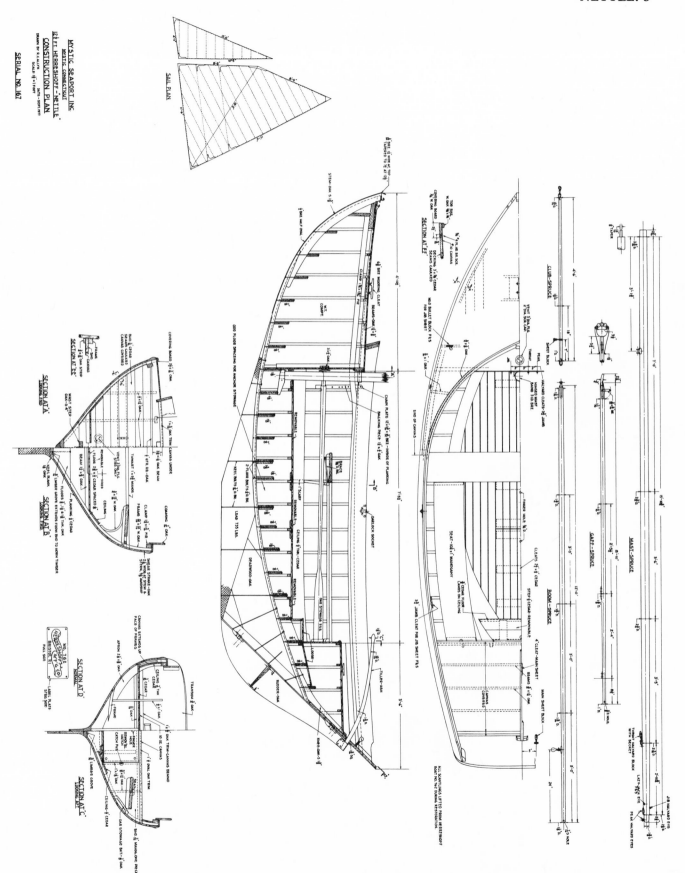

SAIL PLAN

MYSTIC SEAPORT INC.
MYSTIC, CONNECTICUT
12 1/2' HERRESHOFF "NETTLE"
CONSTRUCTION PLAN
DRAWN BY: E. CALVIN   DATE: SEPT. 1977
SCALE: 1 1/2" = 1 FOOT
SERIAL NO. 167

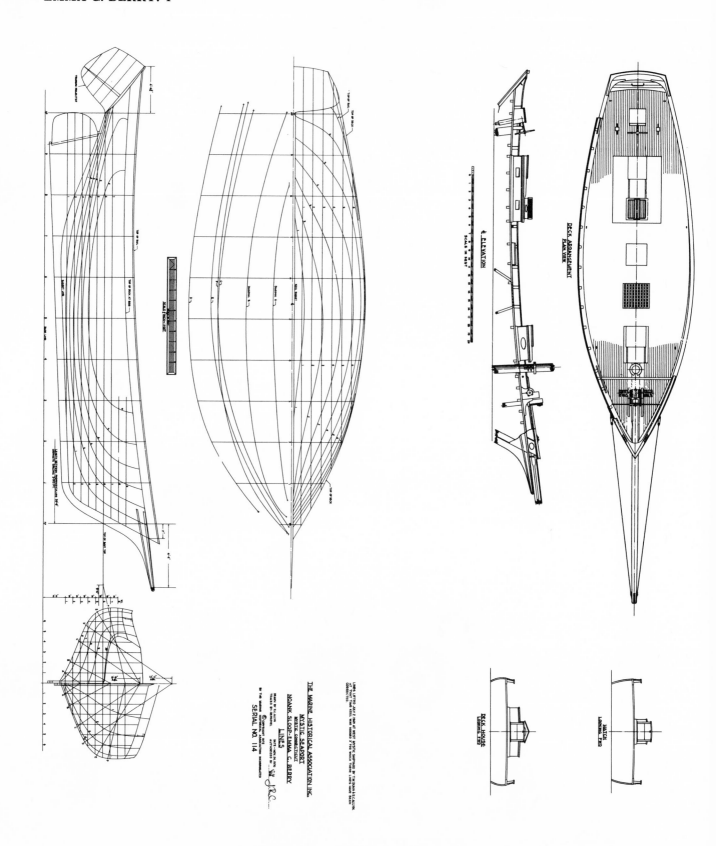

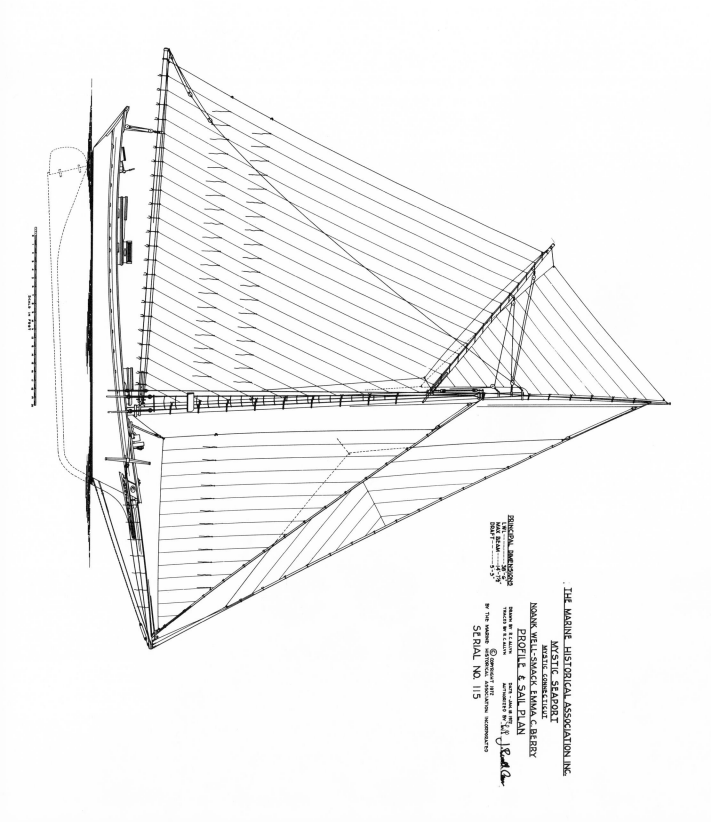

Scale in Feet

PRINCIPAL DIMENSIONS
L.W.L.——————38'-6"
MAX. BEAM——14'-7½"
DRAFT——————5'-3½"

THE MARINE HISTORICAL ASSOCIATION INC.
MYSTIC SEAPORT
MYSTIC, CONNECTICUT
NOANK WELL-SMACK EMMA C. BERRY
PROFILE & SAIL PLAN
DRAWN BY R. C. ALLYN   DATE - JAN. 18, 1972
TRACED BY R. C. ALLYN   AUTHORIZED BY
© COPYRIGHT 1972
BY THE MARINE HISTORICAL ASSOCIATION INCORPORATED
SERIAL NO. 115

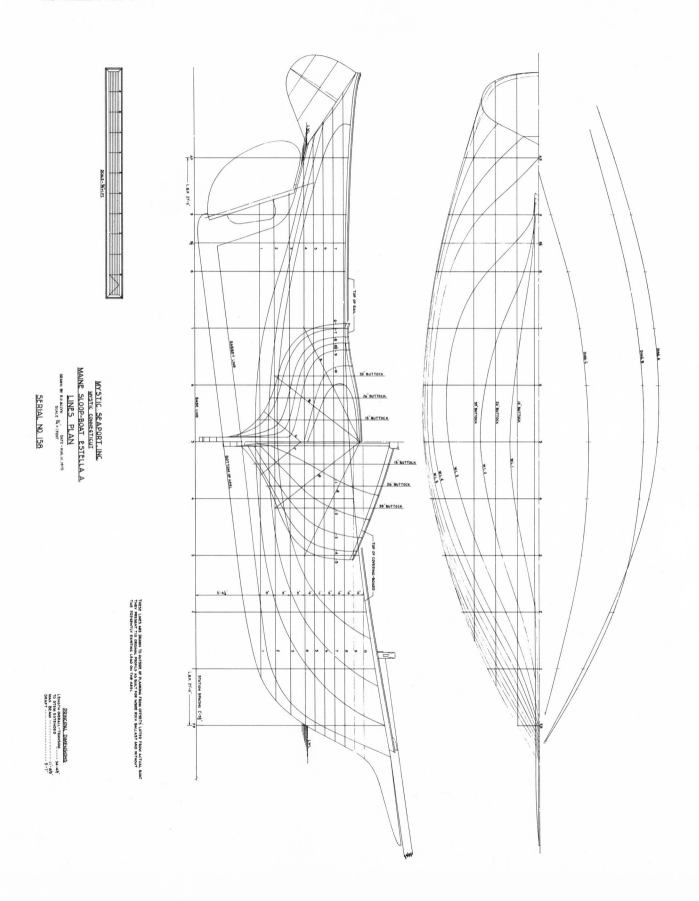

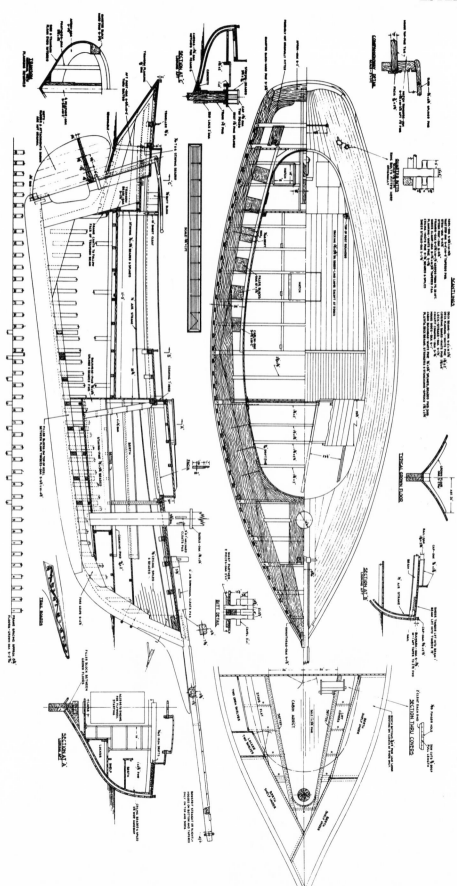

MYSTIC SEAPORT, INC.
MYSTIC, CONNECTICUT
MAINE SLOOP-BOAT ESTELLA A.
CONSTRUCTION PLAN

SERIAL NO. 152

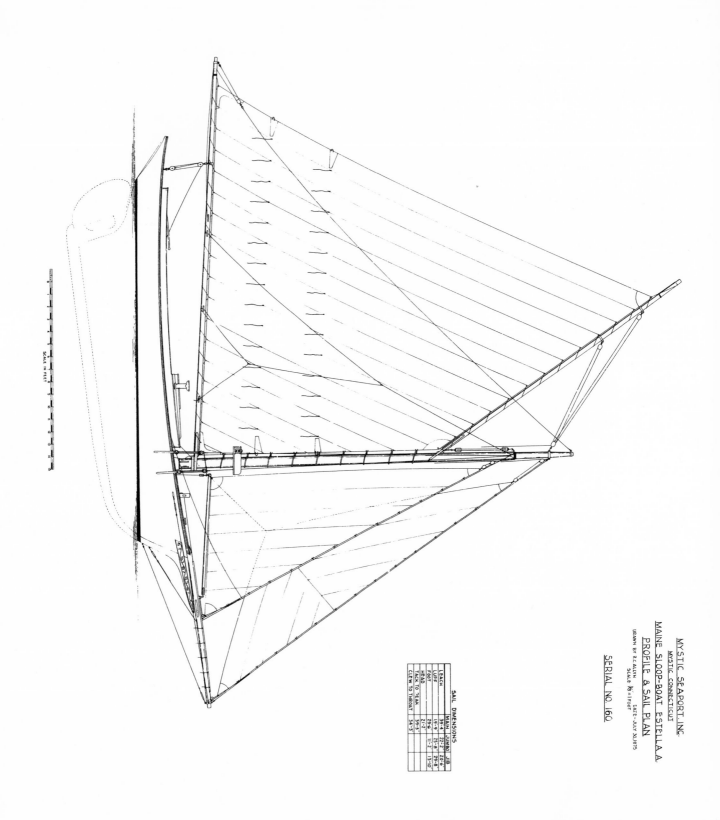

MYSTIC SEAPORT, INC.
MYSTIC, CONNECTICUT
MAINE SLOOP-BOAT ESTELLA A.
PROFILE & SAIL PLAN
DRAWN BY R.C. ALLYN   DATE-JULY 30, 1975
SCALE 3/8"=1 FOOT

SERIAL NO. 160

SCALE IN FEET

SAIL DIMENSIONS			
	MAIN	JUMBO	JIB
LEACH	39'-4	22'-2"	20'-6
LUFF	18'-9	25'-8	29'-8
FOOT	29'-6	11'-2	
HEAD	21'-2		
TACK TO PEAK	39'-3	13'-10	
CLEW TO THROAT	34'-3		

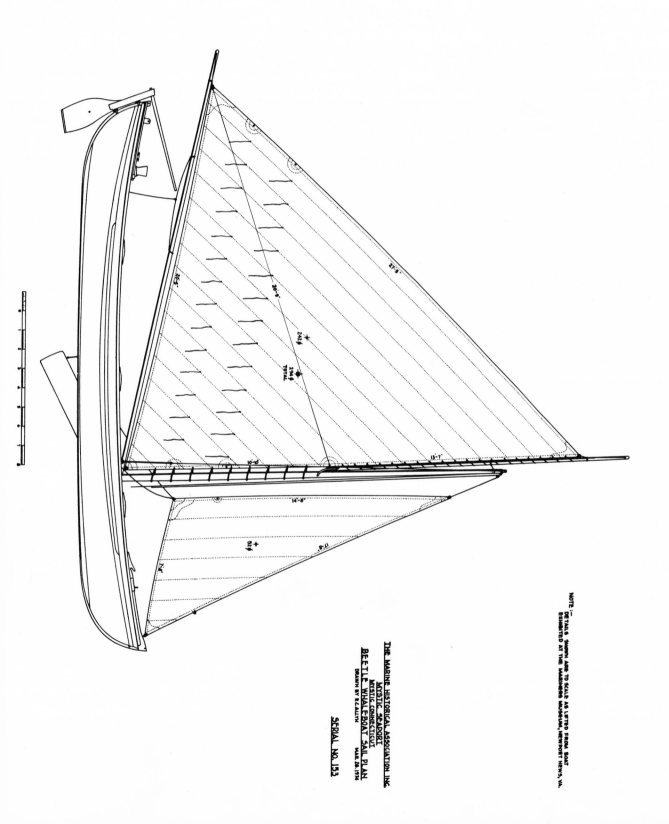

THE MARINE HISTORICAL ASSOCIATION, INC.
MYSTIC SEAPORT
MYSTIC, CONNECTICUT
BEETLE WHALEBOAT SAIL PLAN
DRAWN BY R.C. ALLYN   MAR. 28, 1954

SERIAL NO. 153

NOTE:— DETAILS SHOWN ARE TO SCALE AS LIFTED FROM BOAT
EXHIBITED AT THE MARINERS MUSEUM, NEWPORT NEWS, VA.

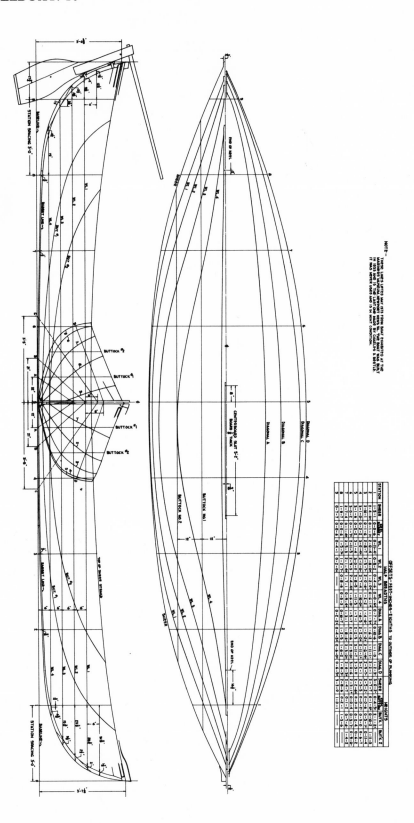

THE MARINE HISTORICAL ASSOCIATION INC.
MYSTIC SEAPORT
MYSTIC, CONNECTICUT
BEETLE WHALEBOAT
LINES & OFFSETS

DRAWN BY E.J. ALLEN
SCALE: 1½=1 FT.
DATE - JUNE 15,1973

SERIAL No. 138

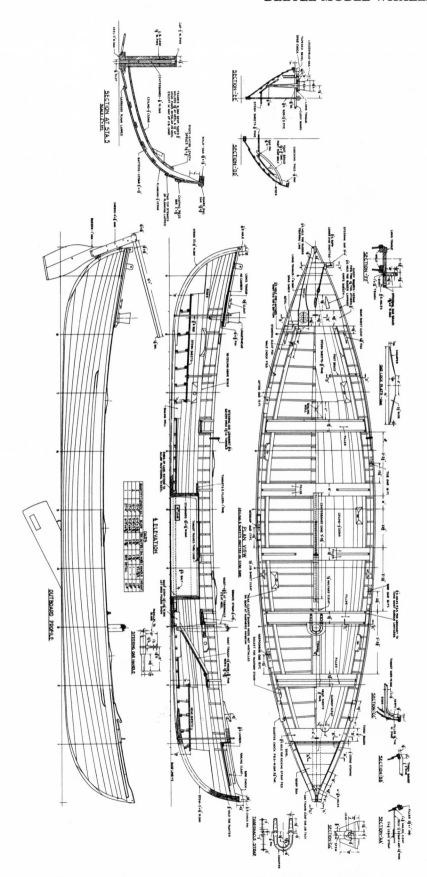

NOMAN'S LAND BOAT: 12

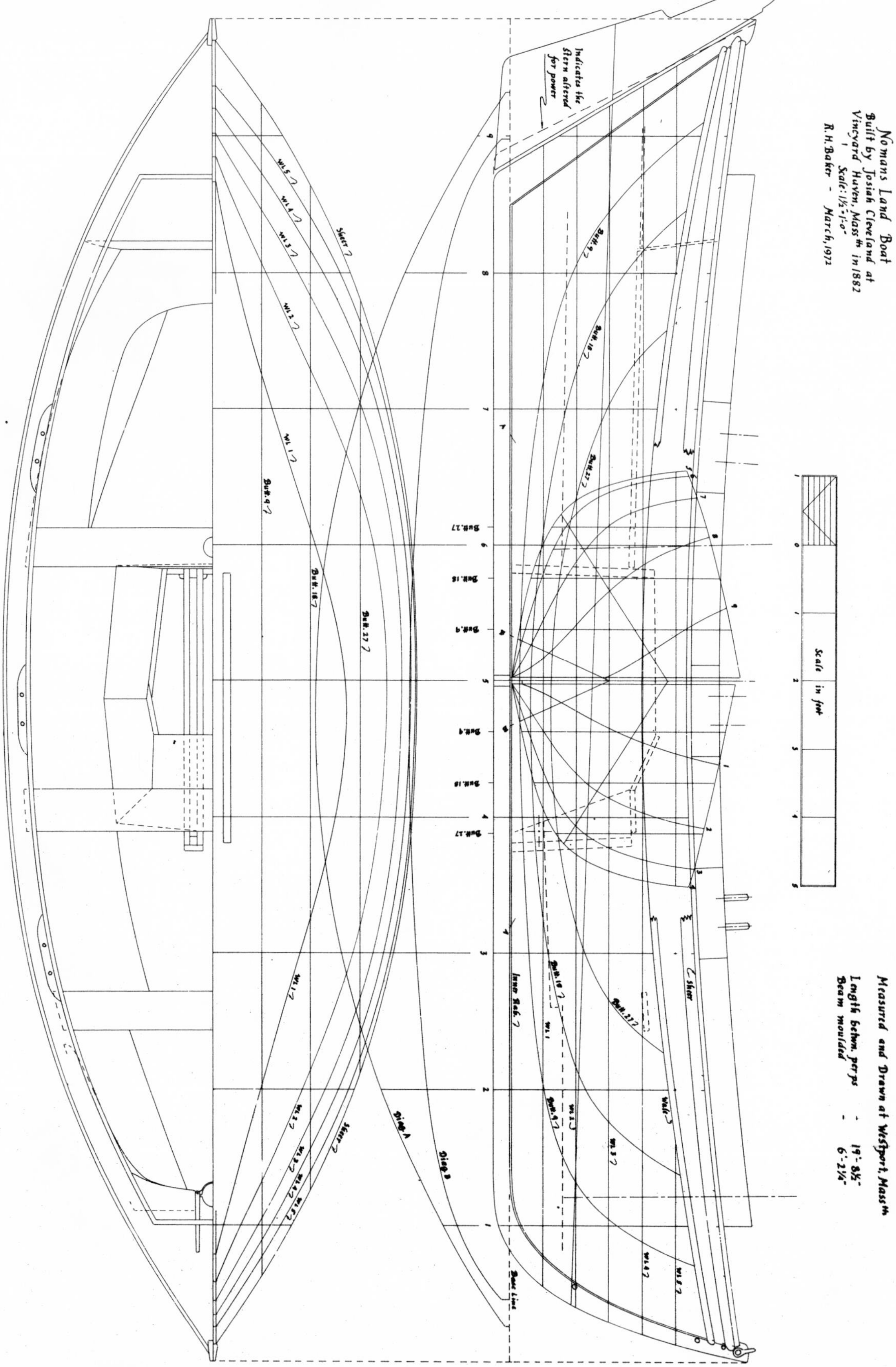
Nomans Land Boat
Built by Josiah Cleveland at
Vineyard Haven, Mass tts in 1882
Scale: 1½"=1'-0"
R.H. Baker - March, 1972
Indicates the stern altered for power
Scale in feet
Measured and Drawn at Westport, Mass tts
Length betwn. perps - 19'-8½"
Beam moulded - 6'-2¼"

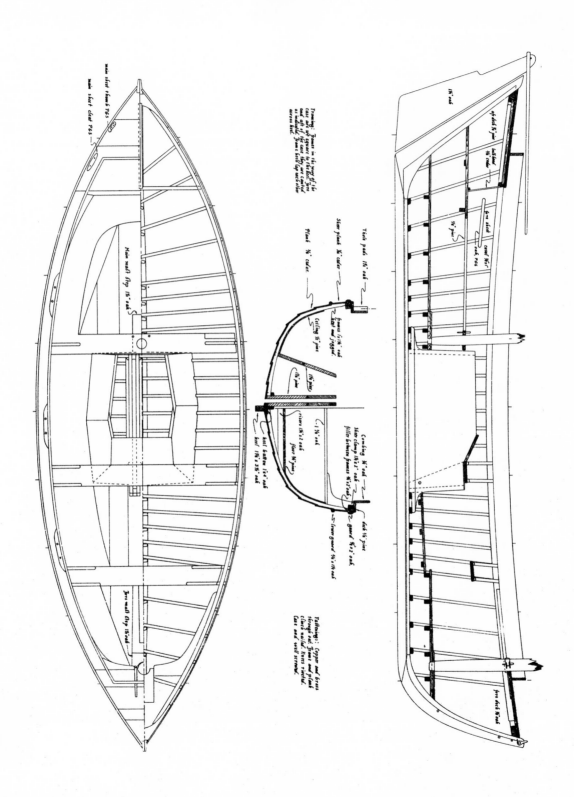

Construction for
Cleveland Nomans Land Boat
R.H Baker – March, 1972
Scale: 1½"=1'-0"

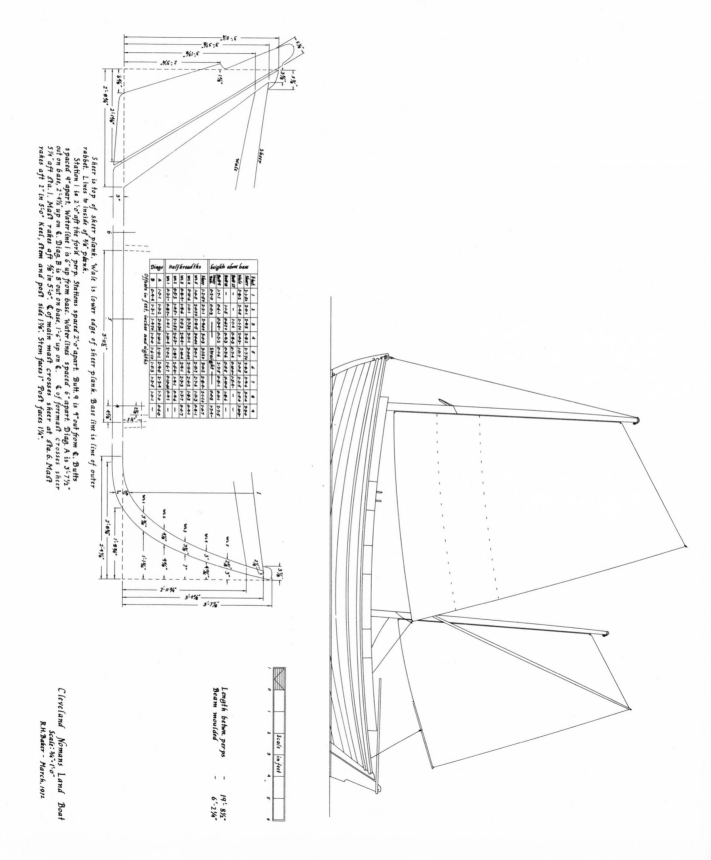

Sheer is top of sheer plank. Wale is lower edge of sheer plank. Base line is line of outer rabbet. Lines to inside of ⅜" plank.

Station 1 is 2'-0" aft the for'd perp. Stations spaced 2'-0" apart. Butt 9 is 9" out from ℄. Butts spaced 9" apart. Water line 1 is 6" up from base. Water lines spaced 6" apart. Diag. A is 3'-7½" out on base, 2'-4½" up on ℄. Diag. B is 8" out on base, 1'-6" up on ℄. ℄ of foremast Diag. crosses sheer 5¾" aft Sta.1. Mast rakes aft ¾" in 5'-0". ℄ of main mast crosses sheer at Sta.6. Mast rakes aft 2" in 5'-0". Keel, Stem and post side 1¾". Stem faces 1" Post faces 1¼".

Cleveland Nomans Land Boat
Scale: ¾"-1'-0"
R.H.Baker - March, 1972

Length betwn. perps   —   19'-8½"
Beam moulded   —   6'-2¼"

Scale in feet

Diags	Halfbreadths	Height abov base								

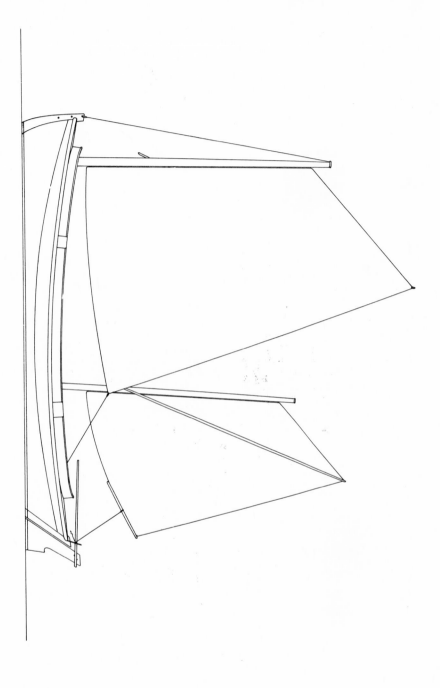

Gay Head Boat of 1882
Scale: ½" = 1'-0"
R.H.Baker - Dec. 1955

Offsets for Gay Head Boat
R. H. Baker - Aug. 1965

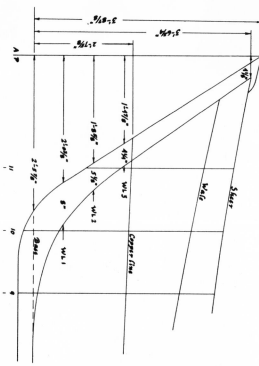

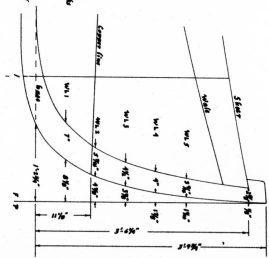

Diag's	Half breadths					Heights above base line					Sta.	1	2	3	4	5	6	7	8	9	10

Offsets in feet, inches and eighths

Station 1 is 2'-0" aft the for'd perp. Stations spaced at 2' apart.
Sta. 2 is 1'-0" aft Sta. 1. Sta. 10 is 1'-0" aft Sta. 9. Sta. 11 is 1'-7½"
for'd the aft. perp. Water line 1 is 6" above base line. Waterlines spaced 6" apart. Diag. A is 3'-11" out on base line, 2'-3½" up on ℄.
Diag. B is 1'-1" out on base line, 1'-9" up on ℄. Lines to outside
of ½ planking. Batten seam construction. Keel sides 2". ℄
of fore mast crosses sheer 2½" aft of Sta. 1. Mast rakes
forward 1½" in 10'-0". ℄ of main mast crosses sheer 1¾"
aft of Sta. 7. Mast rakes aft 3½" in 10'-0". Center board
alongside keel to starboard. Slot 11½" aft of Sta. 1 to 10½"
for'd of Sta. 7.

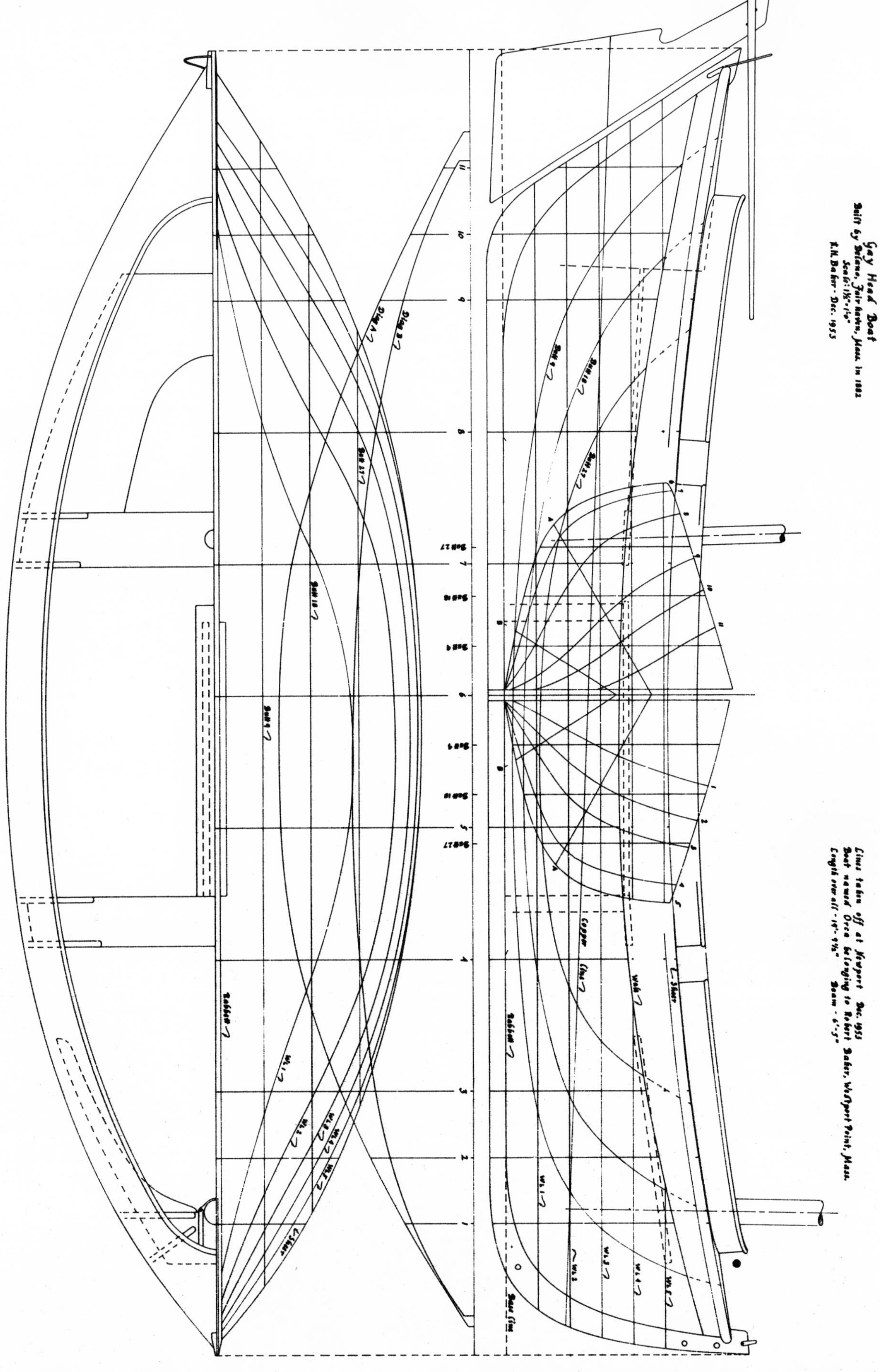

Gay Head Boat
Built by Delano, Fair Haven, Mass. in 1883
Scale: 1½" = 1-0"
E.H. Baker - Dec. 1955

Lines taken off at Mayport Dec. 1955
Boat named Orca belonging to Robert
Baker, Westport Point, Mass.
Length over all - 16'- 9½"   Beam - 6'-3"

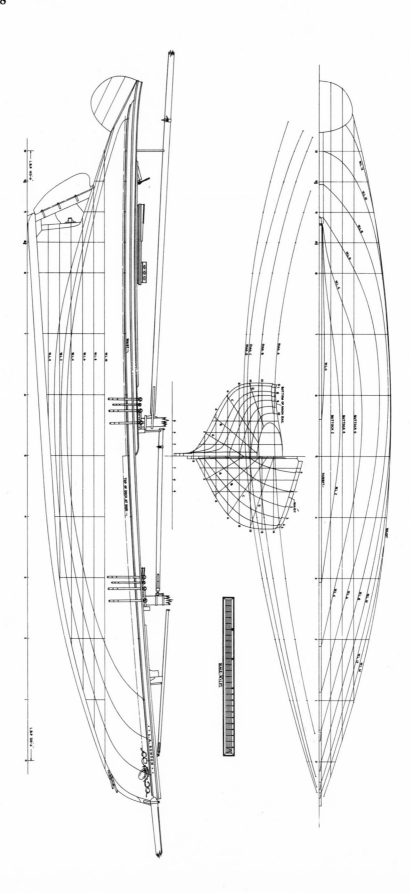

MYSTIC SEAPORT, INC.
MYSTIC, CONNECTICUT
GLOUCESTER FISHERMAN—L. A. DUNTON
LINES PLAN
DRAWN BY R. C. ALLYN   DATE: DEC. 1974
SCALE ¾" = 1 FOOT
SERIAL NO. 155

NOTE: THESE LINES ARE DRAWN TO DIMENSIONS LIFTED FROM ACTUAL SHIP
LINES ARE TO OUTSIDE OF PLANKING

SCALE IN FEET

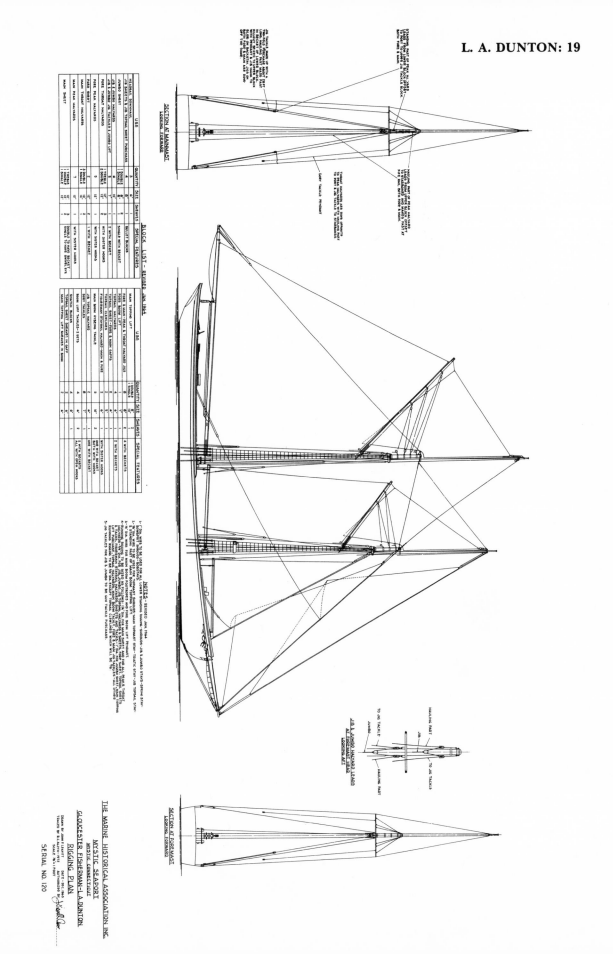

SECTION AT MAINMAST
LOOKING FORWARD

BLOCK LIST — REVISED JAN. 1964

USE	QUANTITY	SIZE	SHEAVES	SPECIAL FEATURES
HEADSAIL DOWNHAUL	5	6"		BULLET BLOCKS
JIB SHEETS & JIB TOPSAIL SHEET PURCHASE	4	8"		SINGLE WITH BECKET
JUMBO SHEETS	SINGLE	8"	2	
FORE BOOM LIFT	2	10"	2	2 WITH BECKET
JIB & JUMBO HALYARDS	5	7"		
FORE & JUMBO JIB TACKLES & JUMBO LIFT	2 DOUBLE	8"	2	2 WITH BECKET
FORE PEAK HALYARDS	1 TREBLE	12"	3	WITH SISTER HOOKS
FORE THROAT HALYARDS	2 DOUBLE	12"	2	WITH SISTER HOOKS
FORE SHEET	2	12"		WITH SISTER HOOKS
MAIN THROAT HALYARDS	2 DOUBLE	12"	2	WITH BECKET
MAIN THROAT	3 SINGLE	12"		1 WITH BECKET
MAIN PEAK HALYARDS	7	12"	1	WITH SISTER HOOKS
MAIN SHEET	1 DOUBLE / 1 SINGLE	12"	2	DOUBLE TO HAVE BECKET SINGLE TO HAVE SHIVE EYE

USE	QUANTITY	SIZE	SHEAVES	SPECIAL FEATURES
MAIN TOPPING LIFT	1 DOUBLE / 1 SINGLE	10"	2	
FORE & MAIN PEAK & THROAT HALYARD	8	8"	2	
FORE BOOM LIFT	2	7"		4 WITH BECKETS
FORE BOW LIFT	2	8"	2	
TOPSAIL HALYARDS	4	8"		
TOPSAIL SHEET—FORE & MAIN GAFFS	2	5"	2	2 WITH BECKETS
TOPSAIL CLEWLINES	2	6"	1	
FISHERMAN STAYSAIL	3	6"	1	WITH SISTER HOOKS
MAIN BOOM STERING TACKLE	2	10"	2	ONE WITH BECKET BOTH WITH HOOKS
JIB TOPSAIL HALYARD	1	7"		ONE WITH BECKET
BOOM LIFT TACKLES—2 SETS	4	6"	2	
BOOM LIFT TACKLES	4	6"	2	2 WITH BECKETS ALL WITH OPEN HOOKS
TOPSAIL SHEET SHEAVE IN GAFF	2	6"	1	
MAIN TOPPING LIFT SHEAVES IN BOOM	2	6"		

NOTES — REVISED JAN. 1964

JIB & JUMBO HALYARD LEADS
AT FOREMAST HEAD
LOOKING AFT

TO JIG TACKLE
JUMBO
JIB
HAULING PART
HAULING PART
TO JIG TACKLE

SECTION AT FOREMAST
LOOKING FORWARD

THE MARINE HISTORICAL ASSOCIATION INC.
MYSTIC SEAPORT
MYSTIC, CONNECTICUT
GLOUCESTER FISHERMAN—L.A. DUNTON
RIGGING PLAN

SERIAL NO. 120

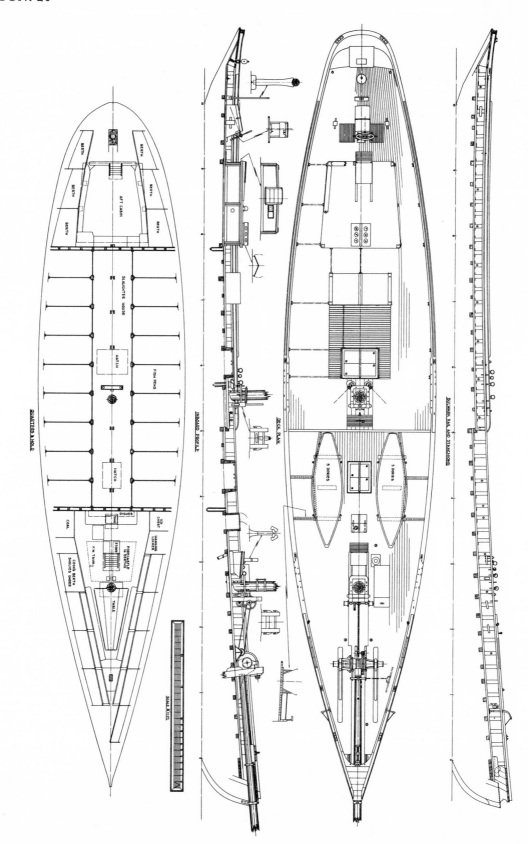

MYSTIC SEAPORT INC
MYSTIC, CONNECTICUT
GLOUCESTER FISHERMAN – L.A. DUNTON
DECKS & BULWARK PLAN
DRAWN BY E.G. ALLYN   DATE – APR. 17, 1973
SCALE ¾" = 1 FOOT

SERIAL No. 157

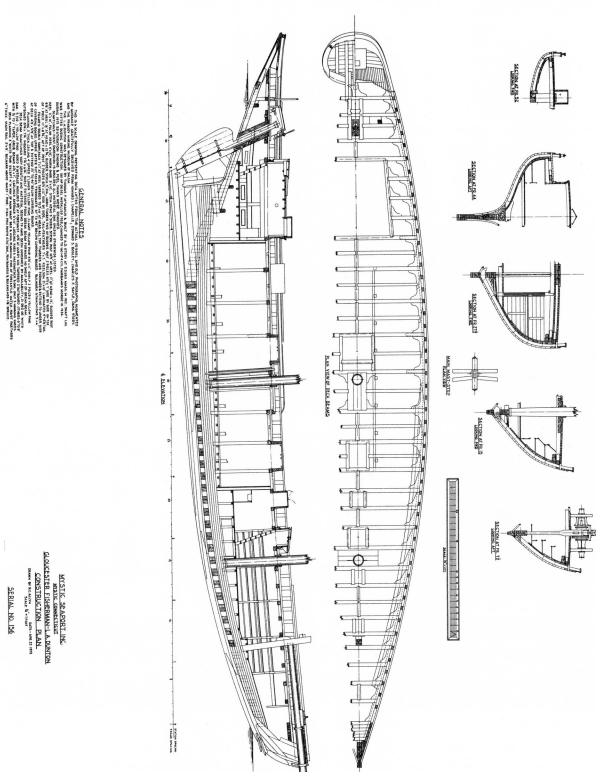

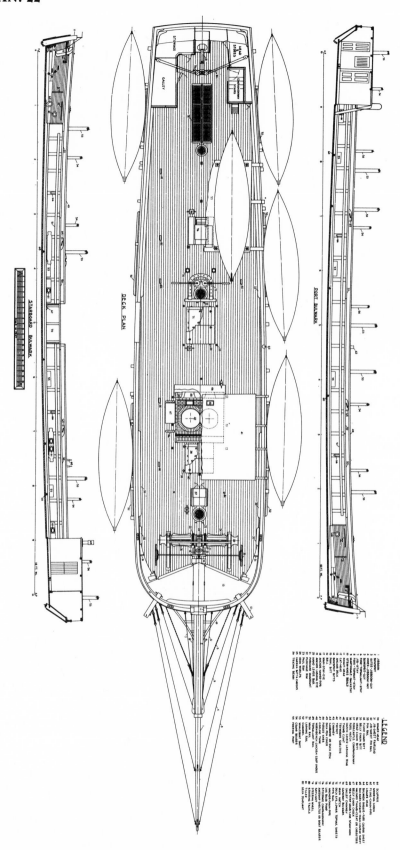

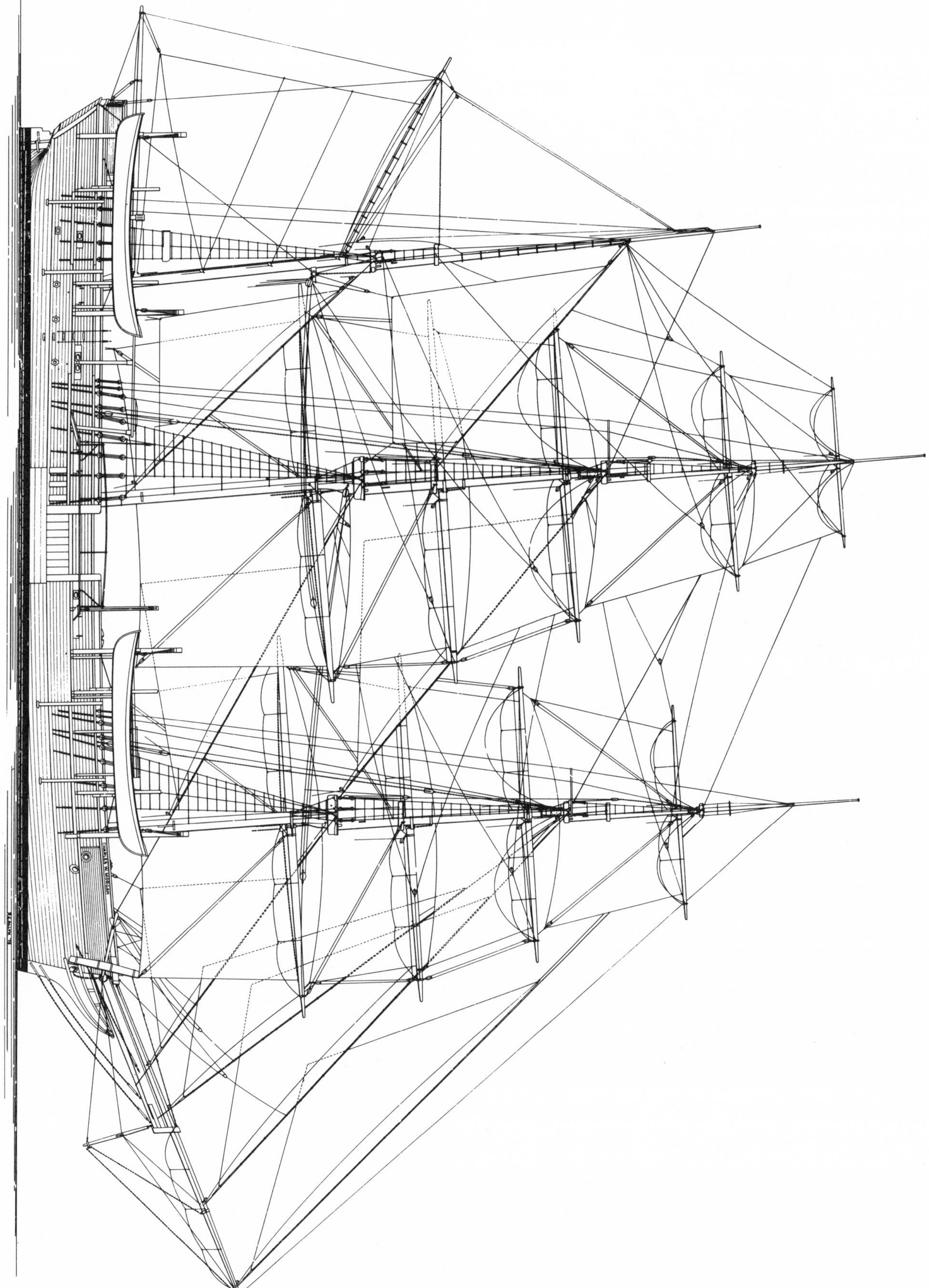

OFFSETS

STATION	HALF BREADTHS WL 2	WL 4	WL 6	WL 8	WL 10	WL 12	WL 14	WL 16	WL 18	WL 20	HALF BREADTHS MAIN RAIL UNDER SIDE	PLANK-SHEER TOP OF	DIAG A	DIAG B	DIAG C
FP	—	—	—	—	—	1-3-0	2-2-5	3-4-1	4-8-1	6-2-6	9-5-1	7-3-6	1-4-3	2-0-7	5-5-5
½	0-9-4	2-0-0	3-4-0	4-8-4	6-0-7	7-4-0	8-5-3	9-5-2	10-4-0	11-1-3	11-11-4	11-4-2	6-7-4	7-4-3	11-0-0
1	2-5-7	4-7-2	6-6-0	8-2-3	9-7-0	10-7-6	11-4-4	11-11-3	12-4-0	12-7-0	12-4-7	12-7-6	9-0-6	10-2-0	13-11-7
1½	3-8-4	6-8-5	9-0-2	10-7-2	11-8-0	12-4-2	12-9-5	13-0-5	13-1-5	13-1-1	12-6-3	13-1-1	10-4-6	12-0-4	15-10-3
2	4-9-0	8-4-4	10-8-4	12-1-3	12-10-1	13-2-6	13-5-2	13-5-5	13-4-5	13-2-7	12-7-3	13-3-5	11-2-0	13-2-3	17-1-1
3	6-2-7	10-2-5	12-2-4	13-1-1	13-6-3	13-8-2	13-8-4	13-7-6	13-6-0	—	12-8-0	13-4-3	11-10-2	14-4-2	17-11-6
4	6-9-3	10-9-4	12-5-5	13-2-7	13-7-6	13-9-6	13-9-7	13-8-5	13-6-5	—	12-7-6	13-4-1	12-0-6	14-8-0	18-1-4
5	6-6-2	10-5-3	12-3-2	13-1-0	13-6-2	13-8-3	13-8-4	13-7-3	13-5-1	—	12-5-3	13-2-3	11-11-5	14-5-2	17-11-6
6	5-4-5	9-2-4	11-5-6	12-7-3	13-2-5	13-5-5	13-6-3	13-5-1	13-2-4	12-11-2	12-1-5	12-11-1	11-5-7	13-9-0	17-6-2
7	3-10-3	6-11-6	9-7-0	11-5-5	12-7-0	13-0-4	13-2-0	13-1-2	12-10-3	12-6-4	11-8-7	12-6-3	10-6-0	12-4-3	16-8-7
8	2-3-6	4-3-0	6-5-5	8-8-5	10-8-4	11-11-6	12-6-4	12-8-2	12-5-6	12-1-5	11-2-7	12-0-1	8-10-5	10-3-7	15-1-3
8½	1-7-6	2-11-1	4-6-6	6-6-2	8-8-5	10-9-1	11-10-7	12-3-6	12-2-3	11-10-3	10-11-1	11-8-1	7-7-4	8-10-0	13-10-4
9	1-1-5	1-9-7	2-8-4	3-10-6	5-8-0	8-1-4	10-7-4	11-9-1	11-10-4	11-6-5	10-7-0	11-3-6	5-11-2	6-10-0	12-1-5
9½	0-8-4	0-11-2	1-2-5	1-7-4	2-3-4	3-4-5	5-8-0	10-5-1	11-4-1	11-1-5	10-2-5	10-10-5	3-6-1	3-11-7	9-2-7
AP	—								10-7-3	10-6-7	9-9-3	10-4-4			
TRANSOM									10-6-2	10-4-3	9-5-0	10-1-0			

STATION	HEIGHTS BUTTOCK NO. 1	BUTTOCK NO. 2	BUTTOCK NO. 3	BUTTOCK NO. 4	BUTTOCK NO. 5	MAIN RAIL UNDER SIDE	PLANK SHEER TOP OF	TOP OF WALE	
FP	13-6-4	17-0-6	19-8-0	—	—	23-9-1	21-2-4	18-2-2	
½	4-0-0	6-11-7	9-11-0	13-2-1	17-5-0	23-7-3	20-8-2	17-5-7	
1	1-7-2	3-5-0	5-5-3	7-8-5	10-8-4	22-10-5	20-4-3	17-1-0	
1½	0-11-0	2-1-6	3-6-3	5-1-0	7-2-4	22-8-5	20-2-3	16-10-5	
2	0-8-0	1-7-3	2-7-3	3-9-3	5-3-6	22-7-3	20-1-0	16-9-0	
3	0-6-3	1-2-1	1-11-2	2-9-3	3-10-1	22-5-3	19-10-6	16-6-5	
4	0-5-5	1-0-5	1-8-5	2-5-7	3-5-7	22-4-6	19-10-3	16-5-6	
5	0-5-7	1-1-5	1-9-6	2-7-2	3-7-3	22-5-5	19-11-4	16-6-6	
6	0-7-4	1-5-0	2-3-4	3-3-4	4-6-6	22-7-3	20-1-4	16-9-2	
7	0-10-6	2-1-5	3-4-5	4-8-6	6-4-6	22-9-6	20-4-2	17-0-5	
8	1-8-2	3-9-0	5-7-2	7-4-3	9-3-4	23-0-6	20-7-7	17-4-4	
8½	2-6-7	5-4-3	7-6-4	9-4-5	11-2-6	23-2-3	20-10-2	17-6-6	
9	4-5-2	8-1-6	10-3-3	11-10-6	13-5-0	23-4-3	21-0-5	17-9-3	
9½	9-3-5	12-8-6	14-1-0	14-10-4	15-9-0	23-6-3	21-3-2	18-0-0	
AP	—	—	—	—	—	23-8-3	21-6-0	18-3-0	
TRANSOM						23-10-5	21-7-5		

REVISIONS

1.- SHEER LINE STATION 2 TO STEM, LOWER PORTION OF STEM, KEEL DEPTH, RAKE OF STERN POST & RUDDER PROFILE REVISED TO SUIT DIMENSIONS LIFTED AT TIME OF HAULOUT. GEN. NOTES 2.3.4 LINED OUT. 6/28/74

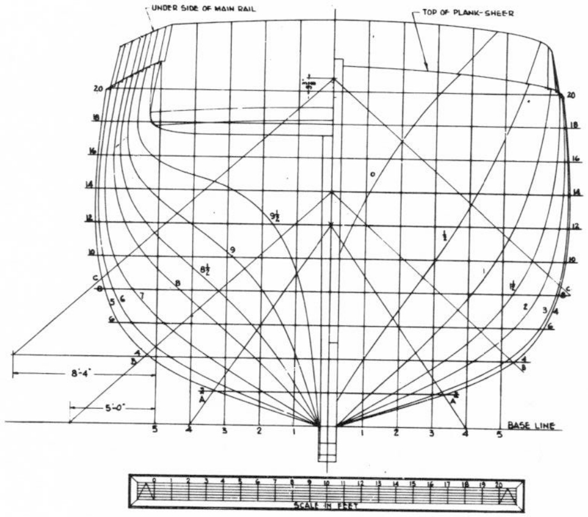

PRINCIPAL DIMENSIONS

LENGTH BETWEEN PERPENDICULARS ______ 103'-4"
LENGTH AT MAIN RAIL ______ 111'-4¼"
MAXIMUM MOULDED BEAM ______ 27'-7½"
DEPTH. RABBET TO PLANK-SHEER AT STA. 5 ___ 19'-11½"

GENERAL NOTES

1.- THESE LINES, DEVELOPED FROM DIMENSIONS LIFTED FROM THE SHIP AT ALL STATIONS, ARE TO OUTSIDE OF PLANKING UP TO TOP OF WALE. OUTSIDE OF PLANKING FROM WALE TO PLANK-SHEER IS 1" INSIDE OF MOULDED LINE. LINES IN WAY OF BULWARK ARE TO OUTSIDE OF PLANKING.

2.- ~~THE SHIP IS PRESENTLY RESTING IN A SAND AND GRAVEL BED. TOP OF THE BED IS 7½ FT. ABOVE BASE LINE AT THE F.P. AND 9½ FT. AT THE A.P. LINES BELOW THIS LEVEL WERE DEVELOPED FROM INBOARD DIMENSIONS TO INSIDE OF SHEATHING SUPPLEMENTED BY STRUCTURAL LAYOUTS AND FAIRING.~~

3.- ~~KEEL SCANTLINGS TAKEN FROM SPECIFICATIONS OF SIMILAR NEW BEDFORD WHALER OF THE SAME PERIOD.~~

4.- ~~PROFILE FOR FOREFOOT AND LOWER PORTION OF RUDDER HAVE BEEN TAKEN FROM OLD PHOTOS OF THE SHIP ON MARINE RAILWAY.~~

THE MARINE HISTORICAL ASSOCIATION INC.
MYSTIC SEAPORT
MYSTIC CONNECTICUT
BARK CHARLES W. MORGAN
LINES PLAN

DRAWN BY - R.C. ALLYN | DATE - JULY 15, 1970
TRACED BY - REPROVEL | AUTHORIZED BY - JRC
SCALE - ¼" = 1 FT

© COPYRIGHT 1972
BY THE MARINE HISTORICAL ASSOCIATION INCORPORATED

SERIAL NO. 100

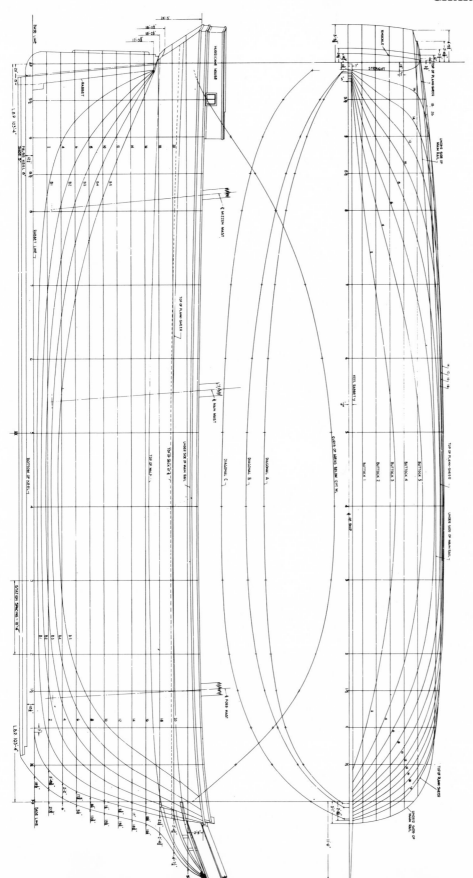

SECTION AT STA. 8½
LOOKING AFT

SECTION AT STA. 1
LOOKING FWD

SECTION AT STA. 5
LOOKING FWD

THE MARINE HISTORICAL ASSOCIATION INC.
MYSTIC SEAPORT
MYSTIC, CONNECTICUT
BARK CHARLES W. MORGAN
CONSTRUCTION PLAN

DRAWN BY: E. CALOYN
TRACED BY: R.F. BROWN
SCALE - ¾" = 1 FT.
DATE - JULY 15 1970
AUTHORIZED BY -
© COPYRIGHT 1972
BY THE MARINE HISTORICAL ASSOCIATION INCORPORATED

SERIAL NO. 10

LEGEND

1. KEEL
2. SHOE
3. KEELSON
4. KEELSON RIDER
5. STEM
6. APRON
7. STEM KNEE
8. BREAST HOOK
9. POINTER
10. DEADWOOD
11. STERN POST
12. STERN POST
13. RUDDER POST
14. RUDDER POST BOX
15. TILLER
16. STEERING WHEEL
17. QUARTER KNEES
18. TIMBERS (FRAMES)
19. DECK BEAMS
20. INTERMEDIATE BEAMS
21. LODGING KNEES
22. HANGING KNEES
23. STANDING KNEES
24. PARTNERS
25. CARLINGS
26. FLOORS

30. DECK STANCHIONS
31. PIN RAILS
32. BULWARK STANCHIONS
33. ANCHOR DECK
34. BOWSPRIT
35. BOWSPRIT HEEL CHOCK
36. JIB-BOOM
37. JIB-BOOM HEEL CHOCK
38. STEM HEAD KNEE
39. KNIGHT-HEAD
40. PAWL BITT
41. BITT
42. WINDLASS
43. FORE LOWER MAST
44. MAIN LOWER MAST
45. MIZZEN LOWER MAST
46. MAST STEP
47. MAST WEDGES
48. MAST COAMING
49. HATCH COAMING
50. HATCH COVER
51. HATCH GRATING
52. COMPANIONWAY LADDER
53. JONES BULKHEAD
54. TRY POT
55. GOOSE-PEN
56. VENT HOLES

60. TRYWORKS SHELTER
61. AFT SHELTER
62. HURRICANE HOUSE TOP
63. SLIDING HATCH
64. FIFE RAIL
65. BILGE PUMP
66. ANCHOR CHAIN LOCKER
67. ANCHOR CHAIN PIPE
68. PLANK-SHEER
69. PLANKING
70. DEALES
71. DECK PLANKING
72. WATERWAY
73. CLAMP
74. CEILING
75. VENT STRAKE
76. LIMBER STRAKE
77. LINING RAIL
78. GARBOARD
79. SHIPS STORES
80. SHIPS STORES
81. GANGWAY COAMING STRIPS
82. SPRUNG BAND
83. FALSE KEEL

NOTE: THIS IS A SCALE DRAWING. SCANTLINGS AND RELATIVE SPACINGS HAVE BEEN LIFTED FROM THE SHIP WHEREVER POSSIBLE.

REVISIONS
1 - STEM, KEEL & RUDDER DETAILS REVISED AS LIFTED FROM SHIP AFTER HAULING 6/17/74

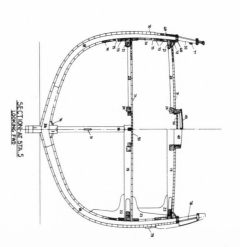

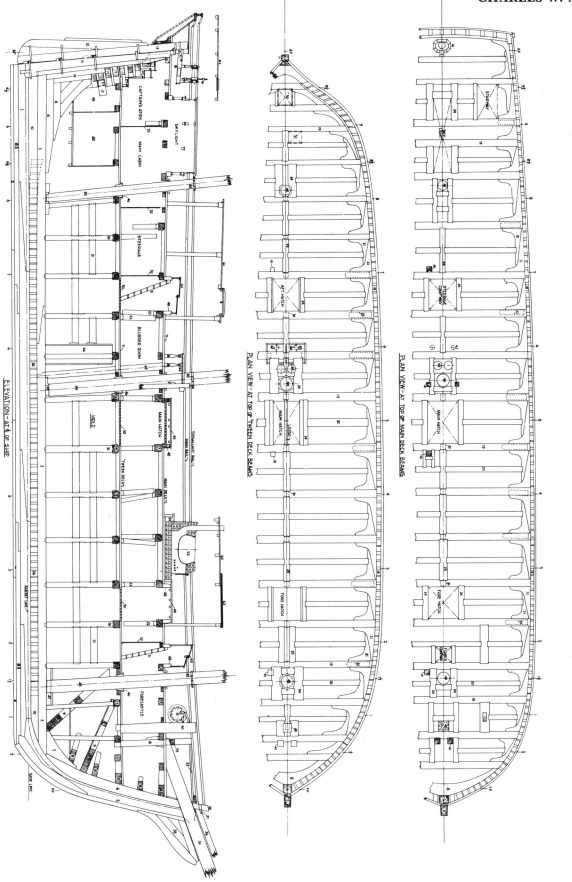

ELEVATION—AT ℄ OF SHIP

PLAN VIEW—AT TOP OF 'TWEEN DECK BEAMS

PLAN VIEW—AT TOP OF MAIN DECK BEAMS

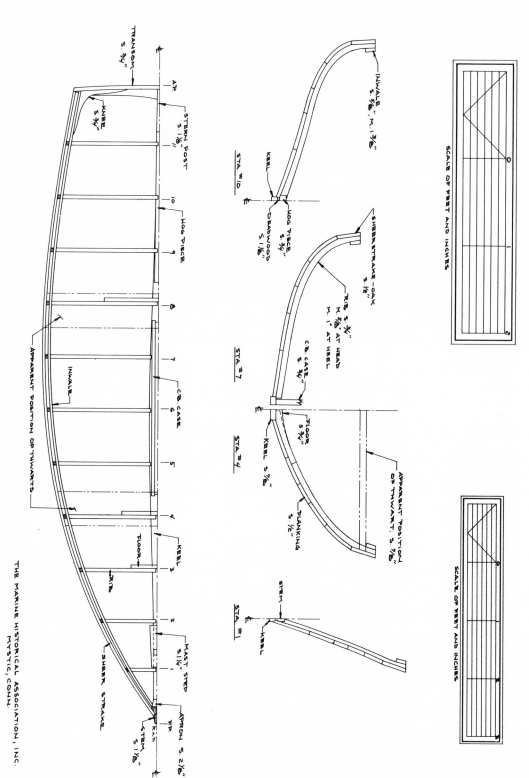

ELEVEN FT SAILING WHITEHALL

CONSTRUCTION DETAILS AS BOAT APPEARS

IN M.H.A. COLLECTION

THE MARINE HISTORICAL ASSOCIATION, INC.
MYSTIC, CONN.

DRAWN BY: R.A.PITTAWAY
DATE: DEC. 26, 1975
SCALE: 2"=1'-0" AND 3"=1'-0"

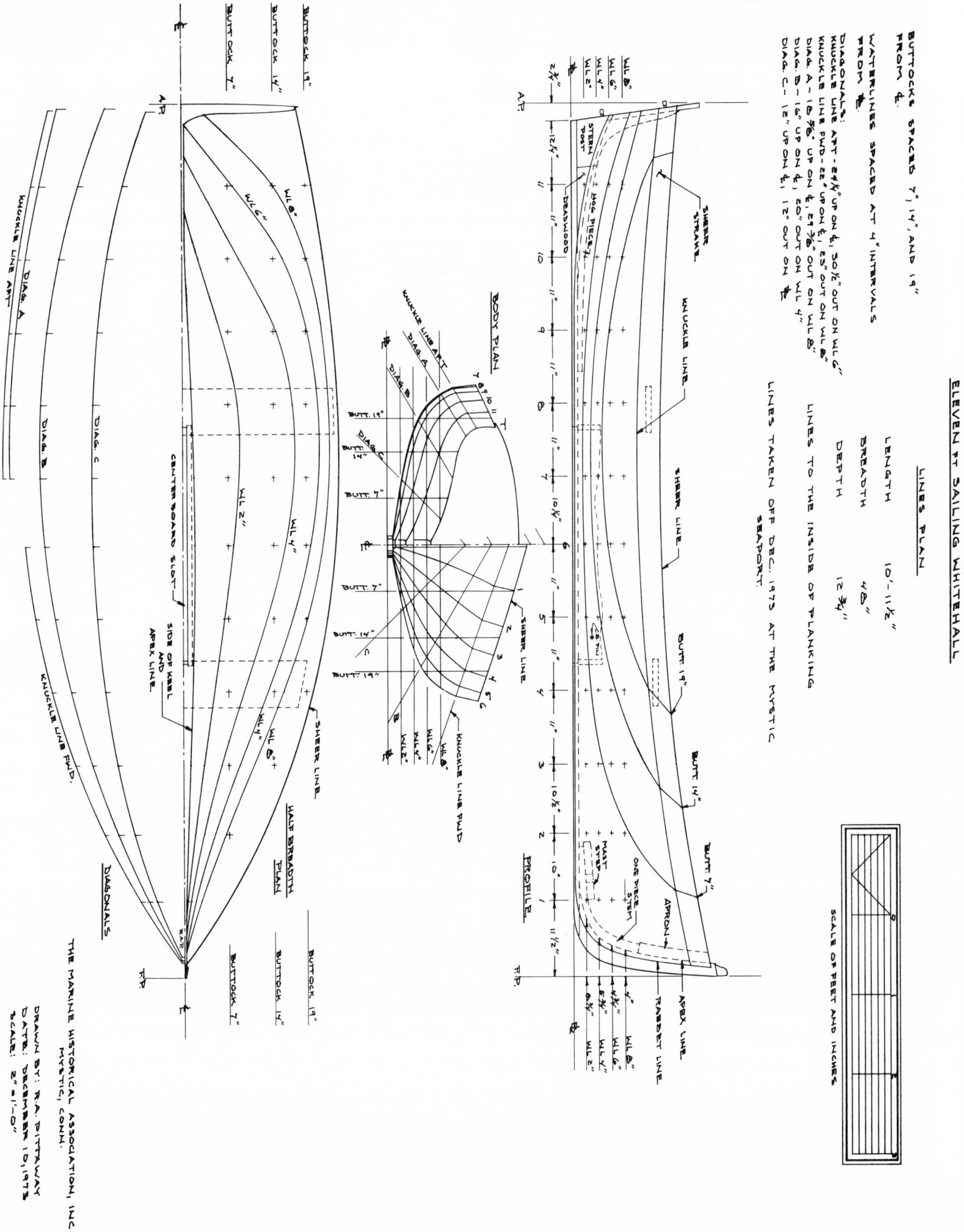

ELEVEN FT SAILING WHITEHALL

LINES PLAN

LENGTH	10'-11½"
BREADTH	48"
DEPTH	12 ¾"

LINES TO THE INSIDE OF PLANKING

LINES TAKEN OFF DEC. 1975 AT THE MYSTIC SEAPORT.

BUTTOCKS SPACED 7", 14", AND 19" FROM ₵.

WATERLINES SPACED AT 4" INTERVALS FROM ₵.

DIAGONALS:
KNUCKLE LINE AFT - 24½" UP ON ₵, 30½" OUT ON WL 6"
KNUCKLE LINE FWD - 22" UP ON ₵, 23" OUT ON WL 6"
DIAG. A - 18 ¾" UP ON ₵, 21½" OUT ON WL 8"
DIAG. B - 16" UP ON ₵, 20" OUT ON WL 4"
DIAG. C - 12" UP ON ₵, 12" OUT ON ₵

BODY PLAN

PROFILE

HALF BREADTH PLAN

DIAGONALS

SCALE OF FEET AND INCHES

THE MARINE HISTORICAL ASSOCIATION, INC. MYSTIC, CONN.

DRAWN BY: R.A. PITTAWAY
DATE: DECEMBER 10, 1975
SCALE: 2" = 1'-0"

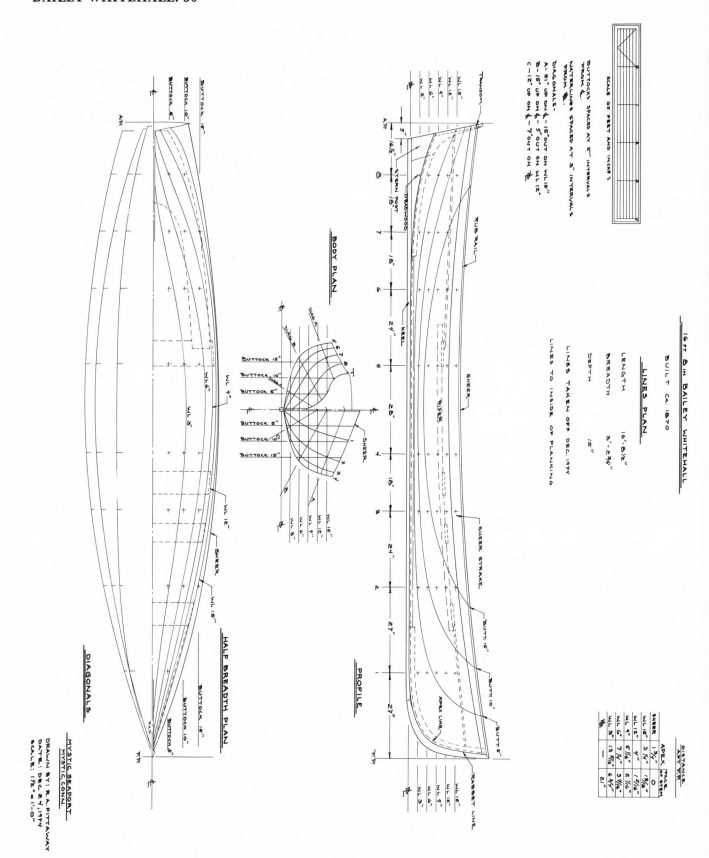

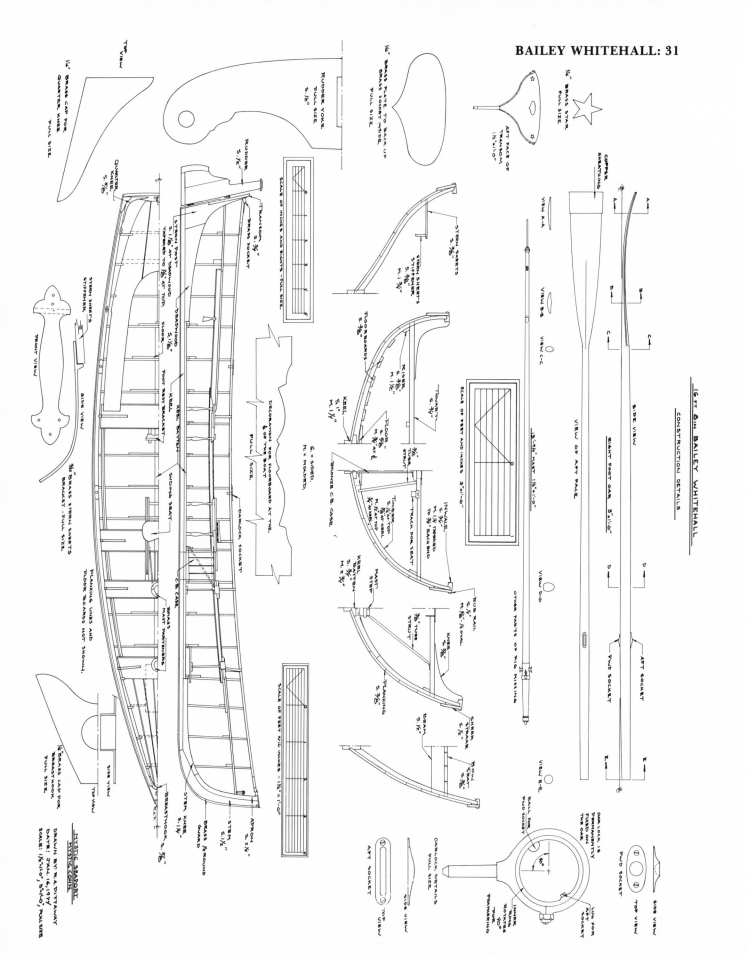

BAILEY WHITEHALL: 31

BOSTON WHITEHALL: 32

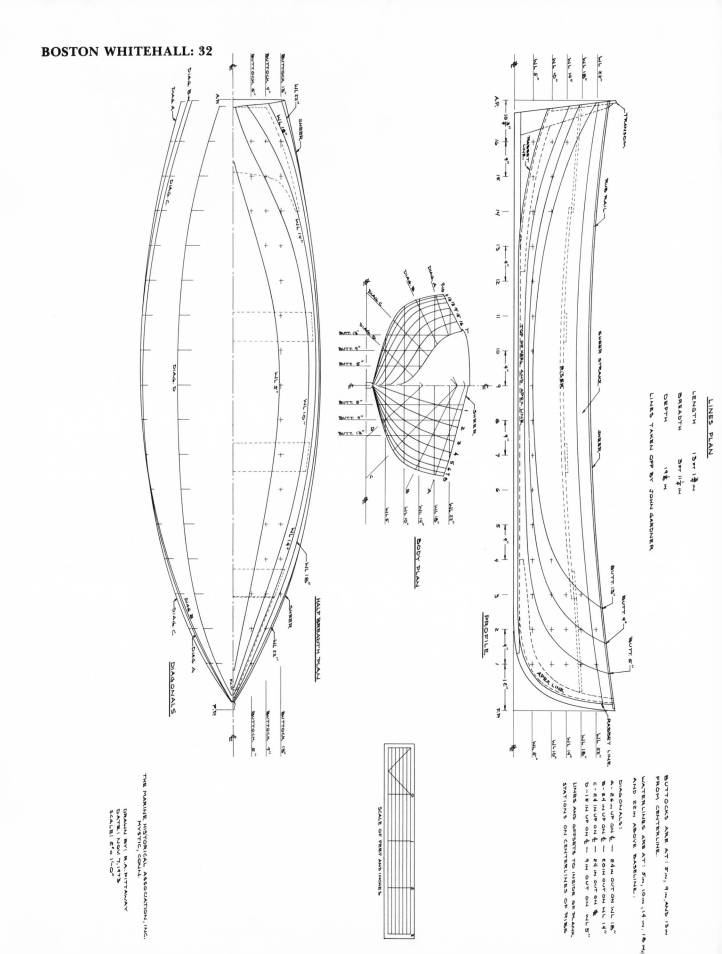

HALF BREADTH PLAN

DIAGONALS

BODY PLAN

PROFILE

LINES PLAN

LENGTH   15 FT 1⅝ IN
BREADTH   3 FT 11¼ IN
DEPTH   19⅜ IN

LINES TAKEN OFF BY JOHN GARDNER.

BUTTOCKS ARE AT: 5 IN, 9 IN, AND 13 IN
FROM CENTERLINE.

WATERLINES ARE AT: 5 IN, 10 IN, 14 IN, 18 IN
AND 22 IN ABOVE BASELINE.

DIAGONALS:
A — 26 IN UP ON ₵ — 24 IN OUT ON WL 15"
B — 24 IN UP ON ₵ — 20 IN OUT ON WL 14"
C — 24 IN UP ON ₵ — 24 IN OUT ON WL 18"
D — 15 IN UP ON ₵ — 9 IN OUT ON WL 5"

LINES AND OFFSETS TO INSIDE OF PLANK
STATIONS ON CENTERLINES OF RIBS

SCALE OF FEET AND INCHES

THE MARINE HISTORICAL ASSOCIATION, INC.
MYSTIC, CONN.

DRAWN BY: R.A. PITTAWAY
DATE: NOV. 7, 1973
SCALE: 2" = 1'-0"

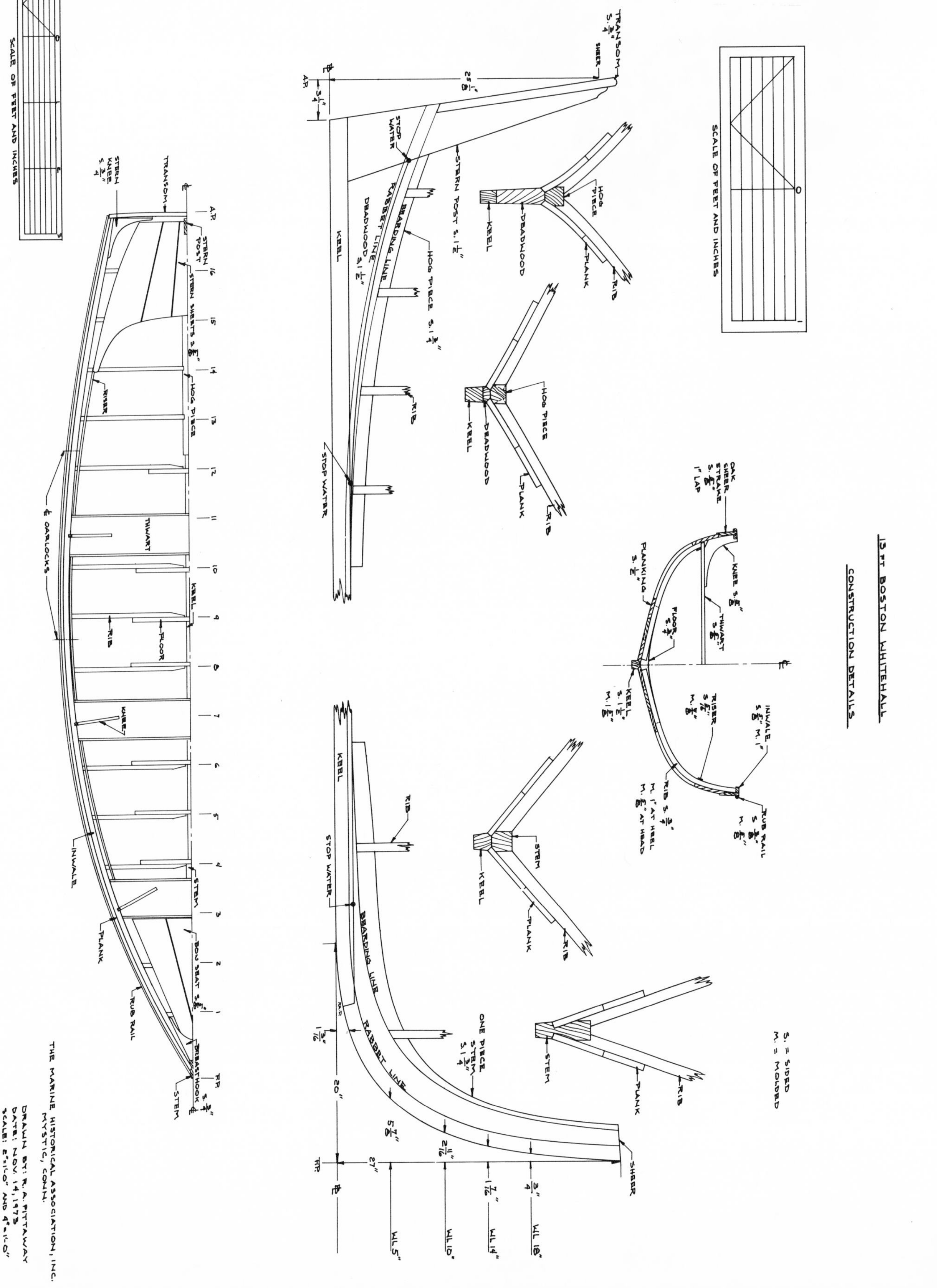
13 FT BOSTON WHITEHALL
CONSTRUCTION DETAILS
S. = SIDED
M. = MOLDED
SCALE OF FEET AND INCHES
SCALE OF FEET AND INCHES
TRANSOM
STERN KNEE S. 3/4"
STERN POST
STERN SHEETS S. 5/8"
HOG PIECE
RISER
THWART
KEEL
RIB
FLOOR
KNEE
STEM
BOW SEAT S. 5/8"
BREASTHOOK
INWALE
PLANK
RUB RAIL
℄ OARLOCKS
A.P.
F.P.
STOP WATER
RABBET LINE
BEARDING LINE
DEADWOOD S. 1 1/2"
HOG PIECE S. 1 3/4"
STERN POST S. 1 1/2"
TRANSOM S. 3/4"
SHEER
ONE PIECE STEM S. 1 3/4"
OAK SHEER STRAKE S. 5/8" 1" LAP
KNEE S. 5/8"
THWART S. 5/8"
PLANKING S. 1/4"
FLOOR S. 3/4"
KEEL S. 1 1/2" M. 1 5/8"
RISER S. 5/8" M. 3/8"
INWALE S. 5/8" M. 1"
RIB S. 3/4" M. 1" AT HEEL M. 5/8" AT HEAD
RUB RAIL S. 3/8" M. 5/8"
WL 18"
WL 14"
WL 10"
WL 5"
THE MARINE HISTORICAL ASSOCIATION, INC.
MYSTIC, CONN.
DRAWN BY: R. A. PITTAWAY
DATE: NOV. 14, 1973
SCALE: 2"=1'-0" AND 4"=1'-0"

WHITEHALL TENDER: 34

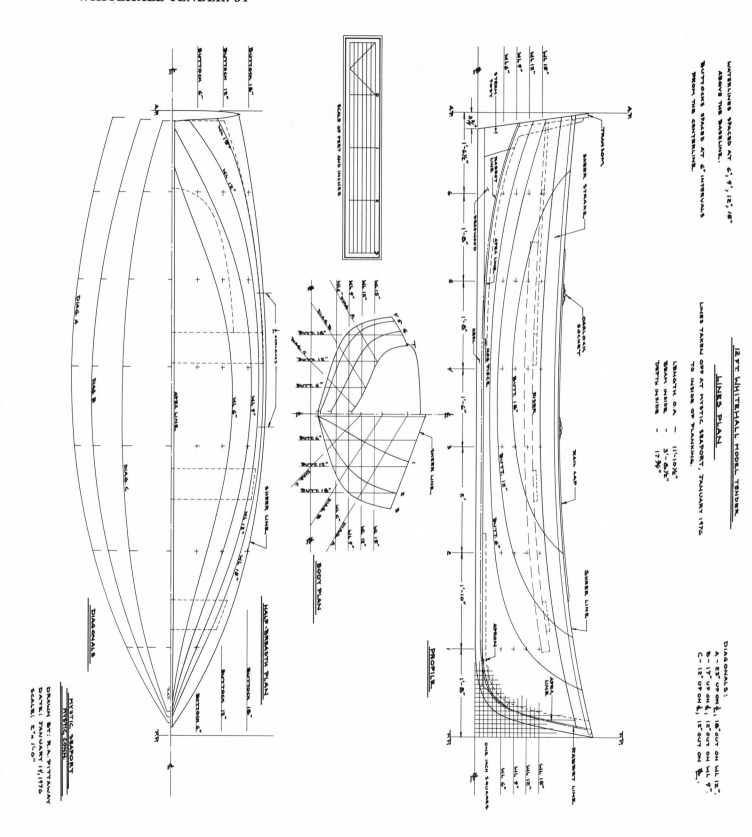

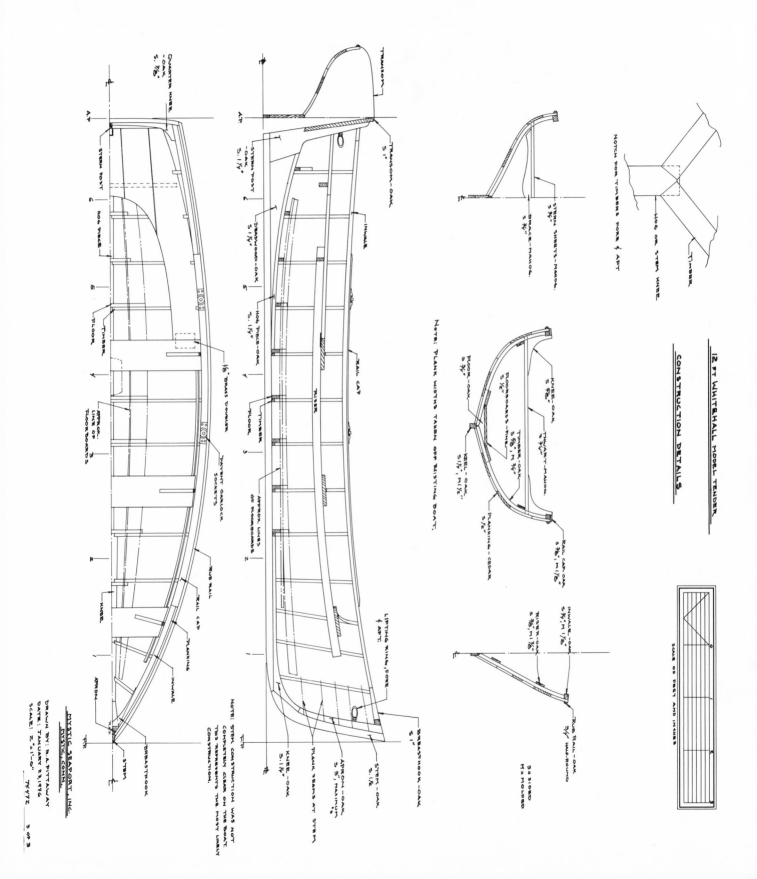

12 FT WHITEHALL MODEL TENDER

CONSTRUCTION DETAILS

SCALE OF FEET AND INCHES

MYSTIC SEAPORT, INC.
MYSTIC, CONN.
DRAWN BY: R.A. PITTAWAY
DATE: JANUARY 13, 1976
SCALE: 2"= 1'-0"
7x/72
3 of 3

NOTE: STEM CONSTRUCTION WAS NOT
COMPLETELY CLEAR ON THE BOAT.
THIS REPRESENTS THE MOST LIKELY
CONSTRUCTION.

NOTE: PLANK WIDTHS TAKEN OFF EXISTING BOAT.

WARDWELL PULLING BOAT: 36

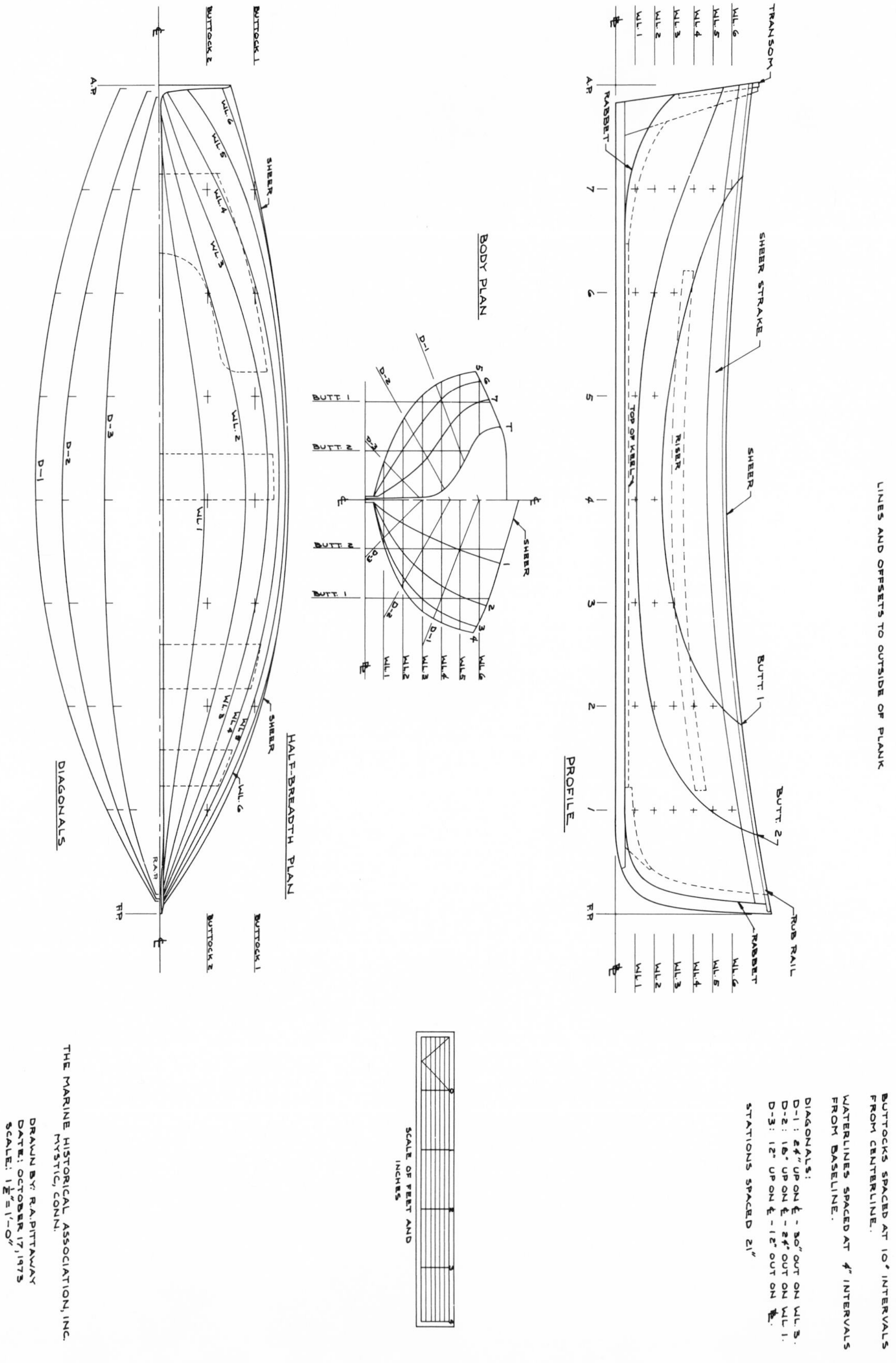
WARDWELL ROWING BOAT
LINES PLAN
LENGTH 14'-0"
BREADTH 4'-6" (OUTSIDE OF PLANK)
DEPTH 1'-8"
ORIGINAL LINES TAKEN OFF BY E.I. SCHOCK
AT THE MYSTIC SEAPORT, MYSTIC, CONN.
LINES AND OFFSETS TO OUTSIDE OF PLANK
PROFILE
BODY PLAN
HALF-BREADTH PLAN
DIAGONALS
TRANSOM
SHEER STRAKE
SHEER
RISER
TOP OF KEEL
RABBET
RUB RAIL
BUTT. 1
BUTT. 2
BUTTOCK 1
BUTTOCK 2
SCALE OF FEET AND INCHES
BUTTOCKS SPACED AT 10" INTERVALS FROM CENTERLINE.
WATERLINES SPACED AT 4" INTERVALS FROM BASELINE.
DIAGONALS:
D-1: 24" UP ON ℄ - 30" OUT ON WL 3.
D-2: 18" UP ON ℄ - 24" OUT ON WL 1.
D-3: 12" UP ON ℄ - 12" OUT ON ℄.
STATIONS SPACED 21"
THE MARINE HISTORICAL ASSOCIATION, INC.
MYSTIC, CONN.
DRAWN BY: R.A. PITTAWAY
DATE: OCTOBER 17, 1975
SCALE: 1 1/2"=1'-0"

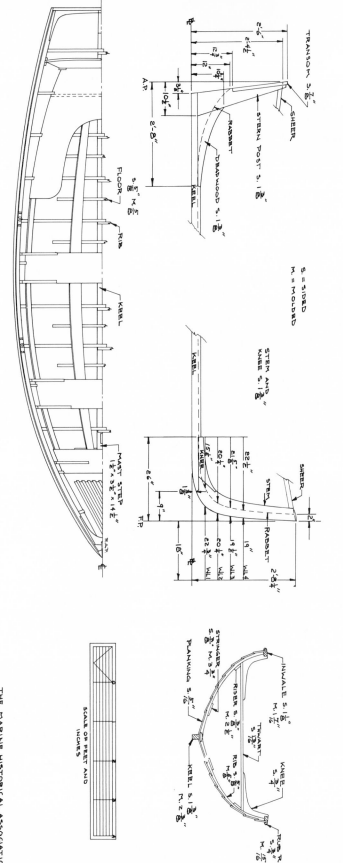

WARDWELL ROWING BOAT
TABLE OF OFFSETS
AND
CONSTRUCTION DETAILS

OFFSETS IN FEET-INCHES-SIXTEENTHS

DIAGS	HEIGHTS FROM ℄		HALF-BREADTHS FROM ℄	STATION	TRANS	7	6	5	4	3	2	1	RABBET
				SHEER	1-2-14	1-8-6	2-0-3	2-2-9	2-3-0	2-1-12	1-8-7	1-0-13	0-0-11
				WL6	1-1-2	1-7-4	1-11-1	2-0-2	2-0-2	1-11-12	1-6-15	0-11-9	—
				WL5	0-6-2	1-5-6	1-11-1	2-0-0	2-1-7	2-0-0	1-7-7	0-10-4	—
				WL4	0-1-11	1-0-10	1-8-7	2-0-0	2-2-6	2-0-15	1-5-7	0-8-11	0-0-11
				WL3	0-0-8	0-7-8	1-3-13	1-9-2	2-0-15	1-10-12	1-2-9	0-6-13	—
				WL2	0-0-6	0-4-0	0-10-4	1-4-0	1-9-0	1-8-1	1-0-1	0-5-7	—
				WL1	0-0-5	0-1-7	0-4-2	0-7-8	0-9-0	0-8-14	0-6-0	0-2-3	0-0-11
			RABBET		0-0-5	0-0-8	0-0-11	0-1-6	0-0-11	0-0-11	0-0-9	0-4-12	—
			SHEER		2-4-10	2-2-4	2-0-8	1-11-6	1-10-5	1-11-1	2-1-12	2-7-5	2-7-15
		RABBET			0-0-8	2-0-0	1-3-7	0-10-13	0-9-9	1-0-0	1-3-9	2-4-10	2-0-0
	B-1				—	2-0-0	0-7-14	0-1-14	0-9-1	1-0-0	1-8-8	—	—
	B-2				0-10-0	0-5-0	0-1-14	—	—	—	—	—	0-0-11
D-1					0-10-6	1-4-7	1-10-0	2-1-13	2-1-7	1-8-3	1-6-13	0-9-8	0-0-4
D-2					0-2-7	0-9-4	1-3-8	1-7-4	1-8-5	1-2-15	1-0-0	0-3-2	0-2-0
D-3					0-0-11	0-5-11	0-9-3	0-11-2	0-11-0	0-7-0	0-4-9	—	0-0-11

R.A.P.

BOTTOM OF KEEL IS THE HORIZONTAL BASELINE

FACE OF STEM AT SHEER IS AT F.P. AND 2'-8½" ABOVE ℄

AFT FACE OF TRANSOM AT SHEER IS 1¼" FWD OF A.P.

DISTANCE BETWEEN A.P. AND F.P. IS 14'-0"

OFFSETS TO OUTSIDE OF PLANKING.

S. = SIDED
M. = MOLDED

TRANSOM S.1½"
SHEER
STERN POST S.1½"
RABBET
DEADWOOD S.1½"
KEEL
FLOOR M.⅝"
RIB
KEEL
MAST STEP 12"x3½"x1½"
STEM AND KNEE S.1½"
STEM
RABBET

INWALE S.1½" M.1½"
RISER S.3½" M.⅝"
THWART S.⅝"
RIB M.⅝"
KNEE S.¾"
PLANKING S.⁵/₁₆"
STRINGER S.⅝" M.¾"
KEEL S.1½" M.2¾"
RUB RAIL S.¼" M.¹⁵/₁₆"

SCALE OF FEET AND INCHES

THE MARINE HISTORICAL ASSOCIATION, INC.
MYSTIC, CONN.

DRAWN BY: R.A. PITTAWAY
DATE: OCT. 19, 1973
SCALE: 1½" = 1'-0"

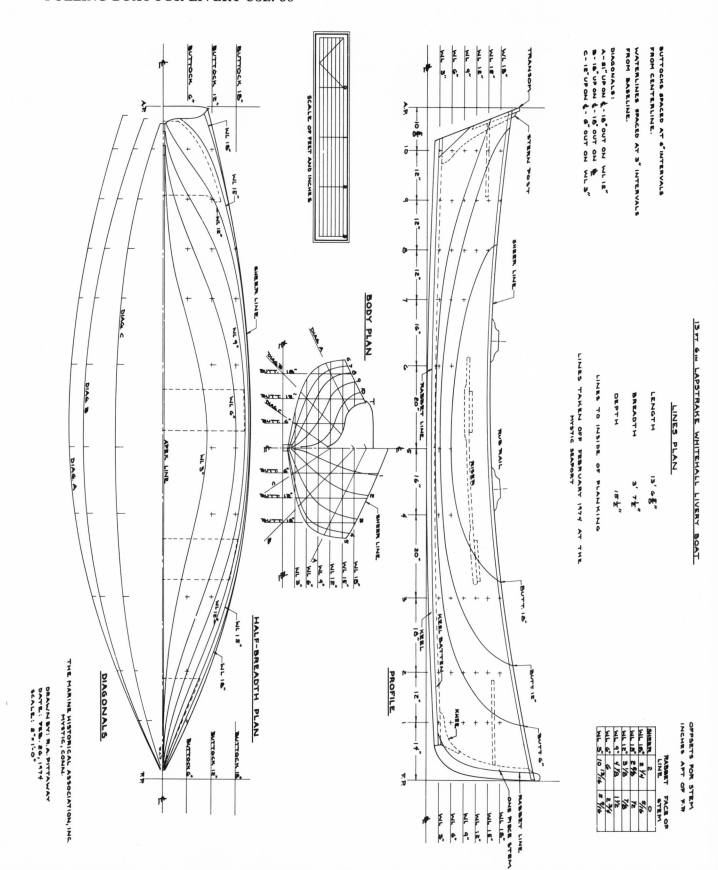

13 FT. 6 IN. LAPSTRAKE WHITEHALL LIVERY BOAT

LINES PLAN

LENGTH 13' 6⅜"
BREADTH 3' 7½"
DEPTH 15½"

LINES TAKEN OFF FEBRUARY 1974 AT THE MYSTIC SEAPORT

LINES TO INSIDE OF PLANKING

BODY PLAN

PROFILE

HALF-BREADTH PLAN

DIAGONALS

SCALE OF FEET AND INCHES

BUTTOCKS SPACED AT 6" INTERVALS FROM CENTERLINE.

WATERLINES SPACED AT 3" INTERVALS FROM BASELINE.

DIAGONALS:
A—21" UP ON ₡—18" OUT ON WL 18"
B—18" UP ON ₡—18" OUT ON ₡
C—12" UP ON ₡—6" OUT ON WL 3"

THE MARINE HISTORICAL ASSOCIATION, INC.
MYSTIC, CONN.

DRAWN BY: R.A. PITTAWAY
DATE: FEB. 26, 1974
SCALE: 2"=1'-0"

OFFSETS FOR STEM INCHES AFT OF F.P.

	RABBET LINE	FACE OF STEM
SHEER	2	0
WL 18"	2 ¼	5/16
WL 15"	2 4/8	½
WL 12"	3/8	7/8
WL 9"	1/8	1/2
WL 6"	6	2 ¾
WL 5 /10	13/16	8 9/16

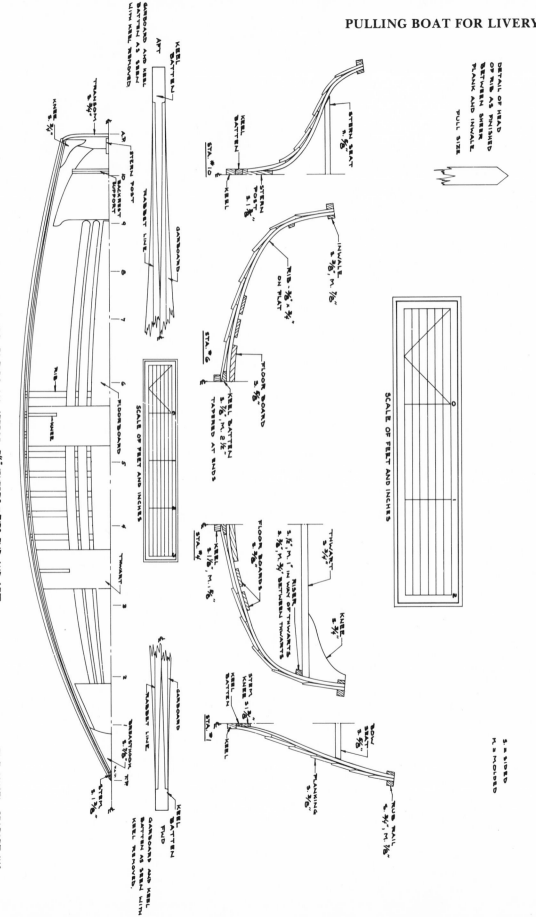

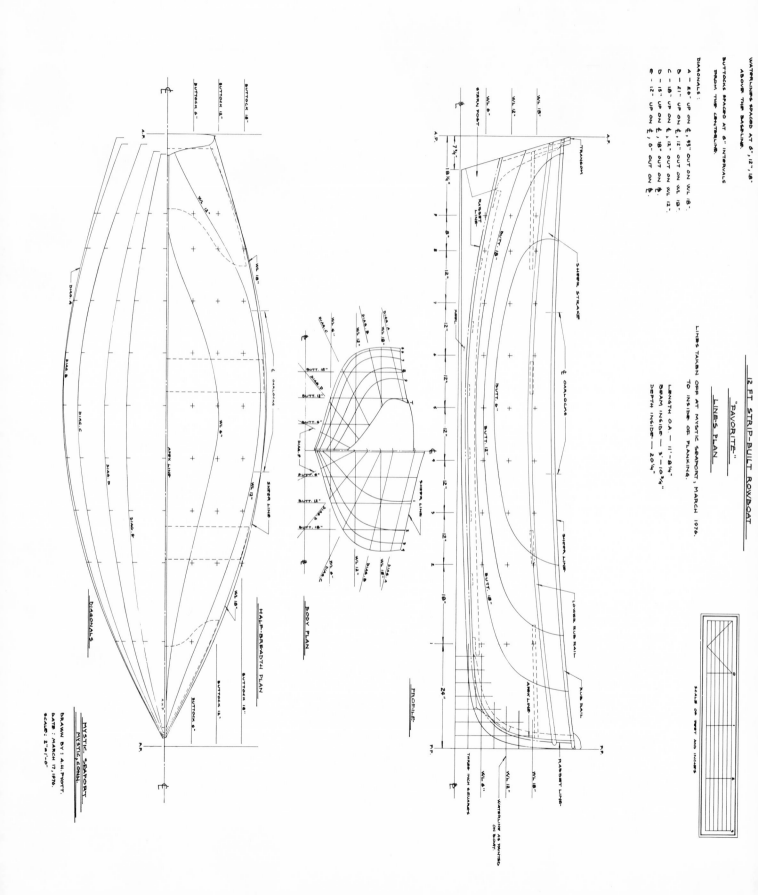

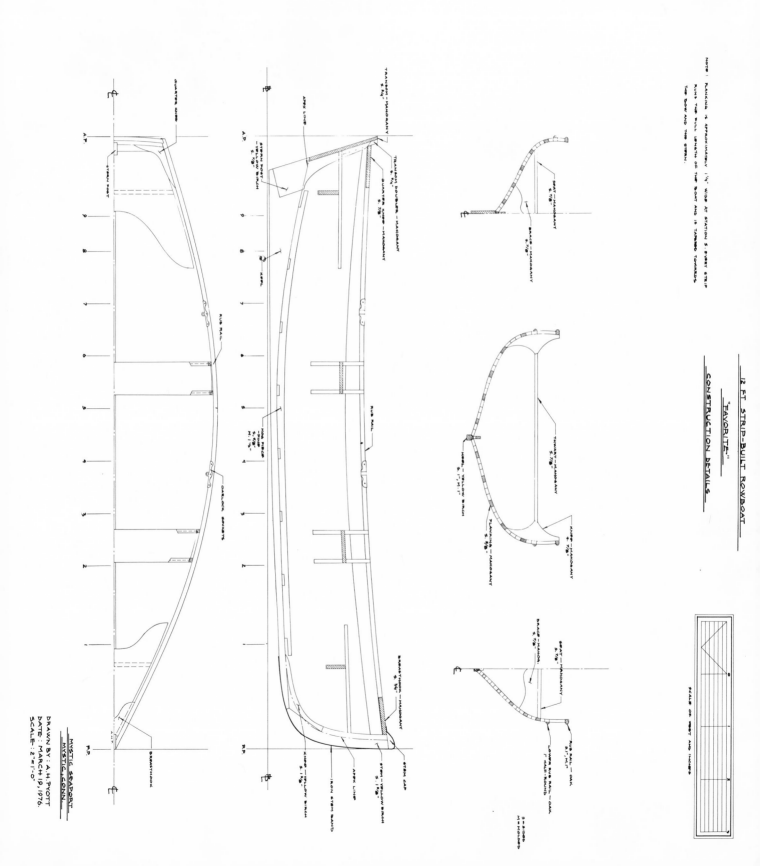

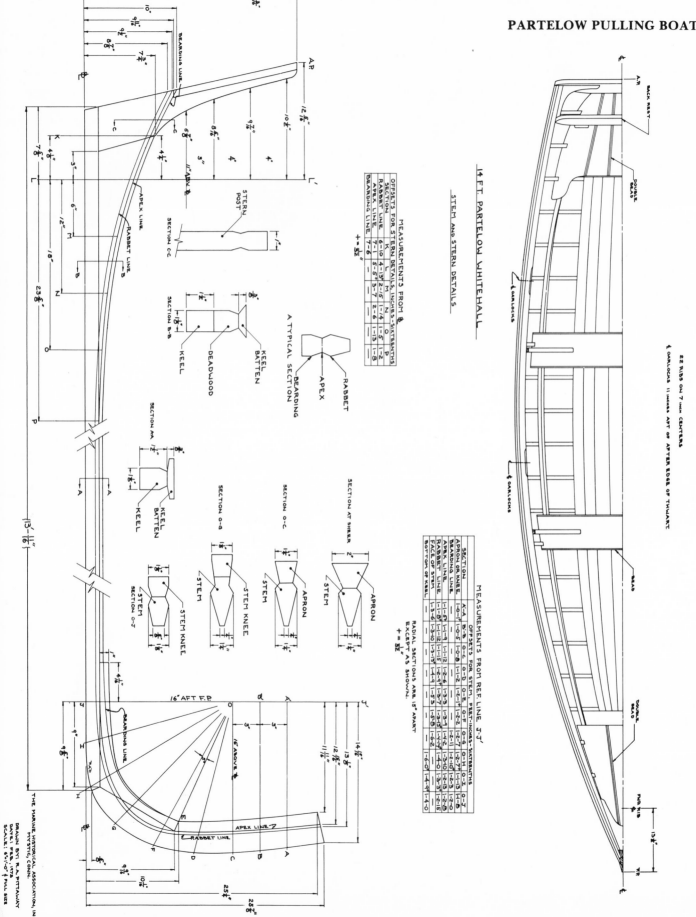

14 FT. PARTELOW WHITEHALL

STEM AND STERN DETAILS

14 FT. PARTELOW WHITEHALL

PLAN VIEW AND SECTIONS

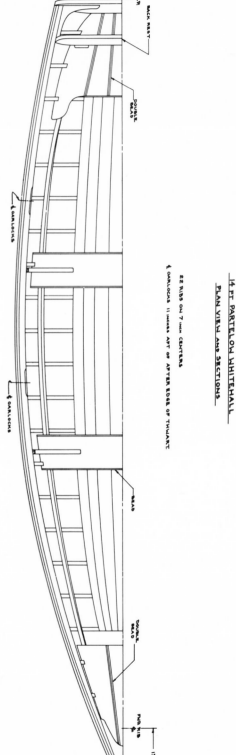

PARTELOW PULLING BOAT: 43

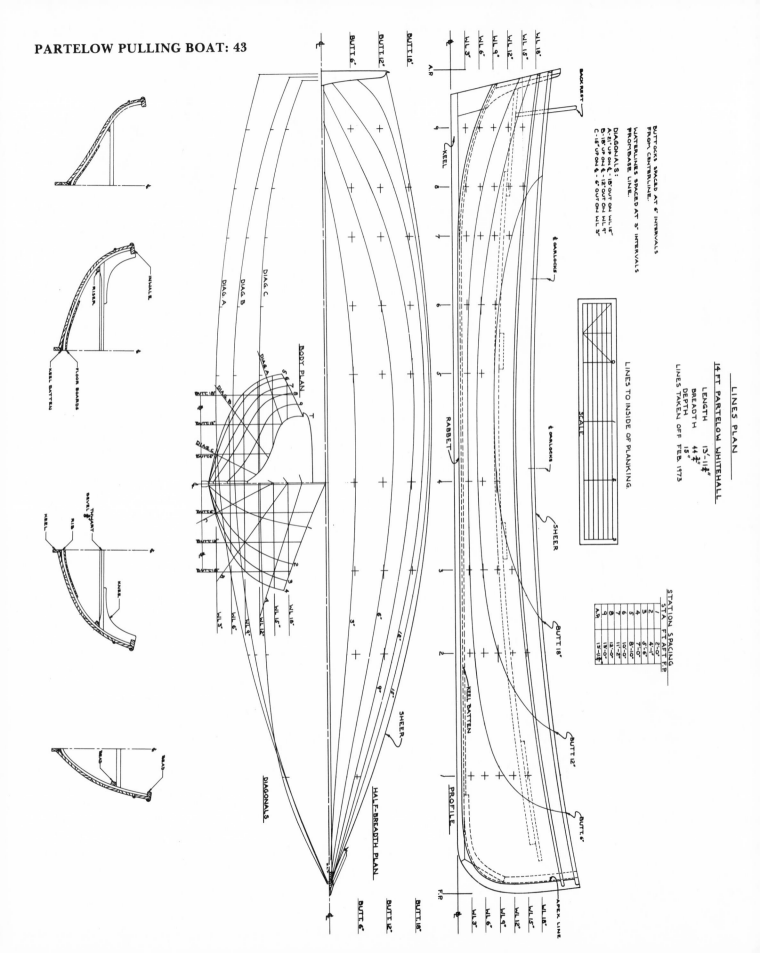

LINES PLAN

14 FT PARTELOW WHITEHALL

LENGTH 15'-11¾"
BREADTH 44¾"
DEPTH 15"
LINES TAKEN OFF FEB. 1973

LINES TO INSIDE OF PLANKING.

BUTTOCKS SPACED AT 6" INTERVALS
FROM CENTERLINE.

WATERLINES SPACED AT 3" INTERVALS
FROM BASE LINE.

DIAGONALS:
A: 21" UP ON ₵ : 18" OUT ON WL 18"
B: 18" UP ON ₵ : 12" OUT ON WL 9"
C: 16" UP ON ₵ : 6" OUT ON WL 3"

STATION SPACING	
STA.	FT.AFT F.P.
AP	0
1	2'-0"
2	4'-1"
3	5'-6"
4	7'-0"
5	8'-10"
6	10'-0"
7	11'-2"
8	12'-0"
9	13'-0"
A.P.	15'-11¾"

BODY PLAN

HALF-BREADTH PLAN

PROFILE

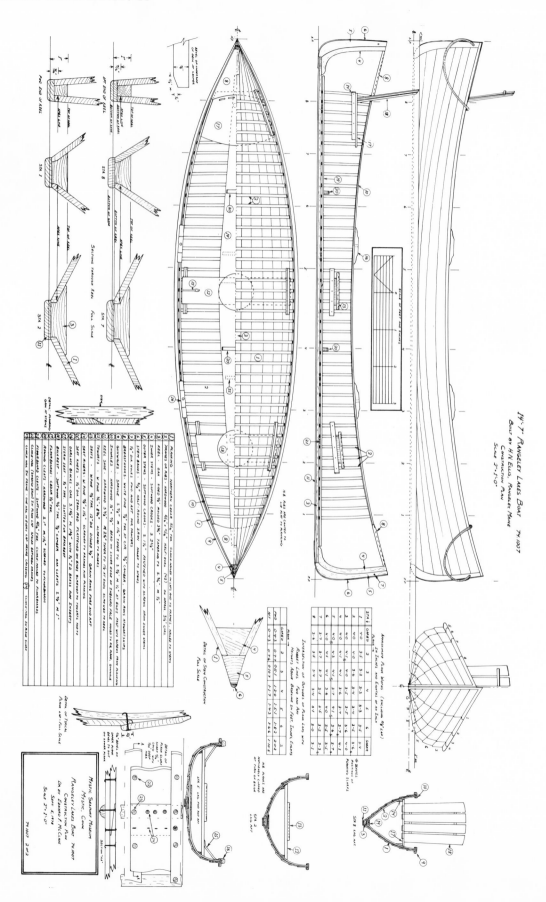

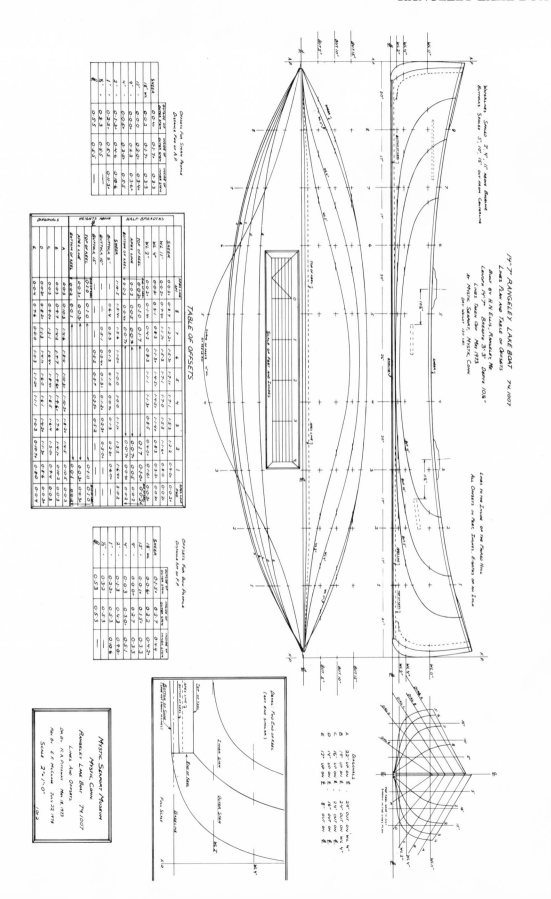

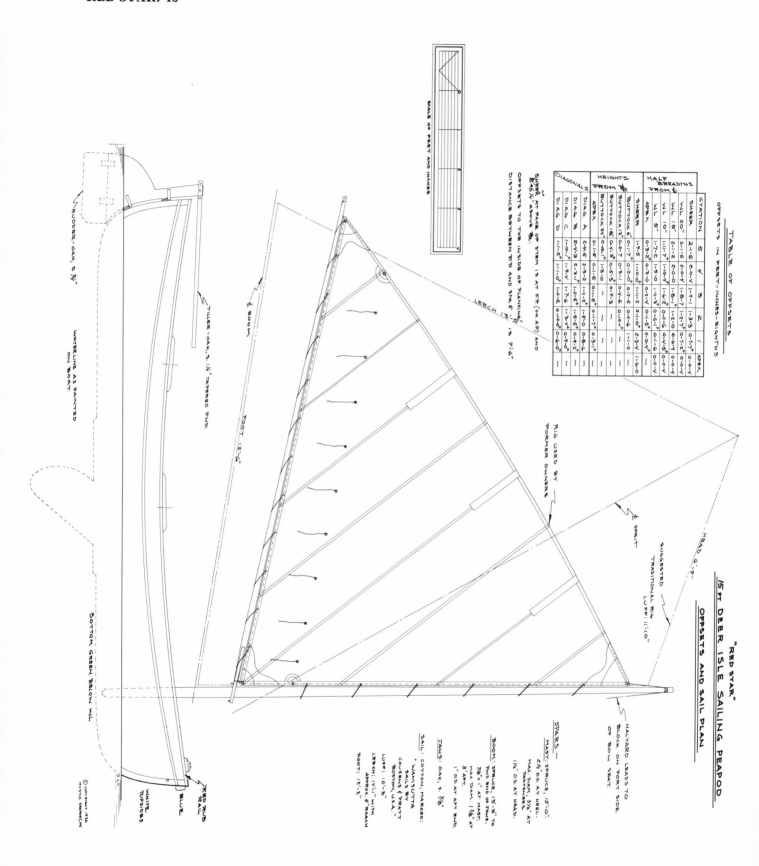

"RED STAR"
15 Ft. DEER ISLE SAILING PEAPOD
OFFSETS AND SAIL PLAN

TABLE OF OFFSETS
OFFSETS IN FEET-INCHES-EIGHTHS

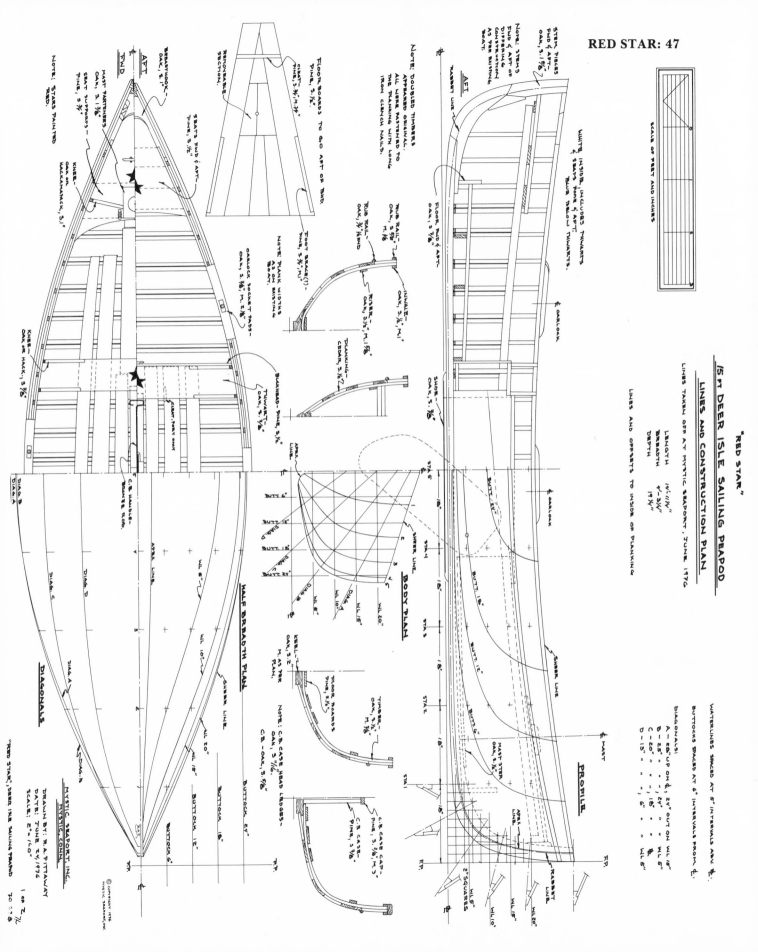

RED STAR: 47

"RED STAR"

15 ft DEER ISLE SAILING PEAPOD

LINES AND CONSTRUCTION PLAN

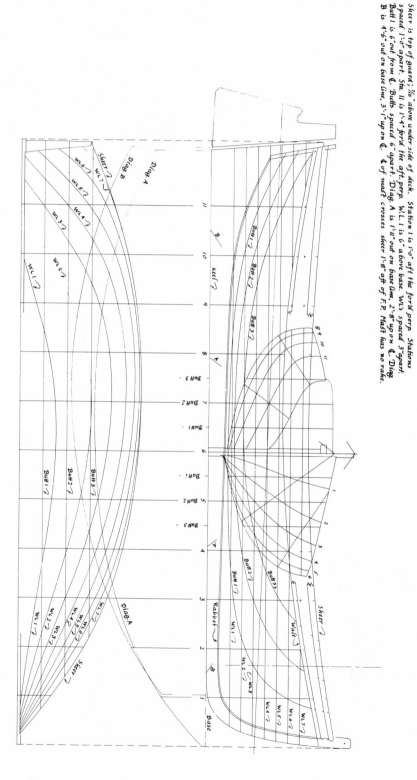

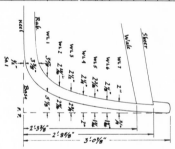

Measured and Drawn at Warren, R.I.
Length betw. perps. — 12'-4"
Beam moulded — 5'-2¾"

Newport Fish & Lobster Boat
Built by Button Swan at
Newport, R.I. about 1870-1875
Scale: 1½" = 1'-0"
R.H. Baker — June, 1975

Scale in feet

Sheer is top of guard; ⅞" above under side of deck. Stations are 1'-0" aft the forw'd perp. Stations spaced 1'-0" apart. Sta. 11 is 1'-4" forw'd the aft. perp. W.L. 1 is 6" above base. W.L's spaced 3" apart. Butt 1 is 6" out from ℄. Butts spaced 6" apart. Diag. A is 1'-11" out on base line, 2'-8" up on ℄. Diag. B is 4'-6" out on base line, 3'-1" up on ℄. ℄ of mast crosses sheer 1'-8" aft of F.P. Mast has no rake.

Offsets in feet, inches and eighths to inside of plank.

Diags			Half breadths										Heights above base			
	B	A	WL1	WL2	WL3	WL4	WL5	WL6	WL7	Sheer	Rab.	Butt1	Butt3	Sheer	Wale	Butt1	Butt3

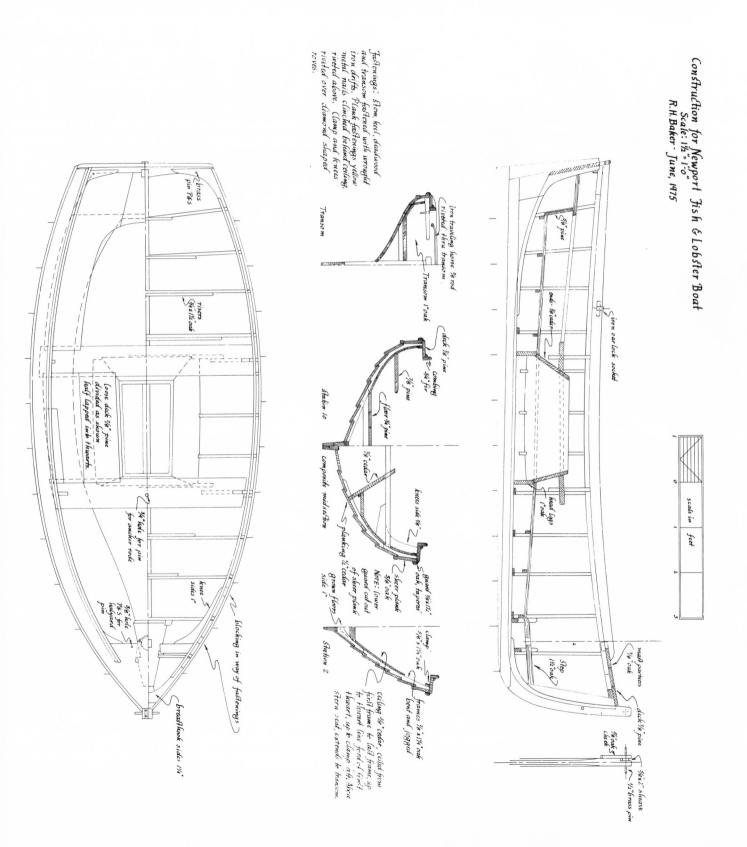

Construction for Newport Fish & Lobster Boat
Scale: 1½" = 1'-0"
R. H. Baker - June, 1975

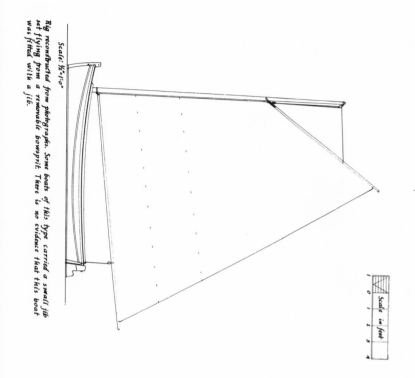

Rig reconstructed from photographs. Some boats of this type carried a small jib set flying from a removable bowsprit. There is no evidence that this boat was fitted with a jib.

Scale in feet

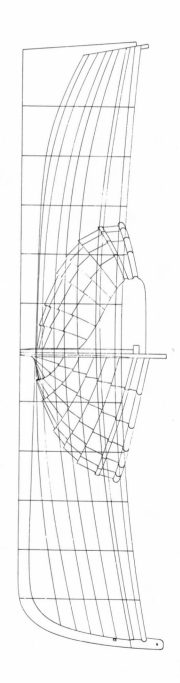

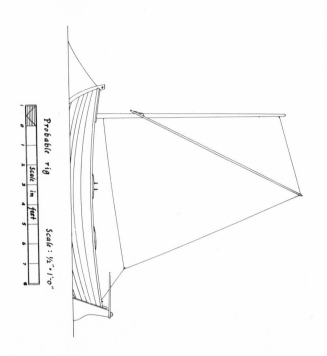

Probable rig

Scale : ½"=1'o"

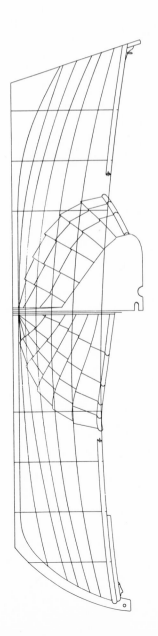

Offsets in feet, inches and eighths to the inside of ½ inch plank.

Station 1 is 1'-0" aft the for'd perp. Stations spaced 1'-0" apart.

Stations 5 and 7 omitted for clarity.

Water line 1 is 4" above base line. Water lines spaced 4" apart.

Butt 1 is 6" out from center line. Butts spaced 6" apart.

Diag. A is 3'-5" up on center line; 3'-7" out on base line. Diag. B is 2'-3" up on center line; 2'-1" out on base line.

Center line of the mast crosses Sheer 1'-7½" aft the for'd perp.

Mast rakes forward ⅜ in 15".

Stem, keel, skeg and post side 1¾". Stem faces 1".

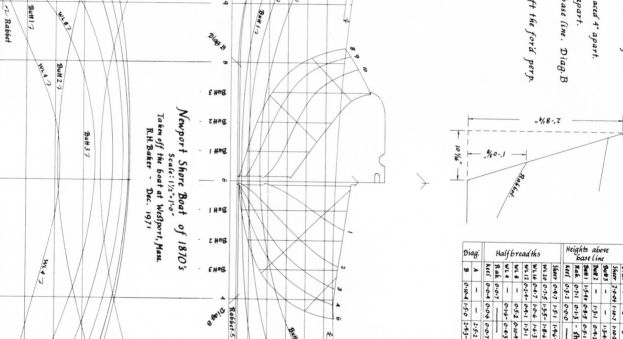

Newport Shore Boat of 1870's
Scale: 1½" = 1'-0"
Taken off the boat at Westport, Mass.
R. H. Baker – Dec. 1971

Scale in feet

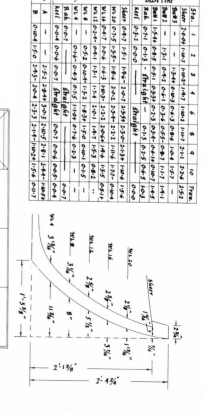

	Sta.	1	2	3	4	6	8	9	10	Trans.
Half breadths	Sheer	2-0-4	1-10-7	1-9-7	1-8-7	1-7	—	1-5-7	2-1-1	2-5-2
	Butt3		1-3-1	0-9-2	0-6-1	0-3-6	0-6-3	0-8-6	1-0-4	1-5-7
	Butt2	1-5-4-4	0-8-5	0-5-1	0-3-6	0-5-5	0-9-7	1-4-5	1-9-1	
	Butt1	0-7-1	0-4-3	0-2-3	0-1-3	0-1-3	0-6-5	1-0-3	1-5-7	
	Rab.	0-3-2	0-1-3	— straight —		0-1-5	0-6-5	1-0-3		
	Keel	0-0-0								
Heights above base line	Sheer									
	WL4	—	—	0-1-6	0-4-3	1-1-0-4	1-6-3	1-8-5-4	2-1-0-5	2-9-1
	WL8	0-2-4-4	0-7-1	0-5-2	0-10-4	1-3-1	1-8-5-4	1-10-2-4	2-4-4	
	WL12	0-4-7	0-6	0-6-3	1-3-1	1-7-4	2-1-2-1	1-5-3		
	WL16	0-7-5	1-3-5-4	1-8-6	2-0-2	2-3-4-4	2-0-6-4	1-4-7		
	WL20	1-4-4-6	2-0-7	2-3-5-4	2-3-5-0	2-1-3-4	1-4-6			
	Rak.	0-5-2	0-7-1	0-2-3	0-3-6	0-4-8	0-6-5-1	0-1-5		
	Keel	0-0-0	— straight —							
Diag.	A	0-0-4	0-0-6	0-0-7	0-0-6	0-0-5	0-0-7			
	B	0-10-4	1-5-0	2-4-3	2-0-4	2-5-3	2-1-4	1-9-2-4	1-5-6	0-11-7

WL4 — 3⅛"
WL8 — 3¾"
WL12 — 2½"
WL16 — 2⅜"
WL20 — 1⅛"
Sheer — ⅞"

2'-13/8"
2'-1¾"

1'-37/8"
11¾"
8"
5½"
3½"
1¾"
⅞"

2'-8⅛"
10⅜"
1'-0⅜"
Rabet

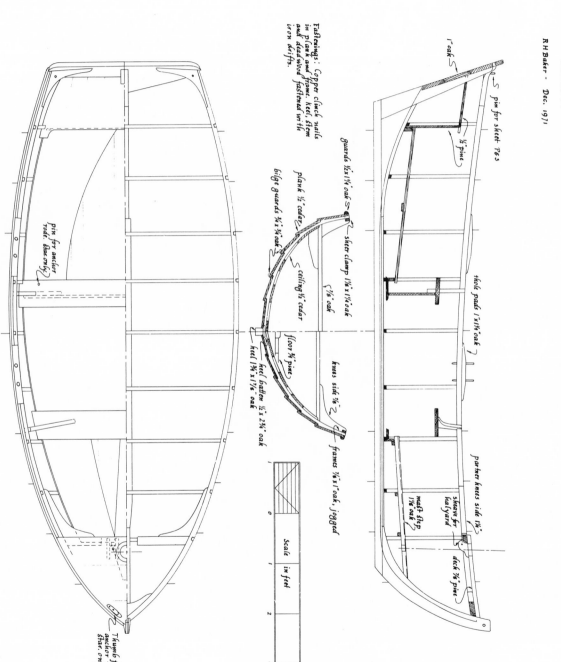

Construction for Newport Shore Boat
Scale: 1½"=1'-0"

R H Baker - Dec. 1971

1" oak

pin for sheet PÉS

½ pine

guards ½×1¼" oak

sheer clamp 1¼×1½" oak

1½" oak

ceiling ½" cedar

plank ½" cedar

bilge guards ½×¾" oak

floor ¾" pine

keel batten ½×2¾" oak

keel 1¾×1⅝" oak

frames ⅝×1" oak, jogged

knees side ⅝"

thole pads 1"×1¾" oak

mast step 1½ oak

sheave for halyard

partner knees side 1½"

deck ⅝" pine

Fastenings: Copper clinch nails
in plank and frame, keel, stem
and deadwood fastened with
iron drifts.

pin for anchor
rode. shar.only.

Thumb for
anchor rode
shar. only.

Scale in feet

0   1   2   3

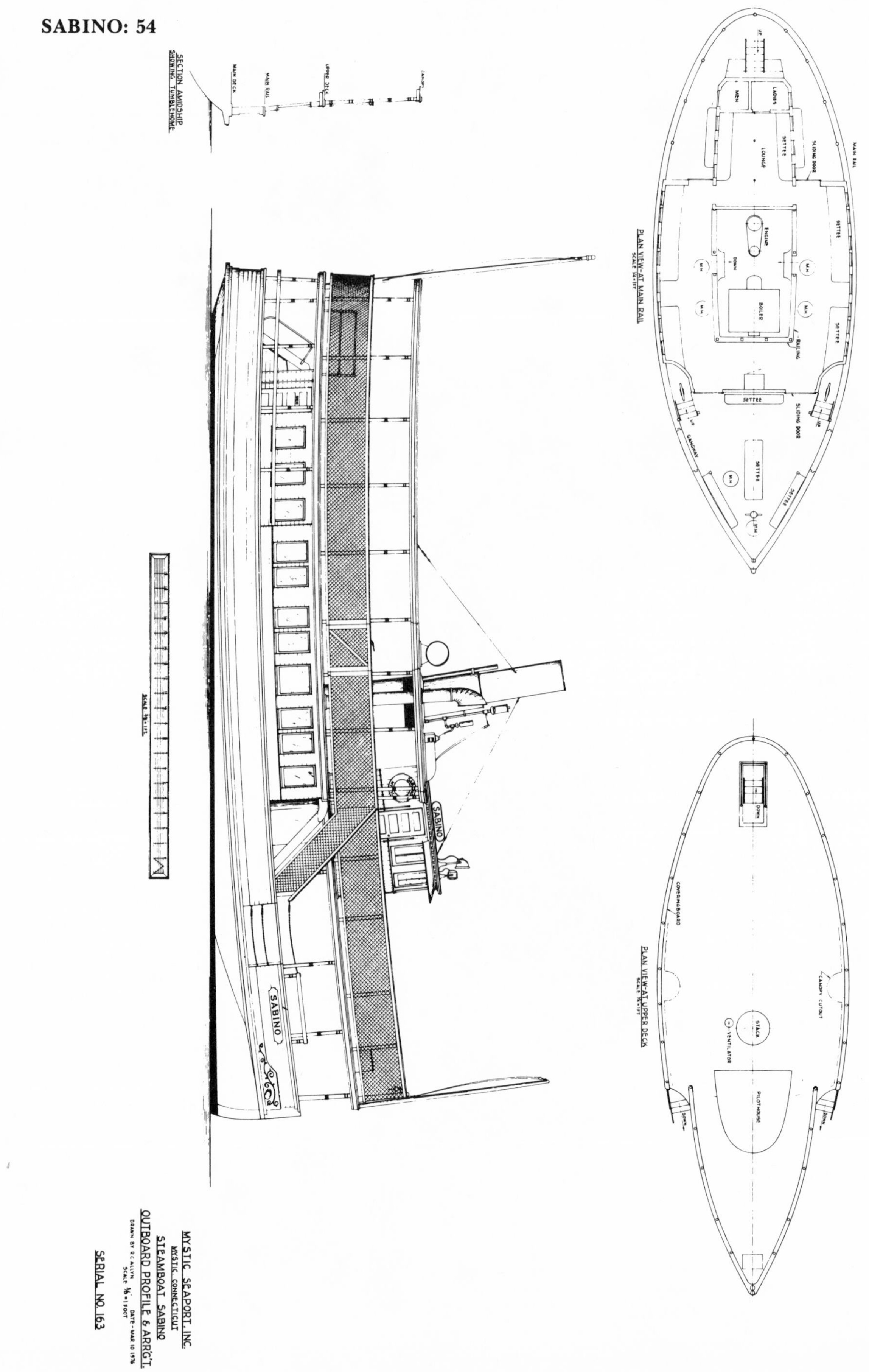

SABINO: 54

MYSTIC SEAPORT, INC.
MYSTIC, CONNECTICUT
STEAMBOAT SABINO
OUTBOARD PROFILE & ARR'G'T.
DRAWN BY R.C. ALLYN
SCALE: 3/8" = 1 FOOT
DATE: MAR. 10 1976
SERIAL NO. 163

SECTION AMIDSHIP
SHOWING TUMBLEHOME

MAIN DECK
MAIN RAIL
UPPER DECK
CANOPY

SABINO

SABINO

PLAN VIEW AT MAIN RAIL
SCALE 1/4" = 1 FT.

MEN
LADIES
SLIDING DOOR
SETTEE
LOUNGE
MAIN RAIL
W.C.
DOWN
ENGINE
W.C.
BOILER
W.C.
W.C.
SETTEE
SETTEE
RAILING
SLIDING DOOR
SETTEE
SETTEE
W.C.
GANGWAY

PLAN VIEW AT UPPER DECK
SCALE 1/4" = 1 FT.

DOWN
COMPANIONWAY
CANOPY CUTOUT
VENTILATOR
STACK
PILOTHOUSE

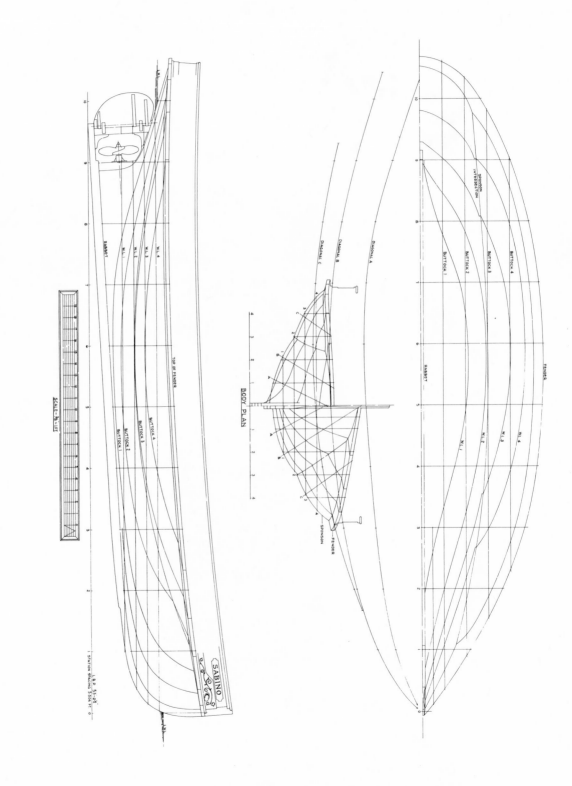

NOTE— THESE LINES DRAWN TO DIMENSIONS LIFTED FROM ACTUAL SHIP
LINES ARE TO OUTSIDE OF PLANKING

MYSTIC SEAPORT, INC.
MYSTIC CONNECTICUT
STEAMBOAT SABINO
LINES PLAN

DRAWN BY R.C. ALLYN   DATE—JAN 6, 1976
SCALE ⅜" = 1 FOOT

SERIAL NO. 162

PRINCIPAL DIMENSIONS
LENGTH OVERALL ————— 57'-0⅝"
MAX BEAM ————— 21'-11½"
MAX DRAFT ————— 6'-3"

SCALE = ⅜" = 1 FT

BODY PLAN

SABINO

TOP OF FENDER

RABBET

W.L. 1
W.L. 2
W.L. 3
W.L. 4

BUTTOCK 1
BUTTOCK 2
BUTTOCK 3
BUTTOCK 4

DIAGONAL A
DIAGONAL B
DIAGONAL C

SPONSON

FENDER

RABBET

L&P 53'-0⅝"
STATION SPACING 5.304 FT

SABINO: 56

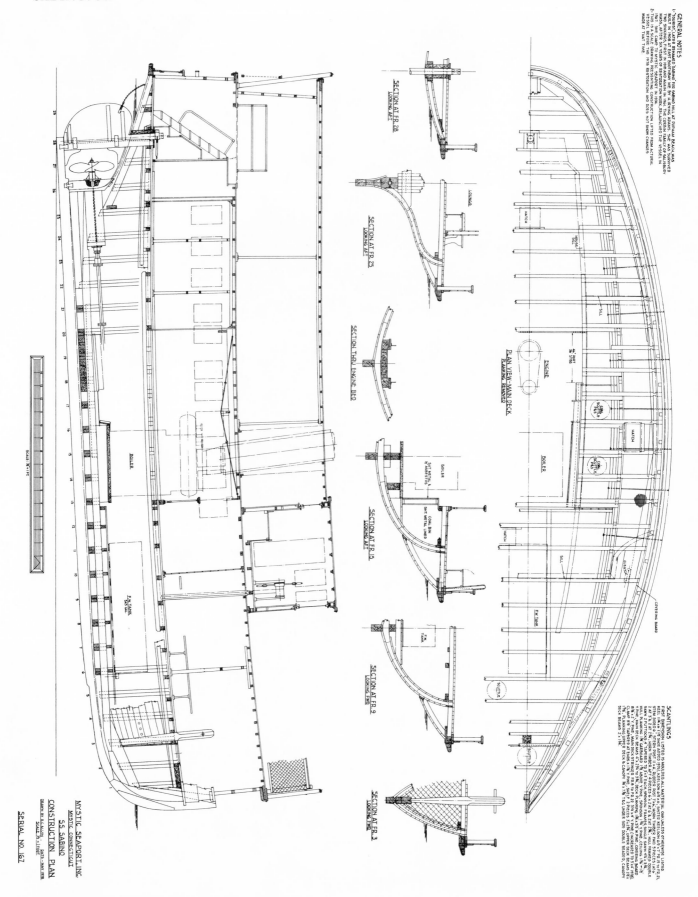

SERIAL NO. 167

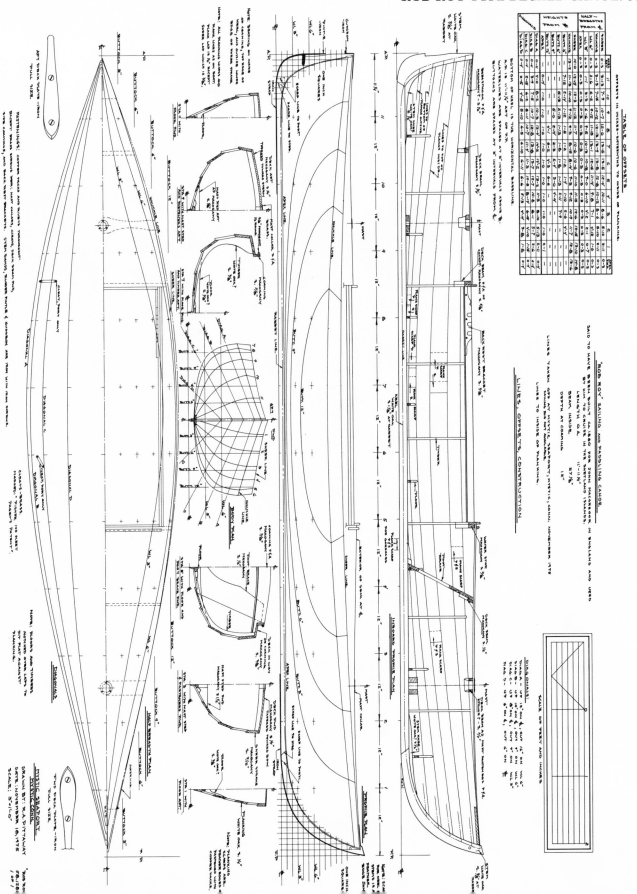

L. FRANCIS HERRESHOFF DUGOUT CANOE: 58

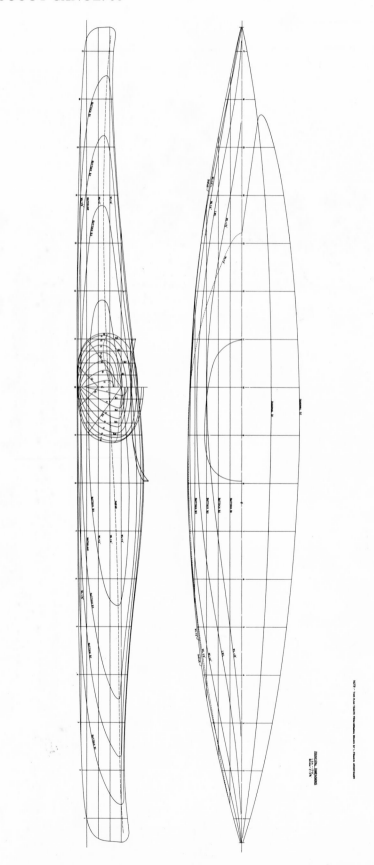

Index

Chronological Index to Accession Numbers

Text set in Bodoni Book,
a typeface known for its compactness and legibility.
Headlines and captions set in Baskerville,
classic and graceful of line as the watercraft it describes.
Typeset and printed by
Connecticut Printers, Incorporated, Bloomfield, Connecticut,
on Mohawk Superfine paper.
Bound by Robert Burlen & Son, Inc., Norwell, Massachusetts.
Designed by Behri Pratt Knauth.